THE

WORK OF THE ROYAL ENGINEERS

IN THE

EUROPEAN WAR, 1914–19

MILITARY MINING

PUBLISHED BY THE SECRETARY,

INSTITUTE OF ROYAL ENGINEERS, CHATHAM

The Naval & Military Press Ltd

Reproduced by kind permission of the Central Library,
Royal Military Academy, Sandhurst

Published by

The Naval & Military Press Ltd

Unit 10, Ridgewood Industrial Park,

Uckfield, East Sussex,

TN22 5QE England

Tel: +44 (0) 1825 749494

Fax: +44 (0) 1825 765701

www.naval-military-press.com

*In reprinting in facsimile from the original, any imperfections are inevitably reproduced
and the quality may fall short of modern type and cartographic standards.*

Printed and bound by Antony Rowe Ltd, Eastbourne

CONTENTS.

PART I.—HISTORICAL.

PART II.—MINE RESCUE WORK.

PART III.—TECHNICAL.

CONTENTS OF CHAPTERS.

PART II.—MINE RESCUE WORK.

CHAPTER III.—MISCELLANEOUS NOTES.

CHAPTER IV.—MINE-LISTENING INSTRUMENTS AND THEIR USE.

CHAPTER V.—MINE SCHOOLS.

LIST OF ILLUSTRATIONS.

PART I.—HISTORICAL.

PART II.—MINE RESCUE WORK.

PART III.—TECHNICAL.

THE WORK OF THE ROYAL ENGINEERS IN THE EUROPEAN WAR, 1914–1919.

MILITARY MINING.

PART I.—HISTORICAL.

CHAPTER I.

DEVELOPMENT OF ORGANIZATION.

1. INTRODUCTION.

Mining is an old and well known branch of Military Engineering, which, before this war, had been regarded as belonging almost exclusively to the deliberate attack and defence of fortresses.

The apparent inability of the mightiest fortresses to withstand long-range bombardment by heavy modern ordnance had led to a natural falling-off in the study and practice of military mining, which were suddenly revived in 1914 by the discovery that stationary trench systems brought back all the old features of fortress warfare.

As in all branches of the military art, the fundamental principles no doubt remained unchanged, but their application to modern conditions led to developments of the most varying nature and widest interest.

At the end of the first battle of Ypres, the opposing armies settled down into trenches, which, in many places on the British front were only 30 or 40 yards apart.

The Germans were the first to begin underground workings, and before the end of 1914 there were at least two definite cases of mines being exploded under our trenches. These gave rise to reports from all parts of the front of suspected mining, and R.E. units, assisted by hastily formed Brigade Mining Sections, commenced work on shallow defensive galleries.

2. FORMATION OF UNITS.

The first recorded demand for special Mining Units came from the IV. Corps at the end of December, 1914, and this was warmly supported by the G.O.C. First Army, who asked at the same time for a similar unit to work on the I. Corps front at Givenchy. Just previous to this, a suggestion had been made to the War Office by

Major J. Norton Griffiths, M.P. (now Sir J. Norton Griffiths, K.C.B., D.S.O.) that coal miners and other underground workers should be specially enlisted for this purpose, great stress being laid on the secrecy and silence with which professional " clay kickers " could work. About the middle of February Major Norton Griffiths was officially authorized to enlist a party of miners for service in France, the first idea being that sections should be formed and attached to Field Companies ; but it was very soon agreed that they should be in distinct units with their own establishment. Major Norton Griffiths at once went to work with the most remarkable energy. The War Office approved the formation of eight companies on the 19th of February, and on the 20th of February the first party of miners actually arrived in France to form the nucleus of the 170th Company, R.E. Five days previously these men were employed on sewer work at Liverpool. Within another fortnight five companies existed in embryo, and were at once engaged in active mining.

Mining became more and more prevalent on all parts of the front, and new companies were continually being formed. Approval was given for the 178th and 179th Companies early in July, 1915, and at the end of the same month the formation of the 180th, 181st and 182nd Companies was authorized. By the end of June, 1916, there were actually 25 Imperial Companies and seven Overseas Companies actively engaged in mining operations, the total force employed in this work being approximately 25,000 men.

The numbers of the Imperial Tunnelling Companies were as follows :—170th, 171st, 172nd, 173rd, 174th, 175th, 176th, 177th, 178th, 179th, 180th, 181st, 182nd, 183rd, 184th, 185th, 250th, 251st, 252nd, 253rd, 254th, 255th, 256th, 257th, 258th.

Overseas Companies.—About the end of 1915 an offer was accepted from the Canadian Government to form two Tunnelling Companies in Canada, a third one being formed meanwhile in France. The 3rd Canadian Tunnelling Company accordingly came into being during December, 1915, the personnel being obtained from Canadian units already in France ; the 1st and 2nd Canadian Tunnelling Companies arrived some three months later.

An Australian Mining Corps consisting of a Headquarters and three Companies arrived in France in May, 1916 ; the 1st and 2nd Companies were allotted to the Second Army, and the 3rd Company to the First Army, whilst the opportunity was taken to make use of the Headquarters in various capacities.

Three additional Tunnelling Companies arrived from Australia in July, 1916, and were distributed as reinforcements for the existing Companies, to raise them to the higher establishment. The increasing use of power plants in connection with mining operations led to the formation in September, 1916, of the Australian Electrical and

Mechanical, Mining, and Boring Company, the nucleus of which was mainly drawn from the original Headquarters of the Australian Mining Corps. A New Zealand Engineers Tunnelling Company commenced work in France early in 1916, and was raised to the higher establishment in September, 1917.

3. SPECIAL MINING STAFF AND ESTABLISHMENTS.

In December, 1915, it was decided to provide the necessary machinery for the application and control of mining personnel, sanction being given by the War Office for the appointment of an Inspector of Mines at G.H.Q., and a Controller of Mines at each Army Headquarters.

Owing to the number of gas casualties caused in the early days of mining, training in mine rescue work was commenced in October, 1915, followed by training in the use of mine listening instruments.

The first Mine School was established in France by the First Army in July, 1916, for the instruction of the personnel of Tunnelling Companies in all branches of mine warfare ; a detailed description of the work carried out at this School is contained in Part III. Similar schools were opened at later dates by the other Armies.

WAR ESTABLISHMENTS.—The establishment of Tunnelling Companies underwent various changes, the approved personnel for the earliest Companies only amounting to nine officers, and 283 other ranks, numbers which were very soon found, especially as regards officers, to be totally inadequate. The following are the War Establishments as finally approved :—

Inspector of Mines.

Brigadier-General (Inspector of Mines)	1
Major (Assistant Inspector of Mines)	1
Captain (Assistant Inspector of Mines)	1
Major or Captain (Mechanical Engineer)	1
Major (Geologist)	1
Medical Officer (Mine Rescue)	1
Total	6
Clerks and Draughtsmen	8

Controller of Mines.

Lieutenant-Colonel (Controller of Mines)	1
Captain (Adjutant)	1
Total	2
Clerks and Draughtsmen	2

Tunnelling Companies. Higher Establishment.

Major (Officer Commanding)	1
Captain (Adjutant)	1
Captains (Os.C. Sections)	4
Subalterns·	12
Medical Officer (Attached)	1
Total	19
Other ranks	550

Tunnelling Companies. Lower Establishment.

Major (Officer Commanding)	1
Captain (Adjutant)	1
Captains (Os.C. Sections)	4
Subalterns	12
Medical Officer (Attached)	1
Total	19
Other ranks	325

Army Mine School.

Captain (Officer Commanding)	1
Subaltern	1
Total	2
Serjeants (Instructors)	2
Corporals (Instructors)	3
Sappers	3
Total	8

Australian Electrical and Mechanical, Mining and Boring Company.

Electrical and Mechanical Company.   Boring Section.

Major (Officer Commanding) ...	1	Subaltern	1
Captain	1		
Subalterns	4		
Total	6		
Other ranks 227		Other ranks ...	50

Attached Infantry.—The question of provision of unskilled labour, in order that the skilled miners should be employed to the best advantage, was always a difficult one. At first the numbers provided were dependent solely on the decision of local Commanders ; but after various changes, it was settled, under orders from G.H.Q., to attach permanently to each Lower Establishment Company 216 infantry, who were drawn from professional miners serving with infantry battalions. This system worked well, and many of the men became highly skilled after a short time. This number was of course not sufficient to do all the carrying and miscellaneous work that was necessary when a Company was working at full pressure, and working parties up to 500 or 600 a day had still to be found by formations in whose area Tunnelling Companies were employed ; so that it was no uncommon thing for the officer commanding a Tunnelling Company to be in control of 1,000 men.

4. DISTRIBUTION OF DUTIES.

The Inspector of Mines at G.H.Q. was charged with the following duties :—

(a). Preparation, under the instructions of the General Staff, of mining schemes which were intended to have a bearing on the principal operations of the campaign, and examination of mining schemes prepared by Armies.

(b). Inspection, for the information of the Commander-in-Chief, of the progress of all mining work.

(c). Advising the Engineer-in-Chief on general questions affecting the personnel, organization, and equipment of the Tunnelling Companies.

The appointment of Inspector of Mines had the most important influence on the co-ordination and systematic development of mining work. Before this time, reports of work had been rendered by Tunnelling Companies to the Division under which they were working, and were forwarded through the usual channels to the General Staff at G.H.Q. From the beginning of 1916, copies of all reports were forwarded through Controllers to the Inspector of Mines, who rendered periodical summaries for the information of the General Staff. A system was instituted under which matters of general interest in any of these reports were circulated to the whole of the tunnelling units, as well as Intelligence Reports and Notes on Technical subjects. These were issued in a regular series of " Mining Notes,"* which continued right up to the beginning of the final British advance in August, 1918.

The Controller of Mines at an Army Headquarters was the principal executive officer for mining operations, and was charged with the following duties :—

(a).—Under the Inspector of Mines : The preparation of mining schemes connected with operations initiated by G.H.Q.,

---

* For classified list of these Notes see *Appendix* C to article on Organization of Engineer Intelligence 'and Information," in the February, 1920, number of the R.E. Journal.

for the technical control and training of the Tunnelling Companies and Army Mine Schools, and for the supply of special mining stores.

(b).—Under the Chief Engineer of the Army :

(i).—The preparation of all mining schemes, and for the distribution and direction of work of the mining personnel allotted to the Army.

(ii).—For the design of tunnelled shelters in the Army area, and for the distribution of labour and stores allotted to the Army for this purpose.

(c).—Advising the Chief Engineer on all questions connected with the appointment, transfer and promotions of officers, on the selection of officers and men from other arms of the service who might wish to join the Tunnelling Companies, so far as the Army to which he was appointed was affected, the grant of half-yearly honours and rewards, and the allotment of leave.

(d).—Assisting the Chief Engineer in the preparation and execution of demolition schemes, if required.

5. GEOLOGISTS.

No Geological establishment ever existed in the British Army. Amongst the headquarters of the Australian Mining Corps, referred to in para. 2, was a distinguished Professor of Geology, who had a large share in raising this Corps. For some time he acted, under the Inspector of Mines, as adviser in Geology to the Controllers of Mines of the First, Second, and Third Armies, and in September, 1916, he was appointed to the Engineer-in-Chief's Staff at G.H.Q., acting during the rest of the war as Geological Adviser to the Inspector of Mines. There was already one geologist attached to the Engineer-in-Chief's Staff, whose work had been chiefly in connection with water supply.

A complete knowledge of the geological nature of the ground to be worked in is essential, particularly as regards water level, for in some parts of the chalk country the difference between summer and winter water levels varies as much as 30 feet. The vital importance of this point is apparent, and it actually happened that deep level galleries were temporarily lost by both sides, on account of insufficient knowledge of this subject during their period of construction.

As a result of investigations by the geological advisers, sufficient data were obtained to enable a table to be drawn up for use by the various Tunnelling Companies, showing where the water level would rise, on the assumption of a maximum rainfall during winter, when evaporation is at a minimum.

The tables were prepared in September, 1916, and proved of the utmost value. As an example, it may be mentioned that at the end of that year the water level rose 18 feet in 15 days at a part of the line near Loos, a possibility for which the tunnellers were prepared, thanks to the geological tables.

So successful was the work of the geologists that they rapidly became an integral part of the mining organization, and their work varied from advising on the best depths and types of ground for all mining work, to investigating the sources of material discovered in captured German pill-boxes.

From captured German records it is clear that they considered a full geological knowledge of high importance. Their organization was a much more elaborate one than ours, and each German Army possessed a complete geological staff, which was responsible not only for advising on suitable sites for mining and dug-out work, but was also responsible for all questions of water supply, location of positions, and the provision of raw material, such as phosphates, road-metal, etc., for the needs of the Army.

A full account of the work of the British Geological Staff is contained in a separate Volume.

6. Personnel and Pay.

Officers.—The officers selected for commissions in the Tunnelling Companies were, generally speaking, mining engineers of wide experience, recruited from all parts of the world, largely by the efforts of the Institution of Mining and Metallurgy, and the Institution of Mining Engineers. Their varied experience proved of the utmost value in all operations of the companies.

Other Ranks.—Owing to the highly specialized nature of the work to be undertaken, special rates of pay were given, as under, which included all emoluments other than rations, clothing, necessaries, and separation allowances :—

    (*a*). *Tunnellers.*—Sappers, 6s. ; Lance-Corporals, 6s. 4d. ; 2nd Corporals, 7s. ; Corporals, 7s. 4d. ; Serjeants, 8s. 1d. per diem.

    (*b*). *Tunnellers' Mates.*—As Sappers, 1s. 2d. per diem, with Engineer pay at 1s. per diem.

The high pay of sappers graded as " Tunnellers " led to a good deal of difficulty. Qualifications were laid down locally, but it was very difficult to reduce men who had been enlisted as " Tunnellers," and who, on trial, failed to come up to the necessary standard ; at the same time, the large number of men sent from England on the higher rate left comparatively few vacancies for equally qualified men drawn from units already in France.

Military mining became a highly technical business, and no man could really be considered a qualified " Tunneller " until he had had

B

some experience of work in the trenches.   Had it been possible to foresee all the circumstances at the time, it would probably have been more satisfactory to have enlisted all men on the lower rate, with the opportunity of rising to the higher rate when properly qualified ; but in view of the urgency of the need, and trade difficulties, this hardly appears to have been a practical proposition in 1915.

Working pay at 1s. per day was authorized for infantry soldiers engaged in mining, and attached to Tunnelling Companies.

Miscellaneous.—Command pay was granted at the following rates :—

Controller of Mines.—5s. per diem.

O.C.   Tunnelling   Company.—Companies under   250,   *nil* ; 250–550, 2s. per diem ; over 550, 3s. per diem.

Chapter II.

DEVELOPMENT OF WORK.

7. Distribution of First Five Companies.

The distribution for work of the first five Companies that were formed is given in the following table, which is a copy of a report compiled at G.H.Q. at the end of March, 1915, from the earliest progress reports which were sent in :—

No. of Company.	At work with.	Strength Officers.	O.R.*	Progress of work.
170	1st Corps	7	80	Givenchy, two headings with connecting galleries—defensive work (16. 3. 15). Latest report (1. 4. 15) gives one heading only, which has been driven 50 ft. ; distance of objective not stated. Cuinchy, three headings with connecting galleries ; No. 1 abandoned, No. 2 driven 216 ft., and No. 3 driven 210 ft., and distant 20 ft. and 10 ft. only from objectives on 1. 4. 15. Work in 1st Div. section has not progressed on account of the difficulties of ground.
173	4th Corps	6	77	Four mines N.E. of Fauquissart started on 3rd and 5th March; ground very wet (16. 3. 15). Two progressing, one driven 110 ft., the other 91 ft., with 380 ft. and 349 ft. still to go (1. 4. 15). Two mines opposite Rue du Bois in sand, which presents considerable difficulty ; objective a house 80 yds. distant occupied by enemy (16. 3. 15).

* Excluding men attached from local units.

No. of Company.	At work with.	Strength Officers.	O.R.*	Progress of work.
174	3rd Corps	5	117	One promising mine at Houplines (16. 3. 15). Six galleries at Le Ruage; No. 1 abandoned, No. 2 44 ft. in, No. 3 40 ft. in, (Nos. 2 and 3 connected by cross gallery), No. 5 108 ft. in, No. 6 136 ft. in, No. 7 just begun (2. 4. 15). Distance of objective not given. In addition certain listening galleries have been driven for defensive purposes.
172	2nd Corps	8	121	Facing Messines Wytschaete Ridge. One mine sunk at trench No. 12 in 5th Div. had to be abandoned. Fresh try being made elsewhere. (16. 3. 15). Mines sunk at trenches G. 1, E. 2, and 14 A. in 3rd Div. section. First promises well, 25 ft. in on 2. 4. 15, objective a farm 120 ft. distant held by Germans. A third attempt is being made at E. 2, heading started on 2. 4. 15. The mine in 14 A. is in difficult ground, objective Hill 76, distance not stated. Mine 15 (N. 36 a.) 23 ft. in on 2. 4. 15, distance of objective not stated.
171	5th Corps	6	165	Work hampered by difficulties of ground in 27th Div. section. Work in 28th Div. section: three galleries in trenches 43, 45, and 32, abandoned on account of bad ground (16. 3. 15). Three galleries in trenches 39, 40, and 49 being pushed forward, objective Hill 60, just N. of Ypres-Comines Rd. Mine No. 1 at St. Eloi (0. 2. 3) started on 25. 3. 15. heading 73 ft. 6 in. in on 2. 4. 15.

* Excluding men attached from local units.

8. EARLY PHASES OF MINING.

Plates I. and II. are copies of the first mining plans made by the 170th Company, the survey of the trench lines being made for the purpose by officers of the Company. All these mines were very shallow, rarely going deeper than 20 feet, and frequently not more than 12 to 15 feet.

This earliest phase of mining may be described as " individual ", depending mainly on the feelings of the Infantry above. The proximity of the trench lines made local objectives, such as important salients, buildings which gave shelter to snipers or machine guns, etc., tempting, and there was frequently conflict of interests between troops who asked only for protection from possible German mines, and those who demanded the destruction of points in the German line. This resulted naturally in a multitude of small underground workings, started in haste, and as often as not, blown with even greater haste. Demands made on the Companies very soon became impossible to comply with, and officers and men were overworked.

Major Norton Griffiths mentions in his diary under the date 15th May, 1915, that during an hour's visit to the C.O. of one Tunnelling Company, three urgent wires arrived from three far separated points on the front, asking for immediate despatch of listeners owing to reported German mining. The listening at this time was primitive, and Commanding Officers always expected it to be done by Tunnelling Officers.

This unorganized or individual method of work was further encouraged by the idea that scattered mining operations all along the front would tend to bewilder the enemy, and conceal the actual objectives of a large offensive which was then under consideration ; thus offensive mines became of primary interest, and in a very short time reports on defensive systems were given up, only those with some definite objective being considered of importance.

The most important offensive operation at this period was that carried out under the 28th Division against Hill 60, and is described in the next chapter.

An interesting example of a successful mining offensive against an enemy salient is illustrated in *Photographs* (I.) and (II.), which show the effect of two mines, each 2,500 lbs. charge, on the Ploegsteert Wood front.

About this same time the urgent necessity for keeping accurate records of all mining work became apparent, and special efforts were made to provide Tunnelling Companies with proper staff of draughtsmen.

The number of shallow defensive systems increased at an enormous pace, the Cuinchy front in June being described as a mass of craters on a front of nearly 1,000 yards, a remarkable development from the three shafts shown on *Plate* I., in the course of little over three months.

On the front that was gradually taken over from the French, similar mining conditions were found, defects of our own systems being exaggerated by narrower galleries, and innumerable small defensive craters close to our own lines.

All through this summer the need for carefully thought out tactical mining schemes in connection with infantry operations above ground was being insisted on by the R.E. Staff at G.H.Q.

During August the first attempt at a deep system was made by the Second Army, when the "Berlin Tunnel" was started against Hill 60 at a depth of about 60ft., but the mistake was made here of going down by means of a long incline, instead of getting straight through the water-logged clay by means of a vertical tub (a much later development), which led to endless trouble with water, and the continual employment of very large pumping parties. Further details about this system will be found in Chapter VI. During August also a scheme on a large scale for the underground attack of the Messines–Wytschaete Ridge was worked out.

After the Battle of Loos in September the active mining front was considerably extended, as the Germans at once commenced mining at the Hohenzollern Redoubt and the Quarries, whilst about the same time the British Third Army took over a broad front from the French stretching as far south as the river Somme, and the German underground workings on the southern part of this front were reported to be deeper and better organized than anything yet met with.

About this same time, the urgent necessity for economizing the number of men employed on listening, and for improving the listening systems and apparatus, became very evident. Special listening schools were suggested, and central listening systems advocated.

9. CO-OPERATION WITH INFANTRY.

During the winter much time and study were expended on improvement of methods, both below and above ground, and considerable training was carried out in the occupation and consolidation of craters. This is a subject which belongs to the study of infantry tactics, and hardly comes within the scope of a history of mining; nevertheless it had been one of outstanding importance during this year of individual mining enterprises, which demanded a very close and most intimate co-operation between the Tunnellers and Infantry. Perhaps the most important point in this connection was the danger of occupying the forward lip of a crater for more than a very brief period, until the defensive galleries had been sufficiently advanced to protect it from enemy underground attack ; but even after a year's crater fighting this point was not always realized.

Another danger that was not always remembered on active mining fronts, was that of siting new trenches without first consulting the local Mining Officer, and there were several cases of new trenches being dug to cut off a salient, or for other reasons, which were immediately blown by the enemy.

An example of lack of co-operation may be quoted. During October there had been several changes of Divisions on a certain front where extensive deep work was going on, in preparation for an offensive. An entirely new system of holding the front was planned, which involved giving up parts of the line, and only holding posts which were strongly wired in. The scheme was already started when it was discovered that the main entrance to a deep system of dug-outs was in the abandoned area. When this was pointed out, it was suggested that the Tunnellers should move their shaft. The existing shaft being over 90 feet deep, it is needless to say that the suggestion was not adopted.

One more point may be mentioned, and that is the possibility of gas remaining in a surface crater for some time after a blow. If the mine is well over-charged and primed, and the explosives have not deteriorated, there should be complete detonation and no gas ; but the danger was always possible, and required explanation to all Infantry raiding or attacking parties.

The appointment of an Inspector of Mines with special mining staffs for each Army, at the beginning of 1916, had a great effect on the development of properly organized mine systems, and from this time onwards can be traced the gradual but steady advance in British mining methods, which gave the British miner the opportunity to prove his complete superiority to such good purpose that by the autumn of 1917 the enemy was reduced underground to a state of absolute passivity on the entire front.

10. MINING ON FIRST ARMY FRONT, 1916.

During the first few months of 1916, the most active mining front was the southern portion of the First Army from Hohenzollern to Carency. In the last week of April, twenty-five mines were fired on this part of the front—13 by the enemy, 12 by us.

Plate III. shows the mining systems on the S. part of the Hohenzollern, and illustrates graphically the intense activity since the battle of Loos.

In the middle of May the enemy captured a salient known as the Kink (S.E. of Hohenzollern), with a fairly complete mining system, and a number of miners. The mines were shallow—16 feet to 23 feet, owing to the water level, and the shafts were all inclines towards the enemy, who therefore did not obtain any great advantage underground.

In the last week of May, 36 mines were blown on this same front—17 by the enemy, 19 by us, whilst in the week ending 1st July, just previous to the Fourth Army attack on the Somme, no less than 51 mines were blown on the First Army front—28 by the British and 23 by the Germans.

Towards the end of July a most successful mining operation was carried out at the Double Crassier, South of Loos. Six charges were blown under the Southern (German) Crassier, which destroyed the whole of the German position from X to Y (see *Plate* IV.). A large gap was created which gave good observation from the British position on the Northern Crassier over German lines ; the German trench A.A. was filled in, together with their mining shafts, and they were compelled to re-start mining from B.B., 100 yards further back.

During all this close fighting underground many cases of heroism occurred amongst the miners, most of which will remain—as must always be the case in war—unrecorded. In Part II. will be found a description of various incidents connected with life-saving by trained rescue men. Just two examples will be given here, both of occurrences at Givenchy.

The first has been described as the bravest action of the war. A shaft in one of the Givenchy mines collapsed ; there was a rush of water, and five men were shut in. The rescue party managed to clear a small passage-way down to the bottom from which they got out three men. Of the other two, one was injured, and being a very big man it was found impossible to get him out through the hole. The fifth man, Sapper Hackett, could have clambered out, but stedfastly refused to leave his mate, who needed attention, and in spite of persuasion by the rescue party, he remained. Desperate efforts were made to enlarge the opening, but there was another fall and rush of clay, and both men were killed. A posthumous V.C. was awarded to this gallant miner.

In the second example damage by an enemy bombardment temporarily stopped the pumps working. Water rose rapidly, and filled to the roof a portion of gallery which sloped down towards the shaft, so cutting off air from a party of men who were at the face. Three volunteers dived through the water a distance of 30 feet to reach the pump house, and after eighteen hours work they succeeded in re-starting ventilation, and effected a rescue.

II. Conditions Towards end of 1916 and early 1917.

During September a decided movement on the part of enemy miners was noticeable, large numbers apparently being withdrawn from the First Army front. This was thought to have been due to nervousness on other fronts, or to shortage of men following on the Battle of the Somme.*

The first week in October was the quietest on record, only two mines being blown on the First Army front, and a total of 12 on the whole British front.

The average weekly footage, which had been 16,000 at the beginning of August, fell during October to just over 11,000, due to quieter conditions generally, and to the smaller working parties provided.

About this period, Tunnelling Companies first began to be regularly employed on the construction of dug-outs, nine companies on the Fourth and Fifth Armies' fronts being almost entirely occupied with this work.

The principal features at the end of the year 1916 were :—

(a).—The state of practical stalemate on the old mining front.
(b).—The development of Infantry subways.

The old defensive mining systems were maintained mainly by pumpers and listeners, whilst deep offensive schemes were going on steadily on the Second Army front, and to a certain extent on the south of the First, and north of the Third Armies' fronts.

Mining policy was by this time thoroughly controlled from G.H.Q., and consequently these schemes, which required many months for their completion, were enabled to be carried through unchecked, in spite of difficulties which were still apt to occur with formation Commanders who considered that Tunnelling units in their area should be at their disposal for new schemes.

The number of men employed underground caused grave concern to the General Staff, and, with the exception of the main offensive schemes just mentioned, strict orders were given that work should be confined to absolutely necessary defensive measures.

The enemy had undoubtedly reduced the number of his men working underground, but made up for this by increased activity above ground, mine shafts being continually subjected to trench mortar fire and raids.

Work was continued in the early part of 1917 mainly on subways and dug-outs. By the end of February nearly 20 miles of subways had been completed on the First, Second, and Third Armies' fronts.

Plate V. shows the details of the Hulluch system of subways.

A strange accident happened during February in Wrexham Tunnel at the Double Crassier. The leads from a power plant were cut by shell fire ; the electrician joined up what he thought to be the broken leads, and started his engine, which immediately fired two

* Ludendorff, in his memoirs, mentions that about this time 125,000 men were sent back to Germany for industrial reasons ; and in May and June, 1917, 50,000 miners were released on the urgent demand of the civil Government.

charges—one at each end of the tunnel. These charges had evidently been laid for defensive purposes some months before, but at this time no one was aware of their existence, and there was no record on paper. Fortunately, the damage done was not very serious, but a useful lesson was taught.

12. CHANGES IN EMPLOYMENT OF TUNNELLING COMPANIES AFTER GERMAN RETIREMENT.

During March, the withdrawal of the enemy south of Arras dislocated the schemes of work on the Third and Fifth Armies' fronts. This is dealt with in Chapter V.

During the enemy's withdrawal, the Tunnelling Companies of the Fourth and Fifth Armies were found especially useful for exploring and removing enemy traps. Several delay action mines went up after periods varying from 8 to 28 days, the best known case being the Bapaume Town Hall, which was totally destroyed during the night of the 25th March—eight days after the occupation by British troops. No crater was formed, and the charge appears to have been concealed in the cellars, which had been converted into lavishly furnished dug-outs, and probably had been used as an enemy Headquarters. They were left in a condition to invite occupation by a similar British unit, but the invitation was not accepted.

After the successful attacks at Arras and Vimy Ridge, the extent of mining areas was still further reduced, and companies were employed on fresh miscellaneous duties, such as recovery of blown wells, road repairs, etc.

At the end of April, 1917, the distribution of Tunnelling Companies was as follows :—

Service.	Equivalent number of Companies.	Percentage
Mining, subways, deep dug-outs, maintenance and listening (N. of Hill 70) ...	$16\frac{1}{2}$	51
Roads (chiefly Vimy–Arras front)	8	25
Recovery of enemy dug-outs, investigation of enemy mining schemes, salvage, etc. (Vimy–Arras front) ...	$2\frac{3}{4}$	9
Reconnaissances for enemy traps, and miscellaneous field works (Fourth and Fifth Armies' fronts) ...	$3\frac{3}{4}$	12
Light Railways	1	3
Total	32	100

The examination of the enemy workings on the Arras-Vimy front showed that their extent was great, but execution and lay-out comparatively poor, and costly in labour. They had shallow and deep systems both on much the same level as our own. A considerable amount of good plant was found. On the whole, the enemy work on this front was decidedly inferior to that in the Somme area, in fact it was surprisingly bad, in view of the anxiety that it had caused us in earlier days. One of the most striking features observed in looking back from the enemy posts was the visibility of our own spoil dumps, especially from the subway systems. Practically the whole of our position on the Vimy front had been completely overlooked by the enemy from a crater in their possession, and the spoil dumps are described as standing up like monuments. There is little wonder that the Germans became nervous, and showed their anxiety by consistent shelling round shaft heads and workings.

The main interest as regards actual mining now centred on the Messines front, and there were many anxious moments before the 7th of June came, and, with it, the successful termination of the greatest mining enterprise of the war.

Subsequent to the Messines operations, which are fully described in Chapter VI., the enemy became highly nervous, and blew a series of 10 mines at Railway Wood, none of which caused the slightest damage to our workings, or casualties to personnel, although the enemy lines appeared to suffer considerably. The German wireless reported that these mines " played havoc with the English position "—actually, we never had any offensive mines in this particular length of front, and the German work was quite wasted.

On the Messines front an enemy deep system was found, which would have been bound, in a short time, to have discovered, and probably wrecked, our own.

During the first week in July not a single mine was blown by either side.

At Hill 70, where some of the most difficult mining on the front had been carried on, most of the German system was captured on the 24th July. The position here had always been one of most peculiar difficulties, and it was only by most strenuous efforts, and great determination on the part of the miners, that the position had been maintained. *Plate* VI. shows the German systems. Hill 70 came completely into our hands on the 15th August, after which date there was no longer any mining north of the Lys, or south of Hulluch.

Plate VII. is the Cuinchy sector, which was the first active mining field on the British front, and remained in our hands throughout the war. An examination of the crater dates shows that a state of absolute stalemate was reached in the early summer of 1916. The *Plate* has been completed by the addition of the German galleries as surveyed after the final British advance.

At the end of August all permanently attached infantry were ordered to the Base, thus reducing Tunnelling Companies to about half their former strength.

In September the connection between the Hohenzollern and Auchy systems was completed, and it was thus possible to patrol underground from the La Bassée Canal to Hulluch, a distance of about four miles, whilst much economy was effected in listening and electric lighting personnel. Listening arrangements had been gradually improved, and during this autumn central listening systems were completed on the whole of the First Army front.

Some interesting work was done during the summer and autumn in the Coastal Sector, at and near Nieuport. The French had decided that subterranean work in the sand dunes was quite impossible. The British tunnelling officers were convinced, however, that the difficulties could be overcome, and after trial shafts had been sunk, both subways and dug-outs were successfully completed, in spite of the greatest difficulties with water and running sand.

At the time when our front line was on the east of the Yser river, two galleries were being run out against the two important salients of the German line, and a subway was in fair way to completion from the river to the front line. The sudden attack on this sector resulted in heavy casualties to the miners, but the subway was a means of saving a considerable number of the Infantry garrison.

Between 3,000 and 4,000 ft. run of tunnels was driven at Nieuport itself, with numerous chambers, and lit by electric light.

The following table gives the numbers of mines blown in 1916 and 1917 on the British and First Army fronts.

	On all British fronts.		On British First Army Front.	
	British.	German.	British.	German.
1916	750	696	466	385
1917	117	106	48	39
Total	867	802	514	424
Most active month.—				
June, 1916 ...	101	126	79	73

Plate VIII. shows the portions of the British front on which minefields existed in June, 1916, when mining was at its height.

During the winter 1917–18 practically the whole of the Tunnelling personnel was employed on dug-out work, in addition to the extension of the subway system at Hill 70, and opening up old caves.

Courses in dug-out work were conducted by the Tunnelling Companies during the winter for the other arms, the R.A. especially being trained so as to be able to do their own work. The main difficulty at this time was the shortage of unskilled labour.

The distribution of the Tunnelling Companies just before the great German attack on March 21st, 1918, was as follows :—

Armies.	Forward Zone. Sections.	Battle Zone. Sections.	Rear Zone. Sections.	
First	10	18	—	(7 Companies)
Second ...	17	19	—	(9 ,,)
Third	5½	16	6½	(7 ,,)
Fifth	½	20½	7	(7 ,,)

Total, 30 Companies, of which the equivalent of 27½ were employed solely on construction of deep dug-outs.

There were no further developments in Tunnelling work ; the employment of the Tunnelling Companies during the rest of 1918 is described in Chapter VIII.

Some of the more interesting of the minor tunnelling enterprises, as well as certain incidents connected with underground warfare, will be described in the next Chapter.

CHAPTER III.

SPECIAL FEATURES DURING TRENCH WARFARE, 1915-16.

13. HILL 60. (See *Plate* IX.).

The earliest mining enterprise of any magnitude, in conjunction with definite Infantry operations, was undertaken against the commanding position east of Ypres, known as Hill 60. This work was organized and carried through by the 28th Division, labour being provided at first from a Territorial Field Company (mostly Northumberland miners), and later by miners drawn from the Monmouthshire Infantry, assisted in the last stages by newly enlisted coal miners from England.

Work was begun on shafts M.1 and M.2 on the 8th March, and was completed on the 10th April, giving an average daily progress of 9 ft. Both these shafts were 12 ft. deep and 4 ft. 6 ins. square in section. The galleries were to commence with :—

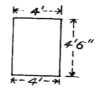

which were reduced to :—

and the branches were further reduced to :—

but this final section was found to be too small, and caused great trouble when the mines were being laid.

M.3 was an old French shaft, only 3 ft. × 2 ft. 6 ins. in section; about 60 ft. of 3 ft. 3 ins. × 2 ft. 3 ins. gallery existed, but was in very bad condition, having many changes of direction and level, and full of corpses.

The soil was good hard sand, and would probably have stood alone, but the galleries were " shored " with frames and sheeting for protection against shake from shell fire. The length of the French gallery was cased and framed.

Chambers.—

M.1, M.1 (a).—3 ft. 6 ins. × 3 ft. 6 ins. × 3 ft. 6 ins. wooden boxes—charge 2,700 lbs. gunpowder.

M.2, M.2 (a).—3ft. 6 ins. × 3 ft. 6 ins. × 3 ft. 6 ins. wooden boxes—charge 2,000 lbs. gunpowder.

M.3, M.3 (a).—Charges laid direct in galleries—500 lbs. guncotton.

The chambers for M.1 and M.2 charges were cut out on both sides of the gallery; boxes were lined with service waterproof sheets; charging was done with 100 lb. bags of powder straight out of the barrel; these were found very heavy for carrying and packing and it is doubtful whether time required for re-filling into 50 lb. bags would not have been well spent.

Tamping.—In every case, except M.3, with sandbags :—

10 feet sandbags	
10 ,, air space	
10 ,, sandbags	50 feet in all.
10 ,, air space	
10 ,, sandbags	

Firing arrangements.—Each of the two charges in each gallery were fired in series, and had double sets of electric leads in case one failed, and each charge had two powder fuzes on each circuit (so that four fuzes had to be fired in series). In addition to the electric firing arrangements, Y-shaped pieces of instantaneous fuze were laid to each pair of charges, with 20 ft. safety fuze attached, and these were duplicated, so that in all there were four separate means of firing. The electric leads were marked with bits of coloured wool, and were run down the galleries suspended on screw hooks, carefully pegged into the parados of the trenches, and finally led into the firing dug-out. A separate officer did the work in connection with each pair of charges, and had his own exploder, all three being accommodated in the one dug-out.

Calculation of Charges.—This was uncertain owing to the great difficulties of survey, which had to be carried out by means of an Abney level, used through a steel loophole plate in the parapet.

M.1 and M.1 (a) were calculated to be 20 ft. to 21 ft. below the enemy trenches; M.2 and M.2 (a), 15 ft.; and M.3 (a) about 12 ft.

The formulæ in the *Manual of Military Engineering* were used, with the co-efficient for hard sand, and aiming for a 60 feet crater.

Craters formed.—M:1 and M.1 (a) were each about 90 ft., and together formed an enormous pit :—

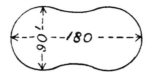

the inside of the hill being literally blown out* ; depth of craters about 30 ft.. The crater formed by M.3 (500 lbs. guncotton) was about 30 ft. across.

Proximity of Enemy.—The enemy was heard working very near the M.3 shaft on April 2nd, and seemed so close that it was feared he might break into our gallery at any time. A charge of 250 lbs. guncotton (increased to 500 lbs. just before firing) was laid as a precaution, but not to be fired except in emergency.

Work on this gallery was stopped, and a practically untamped charge of guncotton laid as silently as possible.

On the 16th April Germans were again heard very close to the junction of M.3 and M.3 (a), and it was subsequently learnt from prisoners that the enemy had intended to blow Trench 38 two days later than our own blow.

Notes on tools, etc.—Ventilation was very difficult : the service blower was found to be much too noisy, and shift was made with blacksmiths' bellows fitted to indiarubber hosepipe.

Lighting was by candles until the mines were charged, then ordinary electric hand torches were used, but were found troublesome, as the batteries lasted such a very short time.

Spoil was removed on specially made silent trolleys, running on wooden rails. The earth was all filled into sandbags which were built into breastwork, and the work was in this way kept quite secret.

Effect.—The mines were fired on April 17th, and undoubtedly produced a great moral effect, the Infantry attack going over with very few casualties.

Debris flew 200 ft. to 300 ft. high, and up to 200—300 yds. away, but all men had been carefully warned, and only one accident occurred—to a man who against orders watched the effect over the parapet. No one was allowed to enter the galleries until reported free of gas, and Infantry were warned not to go down into the craters

---

* In view of later blows this description may seem exaggerated ; it accurately represents, however, the impression that was formed at the time.

for at least half an hour after capture. Two R.E., who entered M.3 shaft without orders 36 hours after the explosion, were killed by gas, due no doubt to the large charge of guncotton used.

The arrangements made for this enterprise have been described in some detail, as they were the first of their kind, and were based on text book teaching, without previous practical experience. The success of the mines was unquestionable, but, from a tactical point of view, the attack was on too limited a scale, and the captured position was rendered untenable by enemy artillery fire.

Plate IX. is a copy of a rough sketch made from memory by the officer who was in actual charge of the mining work.

14. St. Eloi (*Plate* X.).

This was the scene of continuous mining and counter-mining for over a year.

On the 14th March, 1915, the Germans exploded a mine under our line, and captured the whole mound, together with our mine shaft. Mining was re-started at once by a Field Company, and carried on by a Tunnelling Company, two offensive galleries being run out from salients in our new line against the enemy trenches, and against a house which was reputed to conceal snipers.

During the next few months both sides were continually having to blow small charges.

On July 5th one of our offensive galleries, 260 ft. out, broke into a German gallery, and a camouflet was fired. The Germans were heard working underneath us the next day, so work was concentrated on the other gallery, against the snipers' house—two charges (1,200 lbs. and 1,500 lbs. ammonal) were fired on July 10th, completely destroying the house. After this, the enemy was continually blowing defensive mines short of our trenches.

During August a new offensive system at 50–60 ft. depth was started, and was considerably elaborated towards the end of the year as retaliation for the German blows at The Bluff.

In January the Germans again blew a big mine at The Bluff, and a definite offensive above and below ground against the St. Eloi position was prepared in reply.

On the 27th March, 1916, six mines were simultaneously fired under the German salient. The charges were respectively 1,800, 31,000, 15,000, 13,500, 12,000, 600, a total of 73,900 lbs. The enemy front line trenches were completely destroyed over a front of about 450 yds., and the Infantry advanced and dug in 200—300 yards beyond the craters. The sequel was somewhat similar to Hill 60 ; intense artillery fire made consolidation of the craters very difficult, and in the end the Germans regained the whole position. There is little doubt that the enemy was better trained, and more

c

successful in the consolidation of crater positions that we were, and this is graphically illustrated by the photographs on *Plate* X, which were taken some time later, and show very clearly the remarkable work that had been done by the enemy.

15. THE BLUFF. (See *Plate* XI.).

The Bluff, which was just within the British line, consisted of an irregularly shaped mound formed by spoil from the canal cutting, and was about 30 ft. above normal ground level. The Germans blew us here twice in October–November, 1915 ; and in January, 1916, a large blow caused many casualties, and temporarily destroyed the Infantry position.

A proper system of defensive mines was pushed on as rapidly as possible, but the broken ground made work very difficult.

The Infantry position was re-established in March, but on the 25th July the enemy blew four mines simultaneously right behind our trenches, making an enormous crater (450 ft. × 150 ft.) between The Bluff and the canal. Our defensive system was known to be uncertain, and fortunately full warning had been given to the Infantry, who suffered very few casualties. Acting on the warning of the Tunnelling Officer the General Staff had made arrangements for a defensive barrage in the case of a mine being blown by the enemy. The Germans blew, and the barrage came down promptly, which stopped any advance by them to capture the position.

Previous to this we had succeeded, after much trouble, in sinking a deep shaft to 90 ft. below normal level (*i.e.*, 110 ft. below the depth of The Bluff).

At the time of the big blow of 25th July (crater a. on *Plate* XI.) our gallery had reached to within 100 ft. of the near lip of the crater, and about 200 ft. of gallery was damaged, and had to be repaired.

A German gallery was discovered breaking into crater a, and parties of Tunnellers went out several nights running, bored down from the surface, and fired charges with remarkable success, giving us possession of 120 ft. of enemy gallery.

Next, in October, the enemy blew craters c, d, e catching some of our men who were working in the shallow system, but without interrupting the deep work. The enemy system was only 15 ft. deep, and we managed to step down our gallery, and continue the deep workings.

On December 11th, 1916, at about 6.30 p.m., we blew four charges (total, rather over 10,000 lbs.) about 100 ft. apart and connected in series. Ten minutes before the blow two officers and eight men of a Tunnelling Company lay out in a shallow hole in a small crater which had been calculated as directly above the enemy workings.

They started to dig down immediately after the blow, and broke through by midnight to the enemy gallery which they found tamped with sandbags. These were all removed by 10 a.m. next morning, and about mid-day the galleries were entered by men wearing Proto Apparatus—a complete survey was made, and 700 ft. of undestroyed enemy gallery, together with much apparatus, was found to have been captured.

The enemy system was connected to our own shallow workings, and for the first time in its history, The Bluff was reported as absolutely safe from underground attack.

This final operation was a good example of a successful flank attack ; our gallery was well below the enemy, and we succeeded in getting under him and along his front, without being discovered. An interesting sequel occurred here three months later. The enemy was heard working between two of our Listening Posts—we waited for him just too long, and when it was decided to blow, found that he had broken into our gallery and cut the leads. An officer went down and began to untamp, while the enemy was heard untamping on the other side. Both stopped simultaneously when only two layers of sandbags remained between them. The Germans retired hastily, and blew a small mobile charge which partially gassed the officer and three men. We then bored into his gallery from another post, and blew it, destroying the workings and the men at work.

When the position was finally taken on June 7th, 1917, it was found that the enemy had abandoned the original system, and had actually sunk a concrete-lined shaft, 93 ft. deep and 8 ft. diameter, in their support line. This shaft was about 4 ft. out of plumb, and they had just begun to break out a gallery at the bottom. A feature of this shaft was that there was no bomb-proof shelter at the top of the shaft ; it was merely covered with a roof of corrugated iron in a single layer. The construction of this shaft was never suspected by us.

16. Houplines, June, 1915.

A very successful enterprise was carried out here in spite of many difficulties and interruptions. Three offensive galleries had been constructed against a salient and house in the enemy line. When the scheme was nearly complete, the Germans were heard working very close. On the afternoon of the 13th June they were heard immediately above No. 4 (see *Plate* XII.). Nevertheless, it was decided to complete the scheme, and two Tunnelling officers took it in turns to remain continuously listening under the Germans in No. 4.

On the 15th and 16th loud talking was heard, followed on the 17th by silence, which gave the impression that the Germans might blow at any minute.

On the 18th our mines were blown according to plan, five charges being blown at intervals. Nos. 2 and 3 were 100 ft. in under the German parapet, and did specially heavy damage. A camouflet was fired at the point where the German gallery was crossing No. 4, and the German gallery was subsequently entered and examined, several dead Germans being found, and much interesting information obtained.

17. Enemy Entry into Close Timbered Gallery.

A case of enemy miners breaking into a close-timbered gallery within a few feet of a listener aware of the enemy's proximity occurred during February, 1916. Our gallery, as shown on sketch (*Plate* XIII.) had been in contact with the enemy gallery at point (A) and a charge placed. There was solid tamping of 15 ft., an air space of about 5 ft. (B), and then a single row of sandbags. Through this was run a listening tube, (maintaining direct open communication with the German gallery), at the end of which the listener was posted. .

At 10 a.m. on February 11th, the listener heard the enemy removing our gallery timber. He went out to fetch the officers on duty, who were then engaged on another part of the sector. It is uncertain how long altogether the enemy had been working his way through the timber when the officers arrived, but he had penetrated the air space sufficiently to enable him to cut the leads and the listening tube. The officers waited for four hours at the single row of sandbags to hear what the enemy was doing, and they finally began to remove the bags and shot at one of the Germans, whose head appeared through the side of the gallery, wounding him in the jaw. Our men were unable to enter the German gallery, so a charge of 30 lbs. of guncotton was placed inside at the junction and successfully fired. This small charge broke to surface and threw up considerable mine timbers. Our own gallery was little damaged.

18. Experiences of a Tunnelling Company in Main Enemy Gallery.

On 23rd February, 1916, our workings broke into the remaining part of a German gallery destroyed by a charge of guncotton a month previously. Work was continued in the supposed direction of the main enemy gallery, and on March 8th the miners " clay kicking " at the face broke into the top of the German gallery. Two officers, immediately proceeding to the underground magazine, were told that a light had been shown by the enemy through the hole. An emergency charge of 15 lbs. of guncotton was laid on top of the German gallery, tamped with about fifteen sandbags, and was fired. While lighting fuze (two minutes) the enemy was heard apparently trying to enlarge the hole (12.45 p.m.). Three quarters of an hour later the gallery was reported clear of gas, and a further search proved that the blow had formed a chamber (7 ft. in diameter) giving access into the German gallery. Entering, the officer in charge found fragments of one or two Germans, but was affected by gas and had to come out temporarily. Leaving the gallery covered, raiding parties were organized, working with boots off, and carrying four boxes of guncotton. One party went to right and one to the left (5. p.m.). As the former advanced, the enemy turned on the electric lights—but these were connected in parallel, and the officer had cut the leads on his way, so that only the portion occupied by the enemy was in full view. Two Germans were seen coming round the bend in their gallery ; they were fired at and one was seen to fall. Upon pre-arranged signal, parties were then recalled, but one subsequently returned and fired a box of guncotton. During this operation, the lights in enemy portion of gallery were still on, one officer firing at the enemy who was trying to come round the bend.

After the workings had again been reported clear of gas, party returned (8.30 p.m.) and found that the guncotton charge had again made a cavity only. The air was coming through strongly from the enemy side. Another raiding party went forward, this time to a point where, round the turn, the lights were still on and men could be seen moving. Having only 2 min. fuzes, they placed charge of 30 lbs., tamped with German sandbags, and fired.

The workings being again reported clear of gas (1.15 a.m., 9. 3. 16), a party returned to examine galleries. A German mobile charge of about 15 lbs. was found, and a dead German under the debris. The air was still blowing through strongly.

A charge of 240 lbs. guncotton was then carried through the difficult entrance, and the party proceeded until they were fired at with rifles. An officer covered the party while the charge was laid and lightly tamped. It was fired at 4.5 a.m. and, of course, flooded the workings with gas.

The approximate position of the enemy shaft, determined by knowledge of underground workings and by escape of rising gas, was pointed out to Artillery observing officers, and good practice was made upon it by our guns.

No listening apparatus was found. Our miners had been working for five days within 12 ft. of the gallery, and clearly were not discovered until they actually broke into the German workings.

19. ENTRY AND DESTRUCTION OF ENEMY MINES IN CHALK.

Following the explosion of mines under the German trenches on March 2nd, 1916, a raiding party of Tunnellers accompanied the Infantry attack. This party comprised an officer with two N.C.O.'s and eight men. The N.C.O.'s each carried a revolver, electric torch and hatchet, and the men a 15-lb. box of guncotton, with 60 yds. of instantaneous fuze. Detonators were attached but not inserted.

The entrance (*Plate* XIV.) of a German mine was found in the old crater (No. 3 on sketch) which was about 15 ft. deep. The galleries were close-timbered almost throughout with mortise and tenon cases of 9 in. × 2 in. timber giving inside dimensions of 4 ft. 6 in. × 3 ft. The only sign of artificial ventilation was a strong 6-inch diameter galvanized iron pipe from O to H, whilst a 6 inch borehole had been run to surface from X. There were no evidences of tramming. A self-lighting oil hand lamp was found and no sign of candles. There was no electric lighting. Only pick and shovel appear to have been used at the face. The galleries were exceptionally clean and gradients were effected by neatly stepping down the timbers about 2 ft. per set.

The party entered at A and proceeded down a gentle slope to C, placing two sentries at B. From C towards E the gallery was partly wrecked, and at E completely blocked by our explosion of No. 2 crater. On returning to B the party proceeded to W, examining and surveying the side galleries as they proceeded. F—Y was a working face, H—M was wrecked, and at N the tamping and electric leads, from which No. 1 crater had evidently been exploded, were showing. This indicated that 120 ft. of tamping had been used, and clay had been especially brought down for tamping in sandbags and mixed with chalk tamping. From W to O the gallery rose towards the German lines, with a strong draught. As this part of the line was still in German hands, it was considered advisable to destroy this entrance.

A barricade three sandbags thick was first placed, then a charge of 75 lbs. of guncotton, and finally 5 ft. of chalk tamping in sandbags. The charge was fired by two detonators, each with 60 ft. of instantaneous fuze with 4 ft. of time fuze at the end and ignited simultaneously. The place where the charge had been laid was not close timbered, the sets being 4 ft. apart. The ground was chalk with an admixture of clay. The result of the explosion was that a good deal of ground was shaken down, but there was still a way through over the top.

In the meantime, the Germans had recaptured the No. 3 crater, and consequently the entrance A.

The position was serious, as a German charge at E would have destroyed our garrison of No. 2 crater. An incline was therefore started from No. 2 crater to intersect CE. This was successfully done, and an officer and N.C.O. entered. No Germans were encountered, though there were signs that they had been in during the interval.

A charge of 64 lbs. of guncotton was placed at Z untamped.

The ground here was clay and loam, and rather broken by previous explosions. The result was that the timbers were knocked out for 50 ft. and the gallery completely blocked.

At W a charge of 112 lbs. of guncotton was placed, untamped, and exploded. The ground here was chalk, and the result was to bring down a good deal of ground, but at the point of explosion the gallery was merely enlarged to about 7 ft., leaving a clear way through.

The gallery was finally closed at this point by putting a small tunnel of 10 ft. in the side and laying 300 lbs. of ammonal, well tamped. This just blew to the surface and completely sealed the gallery.

20. LISTENING AT GERMAN SHAFT HEAD.

On May 31st, 1916, one of our shallow galleries holed into an enemy shaft head. By means of this direct communication interesting listening results were obtained right up to the time of our firing mines in this, and two other galleries, on June 2nd :—

Date and Time.	Listening Results.	Remarks.
May 31st.		
1 p.m.	Holed into German gallery.	
2 p.m.	Listening with Geophone. Loud laughter and talking—then windlass working, and picking. Interpreter sent for.	German shift comes on. Enemy suspects nothing.
7 p.m.	We fix 2-in. pipe against lagging board and 4 ft. of tamping put in.	
8.5 p.m.	Four or five men sit down opposite pipe. Loud laughter and talking for 30 mins. Stopped by N.C.O. and work begins.	German shift comes on.
11 p.m.	Our interpreter arrives. Pick-work and winch—18 turns up and down.	Shaft is about 36 ft. deep—a total of 50 ft.-60 ft. below ground level.
June 1st.		
12.5 p.m.	Conversation in German—" Who is there? Who is there? Is it the relief? " In English—" Who is there? "	
12.50 a.m. to 1.5 a.m.	Work with pick. 15 mins. of winch.	

Date and Time.	Listening Results.	Remarks.
1.15 a.m.	Winch at work.	
1.45 a.m. to 2.10 a.m.	,, ,, ,,	
2.20 a.m.	Very loud knock.	Timber falling down shaft.
2.50 a.m.	Loud sounds, as if pipe was being touched.	Not understood.
3 a.m.	Voices, and winch starts.	
3.25 a.m. to 4 a.m.	Voices, and winch at work.	
4 a.m.	Conversation in German— " That will soon be deep enough, will it not ? " " Yes —I do not know "—" I will ask the Serjeant-Major."	
5.15 a.m.	Conversation in very low tones.	
5.30 a.m. to 6.15 a.m.	Very loud knocks (12). Continuous work with winch.	Knocking up timber.
6.15 a.m.	Very loud voices. Night shift goes off.	Enemy still un- suspicious.
6 p.m.	Pipe blocked and charge laid (300 lbs. ammonal). Exten- sion fitted to pipe and tamping began.	
9 p.m.	German Officer comes down shaft.	
10. p.m.	German conversation—" Quite right, but it is too heavy." " Very well then, you can have some more people."	Enemy is laying and tamping charges.
11.15 p.m.	Officer comes down and says that men must work more quickly and finish the job. The Germans are unusually quiet to-night.	
June 2nd. 1.15 a.m.	Neighbouring German mine and camouflet fired. Three men working on tamping partly buried, but dug out, and work continued.	Both in shallow system in the clay. They do not affect the shaft.
1 30 a.m.	German conversation not understood.	

Date and Time.	Listening Results.	Remarks.
2.30 a.m.	German conversation—" Well, Bauer, have you found anything ? " " No, sir, nothing at all so far, but they have come further in this direction than I should have thought. We must wait."	Enemy trying to ascertain result of his blow. He may have found an old tamped gallery of ours.
2.45 a.m.	Intermittent conversation in low tones.	
4.15 a.m.	German conversation — two men at winch. " Karl, have you heard from your wife lately ? " " No, she has not written for two weeks." " We shall not get any more leave now." " Why ? " " I have heard it said."	Enemy is satisfied with his blows, but less cheerful than before.
5. a.m.	Working and talking. Not understood. Tamping continued. Nothing heard.	During the morning 93rd Regt. ask 64th if they have been working on the trenches, as something has been heard above the shaft.
9. p.m.	Talking and walking about. Nothing understood. Timber being carried in.	German shift comes on.
10.30 p.m.	Officer or N.C.O. comes down. All work and talking stopped.	Listening period.
12. m.n.	Tapping all round shaft chamber, ends with eight loud knocks.	End of listening. A gallery near shaft head is suspected.
June 3rd. 12.30 a.m. to 6. a.m.	Work continues as usual.	End of night shift.
7.45 a.m.	Pipe stopped and tamping finished. Nothing heard through tamping.	No day shifts worked.
8.55 p.m.	Mines fired.	

21. Rescue of a Miner who had been Entombed for 10 Days.

In June, 1916, 12 men were entombed by an enemy blow near Petit Bois, and the account of the rescue of one is worth recording. The enemy blow destroyed about 150 ft. of the gallery, and great difficulty was found in breaking out and constructing a new gallery for rescue work. The rescue party eventually broke through into the undamaged portion of the old gallery in 10 days. The party discovered bodies of the entombed men, and believing they were all there, and dead, left them while they went off to dinner. Meanwhile one man, a miner by trade, who had kept separate from the others near the face of the gallery, having heard a noise crawled down to the hole which the rescue party had made, and was crawling out, when the party returned from dinner and met him. He owed his life to the fact that the gallery rose slightly to the face, and so the air was purer there. His companions had assembled at the block to listen for the rescuers, and this happened to be the lowest point of that length of gallery. Naturally the bad air collected at this point, and they were all suffocated. The survivor had kept himself alive on half a pint of water which he found in a bottle, and with which he washed his mouth out, then returning it to the bottle. He had a few biscuits but was afraid to eat them for fear of thirst. The experiences of this man during the war had been peculiar. He was wounded in 1914 on this front near Wulverghem ; sent home, and sent out to the Dardanelles ; wounded there, was sent home again, and then sent to France to a Tunnelling Company. Unfortunately he was evacuated from France before he could be interviewed, and the incident passed from notice.

22. Prevalent Hours for Firing Mines.

Tunnelling Companies frequently profited by a knowledge of the enemy's favourite hours for firing mines, which enabled them to regulate their shifts in the danger zones to meet these greater risks. Similarly the enemy studied our customs and habits (sometimes unconsciously regular) to his own advantage. A German mining officer wrote in his note-book, for the benefit of a relieving Company— " the most favourable time for charging is from 5 a.m. "—a recommendation correctly observing the probabilities of the case.

A chart was made to show the time classification, in periods of two hours, for 1,025 mines and camouflets (499 British and 526 Enemy) fired during a period of seven months. The enemy line marked the frequency of blows occurring between 5 p.m. and 9 p.m. and the large number also recorded about dawn. The British line showed a wider range of operations in the evening and early night, but the frequency of these blows around or after sunset was very pronounced. In both curves, the shift from 7 a.m. to 3 p.m. was shown to be comparatively undisturbed.

CHAPTER IV.

THE SOMME, 1916.

23. PREPARATORY WORK.

The programme of underground work for the Somme offensive was worked out in April, 1916, and each of the five Tunnelling Companies that took part was given a working programme to be finished as rapidly as possible with specific latest dates for completion.

The existing defensive systems had to be maintained throughout, and additional Infantry were attached to Companies to cope with the increased work.

The underground operations of this offensive consisted of the following :—

> Mines for destruction of enemy works.
> Galleries to provide advanced emplacements for Machine Guns and Stokes Mortars, to be developed into communication galleries. These were a great feature in the work.
> Galleries for communication purposes only.
> Galleries for emplacements, ammunition, etc., only.

Mines.—The mines were fired as follows :—

   (*a*). Hawthorne Ridge Redoubt. 1 mine—40,000 lbs.
   (*b*). Three mines in the La Boiselle mine System,

                        1 mine—40,600 lbs.}
                        1 mine—36,000 lbs.
                        1 mine—24,000 lbs.}

   (*c*). Three mines in the Tambour Du Clos System,

                        1 mine—15,000 lbs.}
                        1 mine— 9,000 lbs.
                        1 mine—25,000 lbs.}

   (*d*). Two mines, Carnoy.   1 mine— 2,000 lbs.}
                        1 mine— 5,000 lbs.}

These mines were extremely successful, and had great effect, both moral and material.

   (*a*). The charge was at a depth of 65 ft. ; the resultant crater (*Plate* XV., *Fig.* 1) had a high steep rim, but the diameter was much less than was expected from a charge of this magnitude.
   (*b*). The charge of 40,600 lbs. ammonal was at a depth of 75 ft. laid at the end of a gallery over 300 yds. long ; a salient covering 100 yards of enemy line was destroyed ;

many prisoners afterwards stated that the defence was temporarily paralysed by the explosion, which caused 52 casualties.

The two charges, 36,000 lbs. and 24,000 lbs. were fired at a depth of 52 ft. They were 60 ft. apart, but a single crater resulted, circular in plan (see *Plate* XV., *Fig.* 2). This greatly overcharged mine cleared itself to a depth lower than that of the original chambers, and formed remarkably wide rims.

Galleries.—Of the 17 galleries to provide advanced emplacements for Stokes mortars and machine guns, only six were used for communications. This was accounted for by 11 of them being within the area of an unsuccessful attack.

In every case arrangements had been made to complete the trench, and at the end of nearly every gallery there was a Tunnelling officer who was entrusted with the work of breaking through the top of the emplacements for the mortars and machine guns, and breaking out of the end of the gallery to make a starting place for the communication trench, which was to be dug by Pioneers. The experience of these, and of the T.M. and M.G. officers, placed as they were far in front of our lines, and from 40 to 200 ft. from the German line, was probably unique.

As regards the galleries for communication purposes only, of the 20 which were completed to their proper length underground, 16 were connected up with the German line.

The methods adopted in connecting them up were :—

By stepping up to ground level and breaking out and digging.

By placing a charge in a borehole and blowing a crater in the enemy's trenches, then breaking out from the gallery into the crater, and thence into the German trenches.

By making a trench with the pipe-pusher.

Galleries for emplacements or ammunition depôts.—In each case the gallery was broken through at the top without betraying the position of the emplacements. These galleries were used in the first case for signal cables, runners, and ammunition and bomb carriers ; later on they were used for the transport of wounded.

In all cases these underground galleries proved to be of the greatest value, and the application of this form of mining, in conjunction with the attack of a position, was an unqualified success, and from this date was considered an essential adjunct to any important operation.

24. PIPE-PUSHING DURING LATER OPERATIONS.

Further pipe-pushing work was carried out during the operations against Guillemont, and in High Wood.

In the former case, little success was met with—the total result being 120 ft. run of indifferent trench, and it was proved that, even in ideal soil, such work is not practicable if other conditions are really bad. In this case, there were only narrow shallow trenches full of men, and knee-deep in mud. Owing to frequent counter-attacks and heavy bombardments by the enemy, there was no time to build emplacements, and it was impossible to keep the gear properly clean and in working order.

In High Wood eight pipes were forced out, of which four were successfully completed, and fired on September 3rd, when the Infantry attack commenced.

On the same date a tube of 21 pipes was successfully fired just south-east of High Wood, after great trouble and many casualties. The communication trench formed was 50 yds. long, 5 ft. deep, and 12-15 ft. wide at the top. The results achieved, in comparison to the means expended, did not encourage further pipe-pushing under similar conditions, or in woods.

25. MINING AT HIGH WOOD.

In the course of these same operations, some mining work of a novel and hazardous nature was successfully carried out.

During a check in the advance a shaft was sunk and a shallow gallery driven towards a strong post in the enemy's line, which had proved a formidable stumbling block to our advance. The gallery, 310 ft. long and 25 ft. deep, was driven at great speed, and under conditions of the greatest difficulty, especially as regards bringing up material over the devastated battlefield.

A mine was blown on 3rd September, which completely destroyed the strong post, and enabled the Infantry to advance without loss. For tactical reasons the line had to be again withdrawn, and the enemy occupied the crater. Our gallery was rapidly cleared, and on the 9th September a second mine was blown, which destroyed the enemy garrison which was holding the lip of the crater, and this time the advance proceeded unchecked.

The combined craters formed by these two blows were 135 ft. × 85 ft. × 35 ft. deep.

26. DUG-OUTS.

Immediately after the attack on the 31st July, most of the personnel of the Tunnelling Companies engaged were sent back for a rest, this being the first time on record that any Tunnelling Companies had been withdrawn from the line. After a short interval, they were sent forward to commence dug-out work in the devastated area. Rapid progress was made, and before the end of the year underground accommodation had been provided for over 12,000 men in the Fourth and Fifth Armies' areas.

CHAPTER V.

ARRAS–VIMY RIDGE.

27. PREPARATORY WORK.

Towards the end of 1916 orders were received to prepare for an offensive at the Vimy Ridge. A programme of work for the Tunnelling Companies was drawn up and commenced by three companies of the First Army, which were at the Northern end of the Vimy Ridge. The Third Army was also instructed to take measures for an offensive between Arras and Gommecourt, and schemes for tunnelling work were submitted and put in hand.

The proposed offensives in these sectors were subsequently postponed, but early in 1917 orders for operations on the Vimy Ridge–Arras front were again issued.

The mining operations in connection with the attack on the Vimy front on the 9th April were conducted by 4½ Tunnelling Companies. The work consisted of :—

Mines.—Eight mines under the enemy front line ; of these, only two were actually used ; the remainder were not required, owing to the enemy front line being made untenable by our bombardment. These mines had been ready for a considerable time, work actually having been finished the previous October. The largest crater that was formed is illustrated in the frontispiece.

Subways.—Twelve Infantry subways from reserve line to assaulting trenches. These subways averaged half a mile long each, the shortest being 290 yds., and the longest 1,880 yds. They were 6 ft. 6 ins. high and 3 ft. wide, with at least 20 ft. of head-cover, and were lit with electric light throughout, small lighting plants being installed in each subway.

The subways were supplied with dug-outs, assembly chambers, trench mortar and bomb stores, trench mortar emplacements, water tanks, dressing stations, signal offices, and in some cases Brigade and Battalion Headquarters. They had numerous entrances and exits ; the latter were broken out into advanced assaulting trenches on the last night, and the troops were able to file out into their assaulting positions through them. Maps on boards were hung at various points to show the position in the subway in relation to the surface. Tramways were laid in some of the subways, and these were found most useful for carrying up trench mortar ammunition, stores, and rations ; signal cables were carried through the subways, and signal stations were installed in them. The Dressing Stations, being dry and well lit, enabled the wounded to be easily attended to and kept in safety until they could be evacuated. Water mains were also laid in some. Finally, the troops housed in the subways were able to rest in a safe, warm, and dry place, up to the time of the attack.

The subways proved most successful, and, throughout, proof against bombardment; the only damage being done to some of the entrances. These were easily and quickly repaired by Tunnelling Company repair gangs, which were kept in each subway.

The electric light in the subways was installed and run by the Australian Electrical and Mechanical, Mining, and Boring Company. The lights were kept running throughout the whole operation without a breakdown. One plant actually ran 153 hours continuously. Ventilation was good, the only difficulty being in the case of gas attacks, when plenty of ventilation actually increased the danger. Specially appointed traffic officers (not tunnellers) were told off to each subway, and carefully trained beforehand in their duties.

The subways took 3½ months to construct, and excellent footage was maintained by all companies. The weather conditions and enemy trench mortar fire often made the disposal of the spoil a matter of great difficulty.

Photos IV. and V. show typical subway entrances.

28. MISCELLANEOUS WORK.

Bored Mines—Communications.—A number of " bored mines," to blow trenches giving communication across " No Man's Land," were prepared, but only two were actually used.

These " bored mines " when blown formed excellent covered trenches 14 ft. deep and 30 ft. wide. Owing to rapid success of attack, however, they were not extensively used.

Dug-outs.—Considerable dug-out accommodation was provided for troops, by enlarging approaches to mine systems and winch chambers.

Underground Reservoirs.—Two underground reservoirs, capable of holding 50,000 gallons each, and dug-outs for pumping plant in connection with water supply, were built. These reservoirs had over 25 ft. of headcover, and were close timbered and lined with tarpaulins. They were in very hard chalk.

Reconnaissance.—Investigation of enemy subways and dug-outs was carried out by specially detailed parties who followed close behind the attack. Useful work was done in opening up dug-outs and enemy subway entrances, to provide accommodation for troops. One enemy subway was found to be mined, and a charge of 800 lbs. was removed with the assistance of some Germans who were caught in the subway.

29. Preparation and Use of the Arras Caves.

A large portion of the 17th Century Arras was built of hard chalk, from underground quarries in the neighbourhood, at depths varying from 20 ft.–60 ft. These caves were discovered fortuitously towards the end of 1916, and their utilization for the assembly of troops on a large scale was at once considered. Subways across "No Man's Land" were already under construction, and it was determined to make use of the storing capacity of the caves in the best way, by connecting them and the front line subways together. The work was mainly done by the New Zealand Engineers Tunnelling Company. The main galleries driven were 6 ft. 6 ins. high and 4 ft. wide, about 3 miles of gallery being excavated in all. · The caves and galleries were lit electrically throughout by the Australian Electrical and Mechanical, Mining, and Boring Company. Water mains were laid through the galleries, and dug-outs constructed off the tunnels.

A list of the caves prepared and accommodation provided is as follows :—

Cave.	Accommo-dation. (Men).	No. of Entrances.	Remarks.
Nelson	1200	3	Power house.
Wellington	1500	7	Bad high roof.
Blenheim	750	2	Discovered late.
Auckland	300	4	Moderate roof.
New Plymouth	500	3	Mostly passage way. Upper level also.
Russell	50	1	Very small.
Christchurch	4075	10	40 per cent. of floor area not available owing to streets, bad roof, etc.
Dunedin	590	5	Best roof of any cave.
Bluff ..	460	4	
St. Sauveur Caves—			
Total	2000	13	Very low and straggly, with bad roofs.

A plan of caves is given on *Plate* XVI.

CHAPTER VI

MESSINES.

30. PRELIMINARY SCHEMES.

It has already been mentioned in Chapter II., para. 8, that the first idea of a deep offensive in the Messines–Wytschaete area arose during the summer of 1915, when a start was actually made on a deep adit against Hill 60.

During 1916, a commencement was made on various deep galleries, but it was not until the late summer that this scheme began to take shape in its final form. The first interruption from the enemy side came in June, 1916. For some time he had been blowing craters in the re-entrants and salients of his line—sometimes in, and sometimes even behind. his front trenches, on some apparently definite plan. It was thought that his intention was to improve observation and provide flanking positions for covered machine guns, and work did not seem to be directed in any way against our deep system. Unfortunately, one mine fired immediately above our gallery at Petit Bois, damaged 250 ft. length and entombed twelve men. The subsequent escape of one of these men has been described in Chapter III., para. 21.

The next interruption occurred in August at the mine under La Petite Douve Farm ; our charge had already been placed, and a branch gallery which was being driven to a flank, broke into an enemy working. We blew a small charge, and the enemy retaliated, apparently from a deep system, by a mine in " No Man's Land," which wrecked our gallery and cut the leads. Water was let in, and the gallery completely lost. We might have easily blown first, but at great risk of betraying the extent of our deep system. The future entirely justified the abandonment of this mine, the only one to be lost through the whole of the preparations.

About the end of September the enemy was heard working so close to our Hill 60 mine, that it was almost decided to fire this mine in conjunction with a minor Infantry operation. However, the danger was gradually removed by means of some brilliant countermining, and the operation did not become necessary.

31. BERLIN TUNNEL.

The difficulty as regards drainage in the Berlin Tunnel has already been mentioned. At the end of September the water rose to such an extent that the tunnel was completely flooded, and the mine at the end of Caterpillar branch, which had just been charged, was temporarily lost. After several weeks of strenuous work the water was got rid of, and the tamping of the Caterpillar mine completed.

Early in November a new vertical shaft was sunk (see *Plate* XVII.) at point X, and a gallery broken out which was to run from X to Y. When this was finished, the average number of pumpers was reduced by no less than 70. *Plate* XVII. shows the whole of the Berlin Tunnel with its ultimate branches under Hill 60 and the Caterpillar.

32. FURTHER INTERRUPTIONS BY ENEMY.

During February, March, April, and May, 1917, the enemy blew a number of heavy mines and camouflets which were obviously directed against our galleries. At first it was feared he might also have an extensive deep system, but, as time went on, it became clearer from the disjointed nature of his efforts that the blows were from individual deep workings, apparently sunk at random in the hopes of striking our galleries. On the 10th February a very heavy camouflet (or group) was fired in the Hollandscheschuur area. The earth tremor was felt on a three-mile front, and throughout our deep galleries, and considerable damage was done which, however, was fortunately all repairable.

At the end of the month there were several more blows near Spanbroekmolen and Kruisstraat; at the former place our main gallery was wrecked, leads cut, and charges lost. This was an important mine, and more than three months' most strenuous efforts were needed to repair the damage. The chamber was actually only recovered on the 3rd June, when the charges were found to be still in good order, and connections made good; and all was again ready for blowing a few hours only before zero hour.

In the middle of May the enemy was very clearly heard in deep workings at Hill 60. A period of extreme anxiety ensued. By very careful calculation it was estimated that the enemy gallery would just pass clear over ours, and he was allowed to go on working to the end.

33. SCENE AT ZERO HOUR, 7TH JUNE, 1917.

The explosion of the mines containing nearly 1,000,000 lbs. of high explosive was watched by the Inspector of Mines from a dug-out at Kemmel. The scene was described in his diary as follows :—

" 3.10 a.m. A violent earth tremor, then a gorgeous sheet of flame from Spanbroekmolen, and at the same moment every gun opened fire. At short intervals of seconds the mines continued to explode ; period which elapsed between first and last mine, about

30 seconds. I found it difficult to concentrate on looking for the mines, there was so much going on, and the scene, which baffles description, developed so quickly that my attention was distracted. The majority of the mines showed up well with a fine flame. Others merely showed a red glow; this may have been due to their being blotted out by the smoke of the bombardment. The earth shake was remarkable, and was felt as far as Cassel."

34. DETAILS OF MINES.

A complete table of the mines, giving dates, charges, and results is given on *Plate* XVIII., and an outline site plan is shown on *Plate* XIX.

Immediately after the battle every Tunnelling Company concerned made careful reconnaissances, both of our own craters and of what remained of the enemy mining system. From the reports sent in a few examples have been selected. *Plate* XX. shows the details of the craters formed at Hill 60 and the Caterpillar : *Plate* XXI. details of the chamber of St. Eloi mine : *Plate* XXII. details of the switch board for Hill 60, and *Plate* XXIII. typical plan of firing arrangements for two charges.

The chief features of this mining offensive may be summarized as follows :—

(i.) The length of time which had elapsed between the loading and firing of the majority of the mines.

(ii.) The size of the individual charges.

(iii.) The depth of the shafts ; though none of them approach the depth credited to us by the enemy.

(iv.) The great length of the individual galleries.

(v.) The enormous aggregate amount of explosive used, the highest concentration of which was no less than 500,000 lbs. of explosive to 4,500 yards of front, Hollandscheshuur-Ontario Farm.

(vi.) The absence of precedent in military history or civilian experience from which the surface or underground effects of the earth waves, resulting from the simultaneous firing of a number of concentrated mines, could be even approximately gauged.

35. OTHER WORK IN CONNECTION WITH MESSINES OFFENSIVE.

In addition to the actual mining, an immense amount of dug-out work was done before the attack.

Profiting by the lessons learnt in the Vimy offensive, it was decided to provide dug-out accommodation for every headquarters, and this was successfully done for every formation, certainly down to battalions.

After the assault two communication trenches were successfully blown at the Caterpillar by means of bored holes and explosives. Charges consisting of push tube canisters were placed at 6 ft, centres 4 ft. deep, and were blown electrically—28 charges at a time. This work only employed 50 men, and in three hours time two good trenches, each about 200 yds. long, were formed, and were in regular use for long afterwards.

36. SUMMARY.

The success of this great enterprise, probably the most remarkable mining feat in military history, is undoubted ; nevertheless the scheme was by no means universally approved at the time, and at the last minute, when all preparations for the assault were complete, more than one higher commander begged that the men should be allowed to assault without the explosion of mines, the effect of which they could not foresee, and consequently mistrusted.

After the battle the opinions of commanders of all ranks were sought, and were still found to vary considerably. Although some divisions were enthusiastic as to the help given them by the mines, in others, the opinion was by no means unanimous, whilst to the end at least one division insisted that the blows had been a definite hindrance to their attack. The explanation of this may possibly be found in the fact that the assaulting troops belonging to one brigade had not, owing to some oversight, been warned of the presence of mines on their front, and the unexpected explosion of a charge of over 50,000 lbs. at very close range naturally caused a good deal of alarm. Reports were also current that German mines had gone up behind our own front. This mistake is easily understood when the configuration of the line from which our attack started is remembered, and it points an obvious lesson on the importance of giving the fullest information possible to all troops, whenever mines may play a part in the general scheme. In every case where thorough arrangements had been made for the safety and instruction of the troops, practically no damage was caused, and the assistance given by the complete paralysing of the enemy defence cannot be questioned. The best tribute to the work of the miners comes from the enemy himsel , and we cannot do better than give an extract from General Ludendorff s Memoirs :—   " *   *

We should have succeeded in retaining the position but for the exceptionally powerful mines used by the British, which paved the way for their attack, consisting, as usual, of fierce artillery fire supporting a closely massed infantry advance. The result of these successful mining operations was that the enemy broke through on June 7th.

The heights of Wytschaete and Messines had been the site of active mine warfare in the early days of the War. For a long time past, however, both sides had ceased to use such tactics ; all had been quiet, and no sound of underground work on the part of the enemy could be heard at our listening posts. The mines must, therefore, have been in position long before. The moral effect of the explosions was simply staggering ; at several points our troops fell back before the onslaught of the enemy Infantry. *   * ''

37. PREPARATORY WORK FOR FIFTH ARMY ATTACK.

Following on the Second Army offensive the work of the Tunnelling Companies became more general, a large amount of dug-out and subway construction being undertaken in preparation for offensive operations by the Fifth Army on July 31st. All companies suffered heavy casualties, both in officers and men, from shell fire, and gas, amounting to nearly 10 per cent. of effective strength. The completion of the programme of work within the time limit was successfully accomplished in spite of very great difficulties, which strained all resources to the utmost limit.

Subways.—A subway programme was considered, but owing to the short time available, and the difficulties experienced previously in the Second Army front, it was decided to concentrate the labour available on dug-outs. Nearly all the larger schemes had been previously commenced by the Second Army, and the further development of these formed an important part of the programme of work in the various corps areas.

Conditions of Work.—The conditions of work all through the preparatory period were such that no very rapid rate of progress was possible. After the Battle of Messines the enemy pursued a policy of actively interfering with any preparations we might be making for a new offensive, and kept all approaches, forward billets, and dumps under systematic fire, both high explosive and gas shells, especially at night ; and in addition to other projectiles, from the night of 13th-14th July, the enemy employed the new mustard gas shell with considerable effect.

The continual shelling rendered transport of material very uncertain, and added to the delay caused by the difficult nature of the ground. Every site selected had to be tested with trial bores, the soil varying considerably in nature within distances of a few yards. Owing to the patchy nature of the sub-soil, dug-outs were to a great extent grouped in large systems, which, added to the fact that most of the ground was unavoidably in full view from the enemy lines, rendered the concealment of the spoil very difficult.

Canal Banks.—Eighteen subways, 5 ft. × 4 ft. were constructed by a Tunnelling Company through the canal bank near Boesinghe. These were intended for the storage of bridging material for crossings over the canal ; they were to be opened up at zero, and were then to be used as covered approaches to the bridges, when these were built.

The enemy, however, retired from his side of the canal on the 27th July for a distance of 500 yards, and the subways were never used as such. They were extremely useful, subsequently, as dug-outs for troops.

The retirement of the enemy, mentioned above, was due, according to their Intelligence reports, to the fact that some of their troops who had raided our trenches, returned with the information that they had discovered mine shafts on our side of the canal. This may be taken as a good instance of the moral effect of the mines of the 7th June on the German army.

Owing to the withdrawal of the enemy, arrangements were made to form approaches through the canal bank for two pontoon bridges across the canal, which were to take horsed traffic coming along two plank roads from Boesinghe. As the time and labour required to cut approaches to these bridges through the banks would have been very considerable, it was decided to blow gaps in the banks by means of boreholes charged with explosive. The dimensions of the banks were roughly 50 ft. × 9 ft. high, and the gap was required to be 12 ft. wide. Two boreholes, 40 ft. × 6 ins. diameter, were driven through the bank at each approach, and charged with ammonal and blastine, at 6 lbs. per foot, for a length of 20 ft. Boring was commenced at zero hour, and the result of the explosion was so successful, that approaches through the bank were ready at 3 p.m. the same day.

At least 24 hours' work, and a large working party, would have been needed to make similar cuttings by ordinary digging.

Tanks.—One Tunnelling Company was detailed to work with the Tank Corps. Their work consisted of tank crossings over the canal, and over various streams and ditches.

Tramways.—One section of a company was attached to each of the four corps of the Fifth Army on 20. 7. 17, and worked with the Army Tramway Company, laying and maintaining tramways to various battery positions.

38. SUMMARY OF WORK DONE.

Plate XXIV. illustrates the work of the Tunnelling Companies summarized in the following table :—

Corps.	Companies finally allotted.	Dug-outs completed.					
		Headquarters.			Dressing Stations and Aid Posts.	Observation Posts.	
		Brigade.	Battalion.	Artillery.			
XIV. ..	1 Company	3	—	—	—	—	—
	1 Company	1	6	—	—	—	—
Total ..	2.	4	6	—	—	—	—
XVIII. ..	1 Company (Finished by Field Co's.)	3	9	—	—	—	1 Subway 475 feet.
		—	4	—	—	—	
	2 Sections	3	5	2	—	5	1 Subway 590 feet. 1 System for Troops.
Total ..	1½.	6	18	2	—	5	Subways 1065 feet. 1 System for Troops.
XIX. ..	2 Sections	2	4	1	1	—	1 Subway 720 feet.
	1 Company	4	17	—	—	—	
Total ..	1½.	6	21	1	1	—	Subway 720 feet.
II. ..	1 Company	2	8	—	2	—	1 System for Troops.
	1 Company	3	—	4	1	1	1 System for Troops.
	1 Company	2	4	—	2	15	1 System for Troops.
	2 Sections	—	5	—	1	2	1 System for Artillery.
Total ..	3½.	7	17	4	6	18	4 Systems for Troops.
Combined Total ..	8½.	23	62	7	7	23	5 Systems for Troops. Subways 1785 feet.

1 Company R.E. .... Work for Tank Corps.
1 Company R.E. .... Work on Tramways.

Total number of Companies finally employed—10½.

Throughout the later operations against the Passchendaele Ridge Tunnelling Companies were very fully employed on miscellaneous duties in addition to much dug-out work, to which the geologists contributed invaluable help by indicating the most favourable conditions of the ground below the surface. Owing to the continuous heavy artillery fire, many casualties were suffered, but experience was gained which proved highly useful in the open fighting of 1918. This is described in the following chapter.

CHAPTER VIII.

WORK DURING OPEN WARFARE.

39. TUNNELLING COMPANIES IN GERMAN OFFENSIVE, MARCH, 1918.

Before the great German attack opened, many companies were employed in the front and reserve lines making dug-outs, M.G. emplacements, etc. The protection of the R.A. and machine gun detachments was a matter of vital importance, and particular attention was given to providing them with safe cover.

Much work was also done in the preparation of roads, bridges, and water supply for demolition in corps areas.

On the 21st March a number of Tunnelling Companies in Third and Fifth Armies became involved very early, sections at work in forward areas being drawn into the fighting and suffering many casualties. Those further back were called on to organize, and in some cases to hold, defence lines in rear, and this work occupied the full time of some companies for several days, fresh lines being dug and wired as the retirement proceeded.

A large number of demolitions were carried out by Tunnelling Companies, and an equal number were prepared and handed over to other units, both British and French

An estimate of these is given below :—

	Bridges.	Road Craters.	Dumps.	Caves, Wells, Pumping Stations, etc.
Blown	47	15	8	18
Prepared and handed over to other units	61	26	–	—

Demolitions carried out	88
„ prepared and handed over	87

40. WORK OF TUNNELLING COMPANIES, APRIL–SEPTEMBER, 1918.

A number of Tunnelling Companies were employed on rear zone defence line work in the Second and Third Armies during April, May and June :—

<table>
<tr><td>1 company</td><td rowspan="4">⎱ Terdeghem Switch.
Coq de Paille Line.
Boeschepe Line.
Reninghelst Switch.</td></tr>
<tr><td>1 ,,</td></tr>
<tr><td>1 ,,</td></tr>
<tr><td>1 ,,</td></tr>
</table>

1 company	Terdeghem Switch.
1 ,,	Coq de Paille Line.
1 ,,	Boeschepe Line.
1 ,,	Reninghelst Switch.

Berthen Line.

3 companies—St. Omer Line.

2 ,, —Bouvigny–Amiens Line

The companies were employed mainly as follows :—

Supervision of labour.

Rear communications, bridges and roads, and tracks

Causeways and Infantry tracks across marshes.

Drainage of trenches.

Construction of M.G. pill boxes.

     ,,   ,, Splinter-proof shelters.

Inclines for machine guns.

Dug-outs for machine guns.

     ,,   ,, command posts.

Demolitions Reconnaissance, July-September, 1918.—In July a detailed reconnaissance was commenced for the preparation for destruction of all communications and water supply systems in the L. of C. area. The ground to be reconnoitred was comprised roughly in an area West of the line Pointe de Gravelines—St. Omer—Anvin—St. Pol—Frevent—Doullens—Flixecourt—Molliens-Vidame.

This area was divided into four sectors, each sector being in charge of a captain and two subalterns drawn from Tunnelling Companies in First, Second, Third and Fourth Armies.

The following was the scope of the demolitions, of which detailed schemes were duly prepared, including estimates of time, labour and materials :—

(*a*). Roads, including bridges over railways and navigable waterways.

(*b*). Water supply systems, other than purely railway systems.

(*c*). Buildings containing stores and plant on charge of Q.M.G. Directorates in Ports.

(*d*). British installations outside seaports.

The reconnaissance was concluded about the middle of September, as the favourable turn in the military situation rendered the early completion of this scheme unnecessary, and the Tunnelling Officers rejoined their respective companies which were then actively engaged in the operations of our advancing troops.

41. Work of Tunnelling Companies During the Allied Offensive, Aug.–Nov., 1918.

The following is a brief review of the employment of the Tunnelling Companies during the period 8. 8. 18—11. 11. 18 :—

First Army.—From 8. 8. 18 to 26. 9. 19, companies in this Army were employed on the following work :—

> Maintenance of tunnels and the pumping plant at Givenchy. South of the La Bassée Canal in the Cambrin and Cuinchy sectors, the mine and tunnel systems were prepared for defence.
>
> Supervision of the defence work in the localities of Mazingarbe and Les Brebis. Listening patrols were maintained in the Hulluch, St. Elie and Hairpin mining systems.

On the remainder of the Army front in the forward battle zone, through the localities of Vimy, Willerval and Bailleul and thence to Fampoux on the River Scarpe, platoon dug-outs, machine gun dug-outs and emplacements, headquarters dug-outs for battalions, brigades and divisions, were constructed with all possible speed. Shifts were employed day and night continuously.

At the Mine School at Houchin, courses were in progress for instructing Artillery personnel in dug-out construction. The vacancies allotted per course were four officers and 250 other ranks. These courses lasted a fortnight, and were maintained until the termination of the 12th course, 24. 10. 18, and helped appreciably to reduce the demands for Tunnellers to work on battery positions. A record is believed to have been established by one company in August, when a tunnel, dimensions 6 ft. 6 ins. × 2 ft. 9 ins. was driven and timbered to a distance of 62 ft. 2 ins. in 24 hours.

With a view to an advance, all companies received instruction in infantry training and in the duties of " investigation parties," when removing booby traps, landmines and demolition charges.

During the advance in the Arras sectors, a complete reconnaissance was made of all dug-outs in the captured German trenches on Greenland Hill and astride the river Scarpe, including the caves at Roeux, which were first discovered after the Battle of Arras, 1917. Forward roads in the localities of Fampoux and Roeux were repaired.

Investigation parties went forward with each Infantry Brigade advancing and searched villages, bridges, road junctions and railways.

Roads were repaired in the following localities :—

> Pont Fixe–Festubert.
> Vermelles, Hulluch and Loos.
> Liévin and Coulotte.
> Farbus.
> Feuchy–Pelves,

and a light railway track laid from Fampoux along the river Scarpe and Pelves Road.

From 26. 9. 18 the investigation parties remained with the Infantry Brigades during the advance. In addition to searching for booby traps and mines, a daily reconnaissance was made of all dug-outs, cellars, etc., free from gas and safe for immediate occupation.

Delay action mines similar to those left by the Germans in their withdrawal at the beginning of 1917, were first found in the VIII. Corps area, in the localities of Lens, Harnes, Dourge, and Henin Lietard, and later a series of these mines was found throughout the railway system, chiefly at important stations and junctions.

Many cellars and dug-outs in Henin Lietard were found to contain Yellow Cross gas, which at the time prevented a thorough search being made for demolition charges. This locality was placed out of bounds in consequence.

Eighty-four delay action mines were dealt with, including those subsequently reported by the enemy. Mines which were overdue to explode called for exceptional care in their removal ; this was successfully carried out without casualties.

A considerable amount of bridging was accomplished by companies, as follows :—

A five-trestle bridge across the Canal de L'Escaut.
Girder bridges at Marchiennes, Douchy, Saulzoir, Sebourg, Valenciennes and St. Ghislain.
Hopkins bridge at Courcelles.
Inglis bridges over the moat at Condé.

Second Army.—On August 8th five Tunnelling Companies were employed on :—

(*a*). Mined dug-outs.
(*b*). Concrete pill boxes.

This work was being carried on both in forward areas and on the Army lines of defence in back areas. This was continued until the enemy commenced retiring from Kemmel and the Bailleul area towards the end of August. The dug-out work then in hand, which was likely to be of any value, was completed, and the companies gradually became employed on road repairs and the searching for enemy traps and mines.

In the last week of September, when the commencement of the Second Army attack was launched, the Tunnelling Companies were given the difficult task of making good road communications over the old cratered area.

After the river Lys was crossed, the repair and reconstruction of the bridges across the river—all of which had been most effectually destroyed by the enemy—became the important problem, together with the railways. This work continued until the enemy retired from the river Escaut, when the same problem of making good the bridges presented itself again, and it was on this work that the companies were employed when the Armistice was signed on 11. 11. 18.

Third Army.—At the commencement of the advance the companies were mainly employed on completing the construction of machine gun and platoon dug-outs in the forward areas. Detachments of the units were at once detailed to divisions to accompany the infantry advance for the purpose of locating and rendering harmless enemy land mines and traps, and providing underground accommodation as the operations progressed. The detachments remained with the front line troops throughout, and in their reconnaissance of dug-outs and cellars were able to take a considerable number of prisoners. They were followed by other sections employed on the rapid repair and construction of forward roads, and on water supply reconnaissance, which included the cleaning, deepening and equipment of wells for supplying the forward troops.

At an early stage in the operations many Tunnelling Companies were concerned in the construction of bridges, either in conjunction with other units or by themselves.

The British demolitions prepared on roads, culverts and wells in the Army area, after the March retirement, and the anti-tank minefields laid by certain divisions previously, were removed by Tunnelling companies during this period.

Railway reconnaissance extending into the First and Fourth Army areas was carried out by one company, the work of which included the removal of mines and withdrawing timber from, and filling, enemy dug-outs in embankments.

Some 300 miles of roads were constructed or repaired by Tunnelling companies of the Third Army. In addition to the filling in or bridging of craters on main roads, this included making up corduroy branch roads or diversions and re-metalling old roads. In two cases companies opened up quartzite deposits and quarried local stone for the purpose. Forty-three bridges were dealt with; 34 new ones, and nine repaired or converted from single to double road. The work included girder, trestle and pontoon bridges. A Hopkins girder bridge 180 ft. span over a gap 85 ft. deep was built, launched, and completed in 10 days by the New Zealand Tunnelling Company. This was the biggest single span bridge erected during the War.

Fourth Army.—All companies were employed on the following work, at different times :—

Roads—Reconnaissance, maintenance, and repairs.
　　　　Filling craters, construction of plank diversions, etc.
　　　　Removal of mines and obstructions.
　　　　Construction of dry weather tracks.
Bridges.—Construction or repair of bridges.
Railways.—Reconnaissance, and removal of mines.
Wells.—Reconnaissance, clearing and repairs.
Dug-outs, etc.—Reconnaissance and removal of explosive charges.
Tank Traps.—Removal of anti-tank mines, etc.

Among many incidents of interest may be mentioned the following :—

At Albert during two days 105 enemy land mines were removed from the streets without a single accident : all the casualties incurred were caused by the heavy shelling and M.G. fire ; during much of the time work had to be done in gas-masks.

At Lempire, when the progress of tanks was checked by the old British anti-tank minefield, a Tunnelling officer succeeded under a heavy M.G. barrage in removing contact pins from the trench mortar bombs and opening up a clear passage.

At Bellenglise-Magny Tunnel the German engine drivers were seized, and forced to disclose the positions of the charges, which were connected to a switch in the engine-room.

Fifth Army.—From September 2nd till the close of hostilities, work of the Fifth Army Tunnelling Companies may be summarized under two main headings :—

    (a). Searching for enemy mines, etc., in captured areas.

    (b). Restoring communication by rebuilding bridges, and re-constructing roads, railways, etc.

With regard to (a) : two Investigation sections were formed by each company, each consisting of, approximately, 5 officers and 60 O.R., with a G.S. wagon attached to each section for transport. The personnel was specially selected for investigation work. As time did not permit of the men undergoing a special course at the Army Mine School, the men selected were given instruction under company arrangements, in which the working of traps, mines, etc., was demonstrated by models and examples.

With regard to (b) : each company, less the personnel employed on investigation work, was organized for bridging and road construction work. Tunnelling officers with experience of civil engineering were selected as far as possible for this work, and all skilled tradesmen of Tunnelling Companies were retained for this employment. Twenty-six bridges were constructed during the period under review, of which the largest was a 180 ft. span ' Hopkins.' Over 200 miles of damaged roads were cleared and rendered fit for traffic.

In addition to the above, much work was done by the Tunnelling Companies on canals and the river Scheldt, and on railways.

In the case of canals, the work consisted mainly of removing demolished bridges, dams, damaged lock gates, etc., chiefly by blasting.

As regards railways, obstructions (such as railway bridges) were removed, and preliminary work done on the permanent way prior to the arrival of the Railway Construction Companies.

General.—A summary, in statistical form of the work accomplished by the Tunnelling Companies from 8th August—11th November, 1918, is given on the following page.

Summary of Work of Tunnelling Companies during period 8. 8. 18—11. 11. 18.

Description.	First Army.	Second Army.	Third Army.	Fourth Army.	Fifth Army.	Totals.
No. of heavy bridges constructed	65	1	56	5	22	149
No. of light bridges constructed	17	1	12	4	4	38
No. of land mines removed	2,273	1,245	482	883	1,831	6,714
No. of delay action mines removed	37	33	61	109	75	315
No. of other traps removed	132	72	63	180	89	536
No. of enemy demolition charges removed	10,745	3,555	4,231	2,303	3,891	24,725
Total weight of explosives (enemy) removed	386,091 lbs.	445,221 lbs.	453,725 lbs.	379,920 lbs.	976,703 lbs.	2,641,660 lbs.
No. of gas shells removed	2,595	—	—	—	123	2,718
No. of British demolition charges removed	116	199	881	—	235	1,431
Total weight of British demolition charges	48,540 lbs.	67,409 lbs.	394,134 lbs.	—	95,270 lbs.	605,353 lbs.
No. of British anti-tank mines removed	—	—	4,272	—	—	4,272

CHAPTER IX.

CONCLUSION.

42. DISBANDMENT OF COMPANIES.

Immediately after the signing of the Armistice a commencement was made to release men who were essential to home industries, and amongst the first to be asked for were the coal miners.

Tunnelling Companies were rapidly disbanded, and in a very short time no longer existed as units.

The lessons of the past, and the problems of the future were summed up in a letter addressed by the Engineer-in-Chief to the Chief of the General Staff, France, at the beginning of 1919. This letter gives a review of the whole subject, and is here reproduced ' in extenso.'

43. LETTER FROM E.-IN-C. TO C.G.S., JANUARY, 1919.

" The Tunnelling Companies have acquired a great reputation in the War for efficiency, stout-heartedness and general usefulness, apart from their proper rôle in which they have always had the upper hand over the enemy.

These good results are due to the following causes :—

(*a*). Each company has a large number both of officers and men, and a considerable transport on its establishment ; Field Companies on the other hand have always been short in these respects, and have been like a man with a head and body, but only one arm and one leg.

(*b*). There has been great *esprit de corps*, fostered by the organization which gives Tunnelling Companies official fathers and mothers, in the persons of Controllers and the Inspector of Mines, whose duty it is to look after the interests of the companies in addition to co-ordinating, organizing and controlling their work. Moreover the companies have remained in the same areas for long periods, and acquired local experience of the utmost value. Contrasted with Army Troops Companies, for instance, who have been nobody's children and have been moved from Corps to Corps—each of which has been inclined to get the utmost out of them—the lot of the Tunnelling Companies has been a happy one.

2. The close of the War and the needs of the coal-fields at home are causing all the Tunnelling Companies to disappear rapidly, and it is desirable to consider the needs of the British Army in the future as regards mining and tunnelling.

DI

3. Mining is essentially a feature of stationary warfare, a phase of War which every commander will strive to avoid unless he is in such a position that mobile warfare is impossible. While, therefore, the study and practice of the art of mining and counter-mining is necessary, it is not desirable that any special units for this purpose should compose a part of the regular Army. The objections to this being the case are almost insuperable. To attain and maintain the highest degree of efficiency—and only this standard can justify a specialist unit—the miner must work continually at his trade ; to attract men of the proper class the pay must be commensurate with the wages earned in civil life ; and further, the prejudices of the miner would have to be studied, *e.g.*, his preference to associate with men of his own trade only, and to work under officers who are miners also ; in fact, the maintenance of efficient mining units as part of the regular Army is impracticable.

4. The question which will have to be dealt with, therefore, is how—when the necessity arises—will it be possible to provide trained men for mining or for dug-out work in difficult ground. The best solution would appear to be the raising of Tunnelling Companies on a territorial basis as part of the Territorial Force? These companies would be trained annually, and their training would include all branches of ordinary Field Engineer work. The annual training would be carried out in conjunction with that of other branches of the service, to prevent any system of water-tight compartment ideas as to work.

5. A difficulty would arise as to officers, for the bulk of officers and the best ones in Tunnelling Companies are metal miners employed abroad, whilst most of the men are coal miners employed at home. This difficulty could probably be got over by giving each company a cadre of officers formed from those employed in Great Britain, and as far as possible in the company's territorial area, who would train annually with their company, while suitable officers serving abroad would be borne on a special list and be liable to be recalled home on mobilization for posting as required. Any such officers who happened to be in England during the training season would be posted to a company for training with it.

It would be necessary to include special medical officers on the establishment of these Tunnelling Companies, as has been done in France, drawn from suitable doctors practising in Mining areas in Great Britain. The part played by the M.O.'s of Tunnelling Companies in keeping the companies efficient and up to strength is not generally known. It is no exaggeration to say that the Tunnelling Companies would have wasted away rapidly, had it not been for the special knowledge of miners' characteristics, habits, and ailments possessed by their M.O.'s. Their retention on the establishment is an essential part of the scheme.

6. While the above scheme would provide the organization and personnel for war purposes, it must not be forgotten that progress and improvement in the science of military mining is necessary if efficiency in the field is to be expected.

At Chatham, therefore, a Mining School should be established as part of the S.M.E., where experimental work could be carried on, and the young officers of the regular R.E. be trained in the principles of mining and dug-out work.

7. It will be noticed that very little reference has been made to dug-outs.

Whatever may be the future of military mining, there is no doubt that modern warfare will impose the necessity of providing underground cover, on an ever increasing scale. Protection from bombing will be required more and more, apart from the question of artillery methods and fire.

To meet this demand for cover it is essential that all arms should be trained to make their own cover in ordinary ground with R.E. supervision and assistance only. It is not a practicable proposition to make the R.E. responsible for providing all such accommodation that may be required. It is recognized now that trench work, field works, wiring, etc., are part of the duties of the soldier and that the R.E. unit, which it is possible to provide, is more than fully occupied with assisting and supervising the other arms in these duties, and in carrying out special work which it is impossible for anybody else to do.

In the same way it will be recognized in time that, in suitable ground, ordinary dug-out work is part of the ordinary soldier's duty, supervised and assisted by the R.E., and it should become, therefore, part of his training. Field Companies should be trained to a much higher degree of efficiency in it than is at present sometimes the case, and "miner" should be an authorized trade. The good results obtained with little trouble by certain Chinese Labour Companies composed of agriculturists show how easy this is; the degree of proficiency in face work, timbering, etc., attained in a short time, in ordinary ground, was remarkable.

The experience of Army Mine Schools in France (especially the First Army Mine School), where classes of all arms, and all ranks, received instruction, was equally satisfactory; and it would be a distinct loss if we failed to profit in the future by the experience gained in this war.

Selected classes of all arms and all ranks (especially the R.A.) should receive instruction in dug-out work at the S.M.E., Chatham: where in addition all young regular R.E. officers would be instructed, and experimental work with new instruments, plant, etc., carried out, and new methods tried."

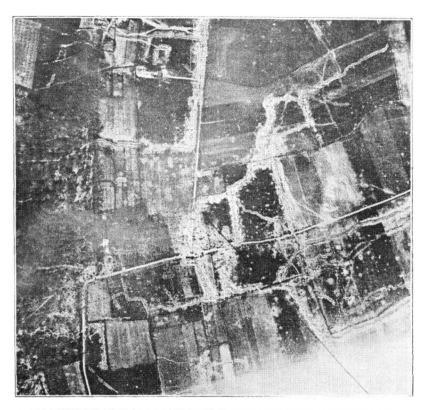

Photo I.—East of Ploegsteert Wood.   Before the " Blow."

Photo II.—East of Ploegsteert Wood.   After the " Blow."   Showing the Craters.

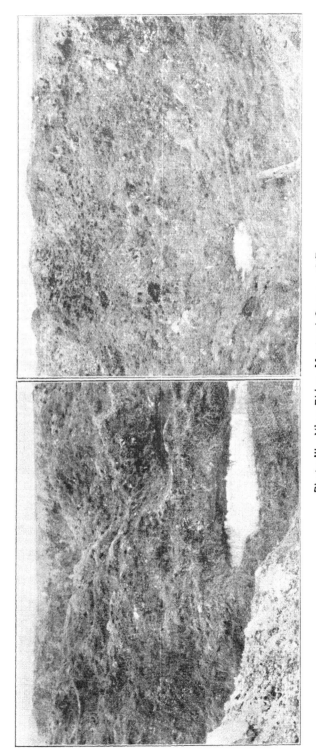

Photo III.—Vimy Ridge, Montreal Crater, 1917.

Photos IV. and V.—Vimy Ridge.   Entrances to Subways.

PLATE I.

CUINCHY BRICKFIELDS,
SHOWING POSITION OF MINES.

Mines— { Nº1, Nº2, Nº3 }
Trenches ————
Brickstacks ... ■

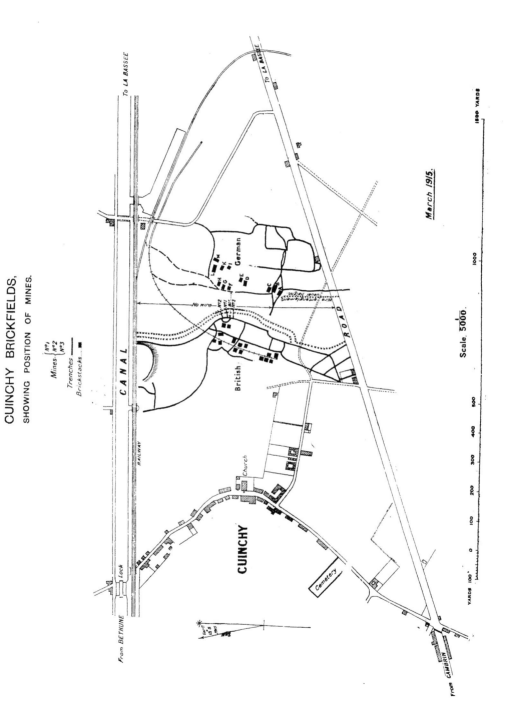

March 1915.

Scale, 5000.

YARDS 100' 0   100   200   300   400   500   1000   1800 YARDS

PLATE II.

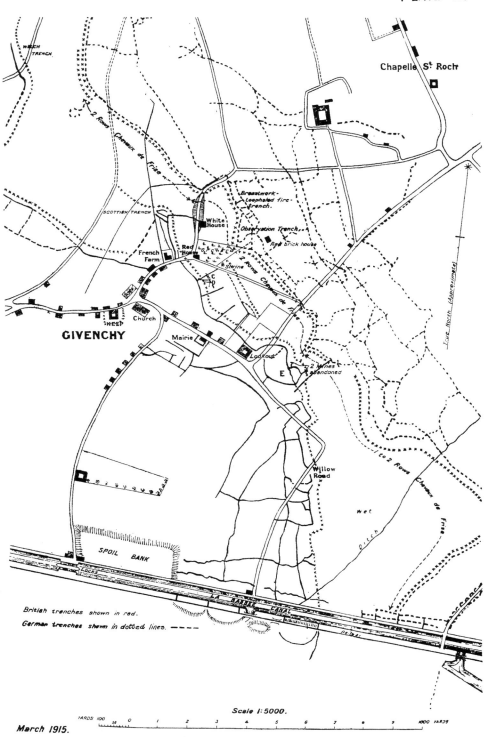

Chapelle St Roch

WELCH TRENCH

2 Rows Chevaux de Frise

SCOTTISH TRENCH

Breastwork-Loopholed fire-trench.

White House

Observation Trench

Red brick house

French Farm

Red House

Shrine

Chapelle de

C

D

KEEP

Church

GIVENCHY

Mairie

Lookout

E

2 Mines abandoned

True North (Approximate)

Willow Road

1 to 2 Rows Chevaux de Frise

Wet Ditch

SPOIL BANK

LOCKS

LA BASSÉE CANAL

British trenches shown in red.

German trenches shown in dotted lines. ————

Scale 1:5000.

YARDS 100 50 0 1 2 3 4 5 6 7 8 9 1000 YARDS

March 1915.

PLATE III

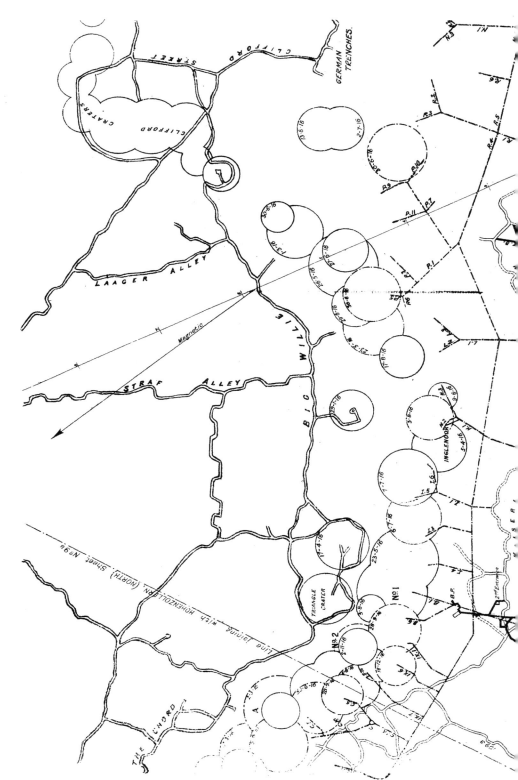

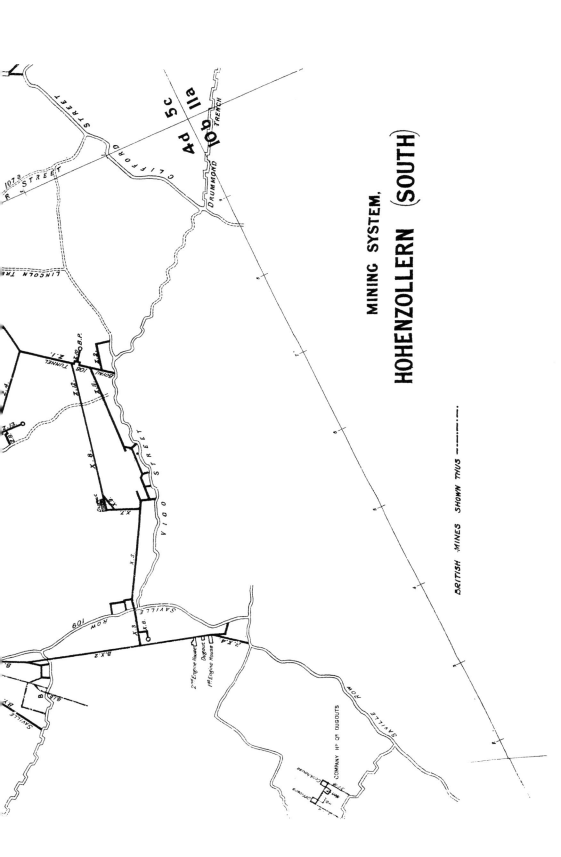

MINING SYSTEM.

HOHENZOLLERN (SOUTH)

BRITISH MINES SHOWN THUS — — — — —

PLATE IV.

BULLY-GRENAY DOUBLE CRASSIER.

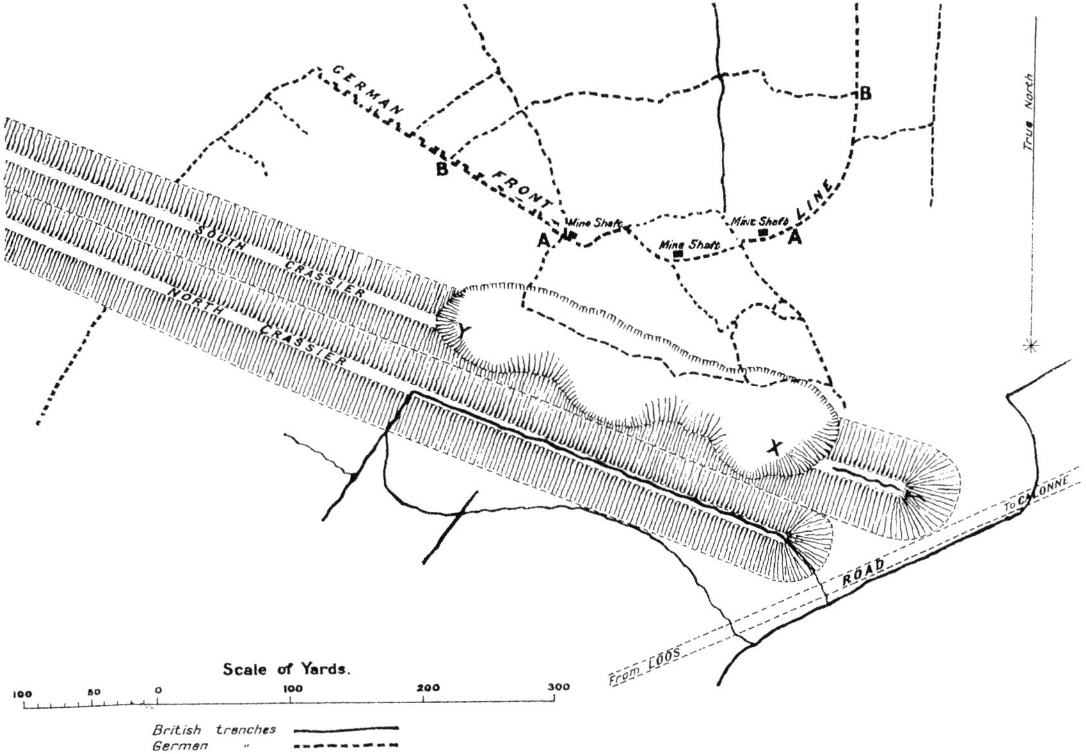

True North

GERMAN FRONT LINE

SOUTH CRASSIER

CRASSIER

NORTH CRASSIER

A
B

Mine Shaft
Mine Shaft
Mine Shaft

ROAD

To COLONNE

From LOOS

Scale of Yards.

100   50   0   100   200   300

British trenches
German   "

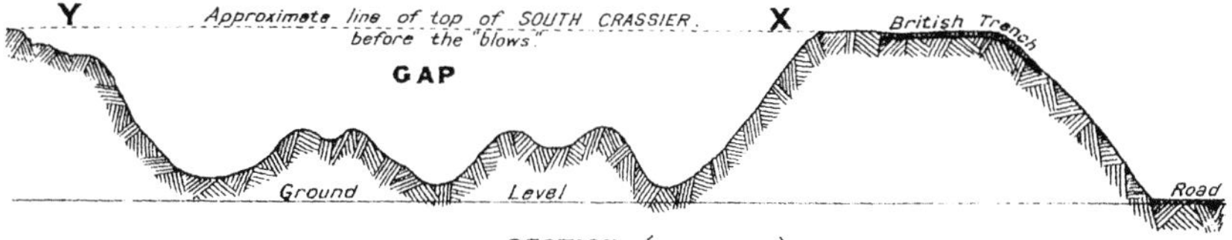

Approximate line of top of SOUTH CRASSIER before the blows

GAP

Ground Level

British Trench

Road

Y   X

SECTION. (Not to scale)

August 1916.

PLATE V

HULLUCH SUBWAYS.

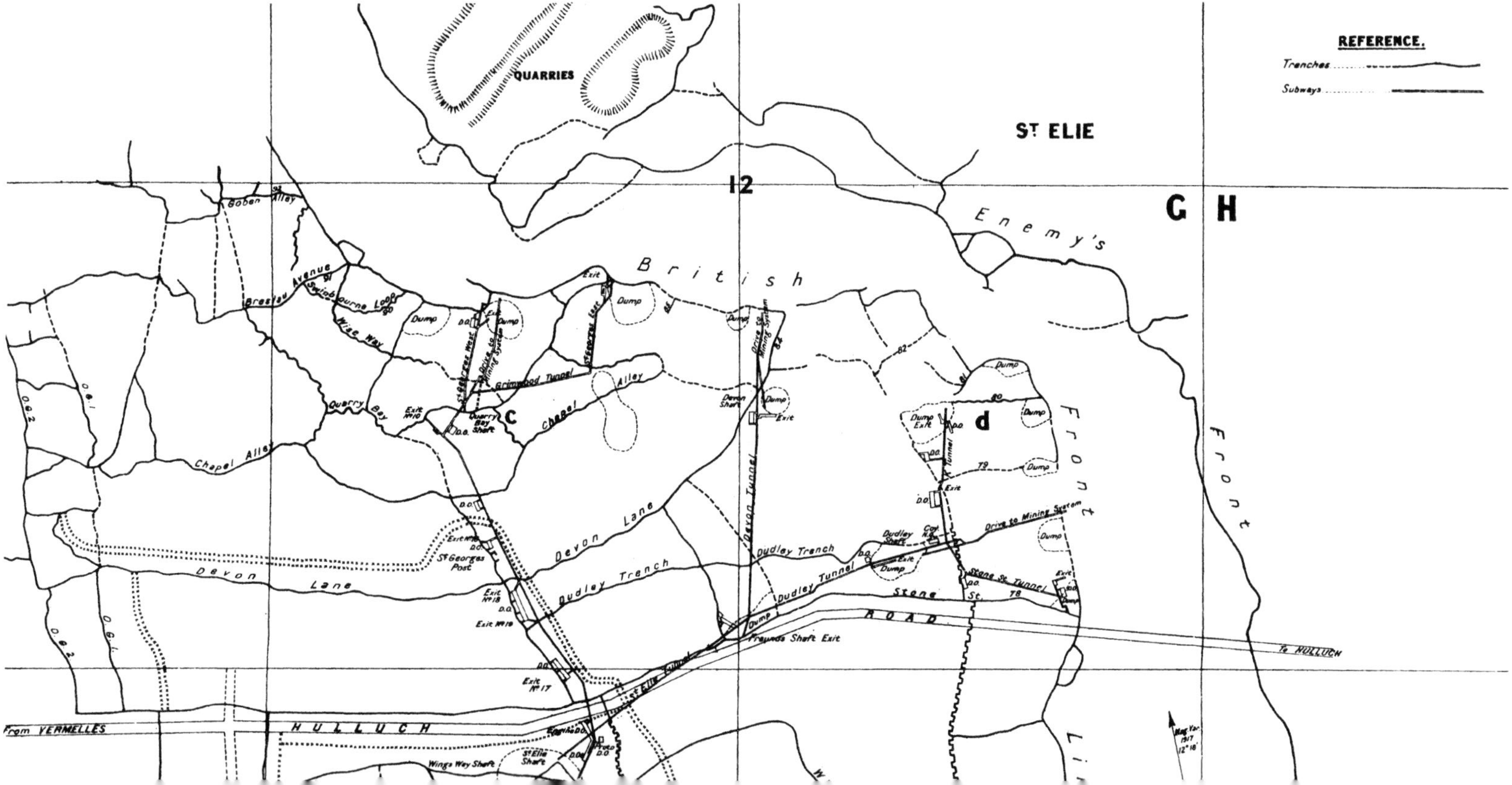

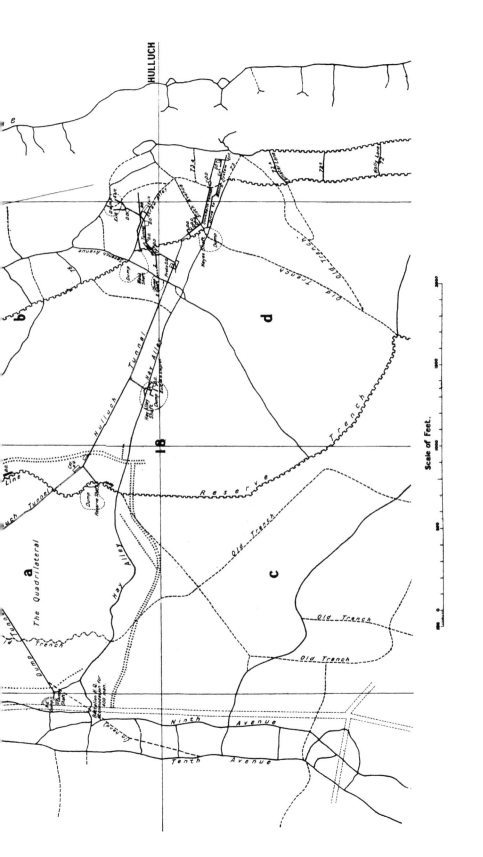

HULLUCH

The Quadrilateral

Hulluch Tunnel

Reserve Trench

Hay Alley

Ninth Avenue

Tenth Avenue

Old Trench

Old Trench

Old Trench

Old Trench

Research Avenue

Scale of Feet.

a
b
c
d
e
18

PLATE VI.

HILL 70.
SKETCH SHEWING POSITIONS
OF THE GERMAN GALLERIES
CAPTURED ON 24.7.1917.

GERMAN GALLERIES SHOWN THUS ⌐⌐⌐⌐⌐

NASH ALLEY

Cameron Alley

Scale 1:0" = 800-0"

Between A, B, C & D. leads
2 double electric leads
2 single electric leads
Between D. E & F.
2 double electric leads
2 single electric leads

Note:- at line E. Crater was blown by enemy
British line ran from X to Y.

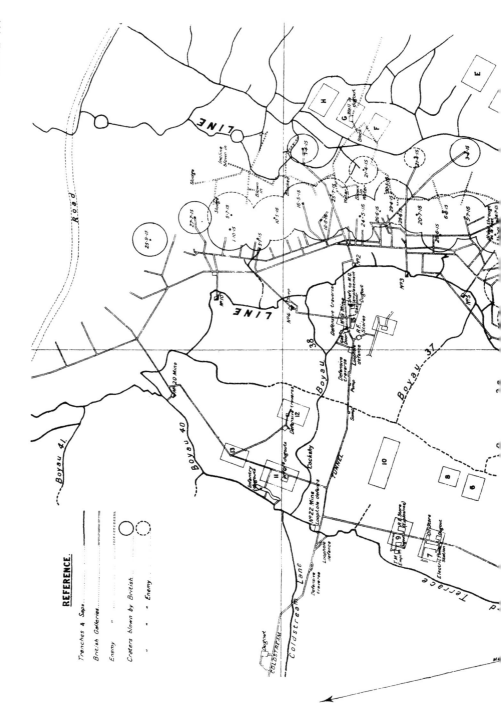

CRATERS on CUINCHY FRONT.

PLATE VII

REFERENCE.

Trenches & Saps
British Galleries
Enemy
Craters blown by British
"   "   Enemy

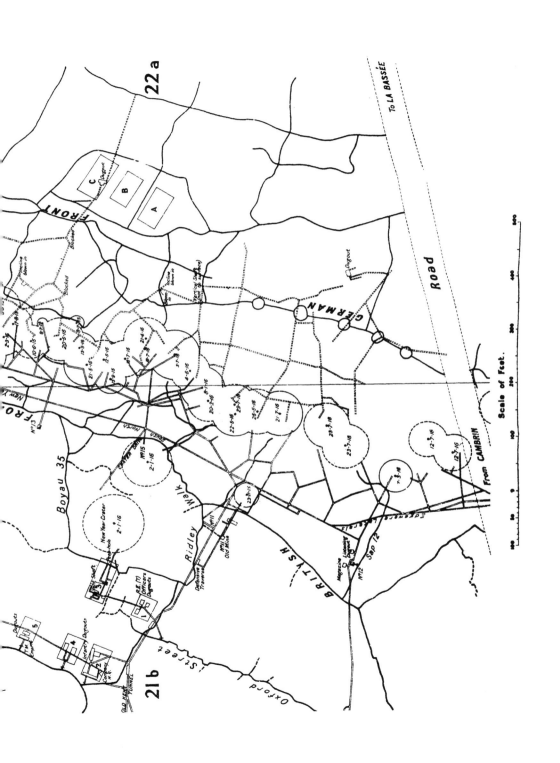

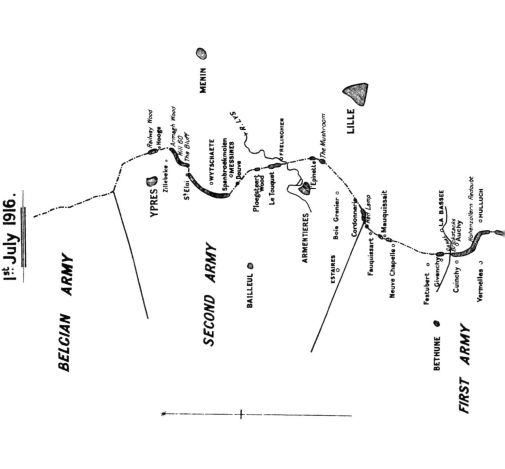

MINING AREAS ON BRITISH FRONT
1st July 1916.

BELGIAN ARMY

YPRES
Railway Wood
Hooge
Zillebeke
St Eloi
Hill 60
The Bluff
Armagh Wood

MENIN

WYTSCHAETE
Spanbroekmolen
MESSINES
Douve
R. LYS
FRELINGHIEN

SECOND ARMY

BAILLEUL

Ploegsteert Wood
Le Touquet
Epinette
The Mushroom

LILLE

ARMENTIERES

Bois Grenier
Cordonnerie
Red Lamp
Mauquissait

ESTAIRES

Fauquissart
Neuve Chapelle
LA BASSEE
Canal
Brickstacks
Auchy

BETHUNE
Festubert
Givenchy
Cuinchy
Hohenzollern Redoubt
HULLUCH
Vermelles

FIRST ARMY

PLATE VIII

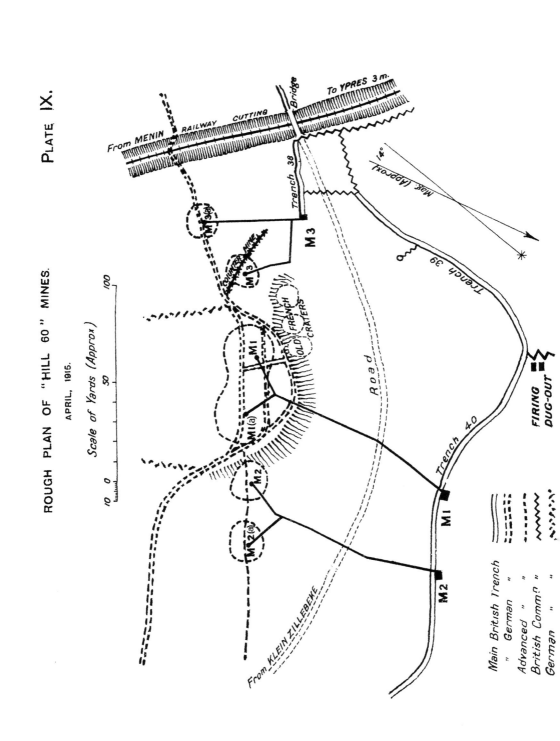

PLATE IX.

ROUGH PLAN OF "HILL 60" MINES.

APRIL, 1915.

Scale of Yards (Approx)

10 0   50   100

From MENIN   RAILWAY   CUTTING   Bridge   To YPRES 3 m.

Trench 38

M 3(a)

M 3

COUNTER MINE

OLD FRENCH CRATERS

M1

M1(a)

M2

M2(a)

From KLEIN ZILLEBEKE

Road

Trench 39

Trench 40

M1

M2

Mat. (Approx)

14°

FIRING DUG-OUT

Main British Trench
"   German   "
Advanced "   "
British Commⁿ "
German "   "

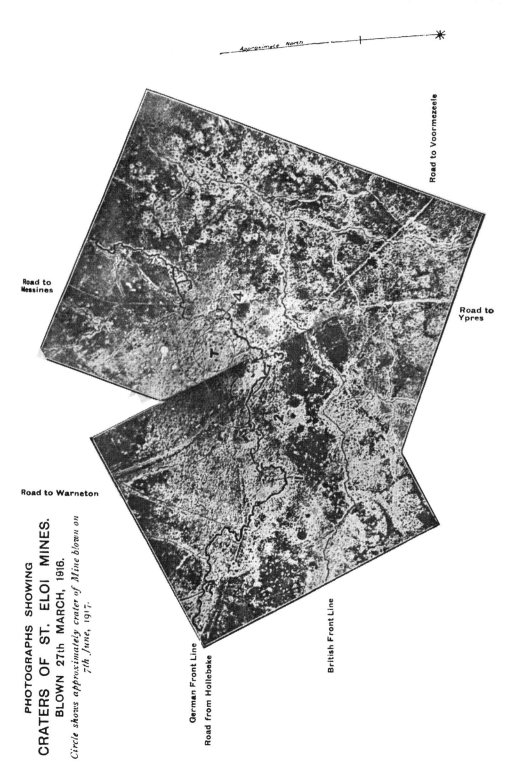

PLATE X.

Approximate North

Road to Voormezeele

Road to Ypres

Road to Messines

Road to Warneton

German Front Line
Road from Hollebeke

British Front Line

PHOTOGRAPHS SHOWING
CRATERS OF ST. ELOI MINES.
BLOWN 27th MARCH, 1916.
Circle shows approximately crater of Mine blown on 7th June, 1917.

PLATE XI.

THE BLUFF.

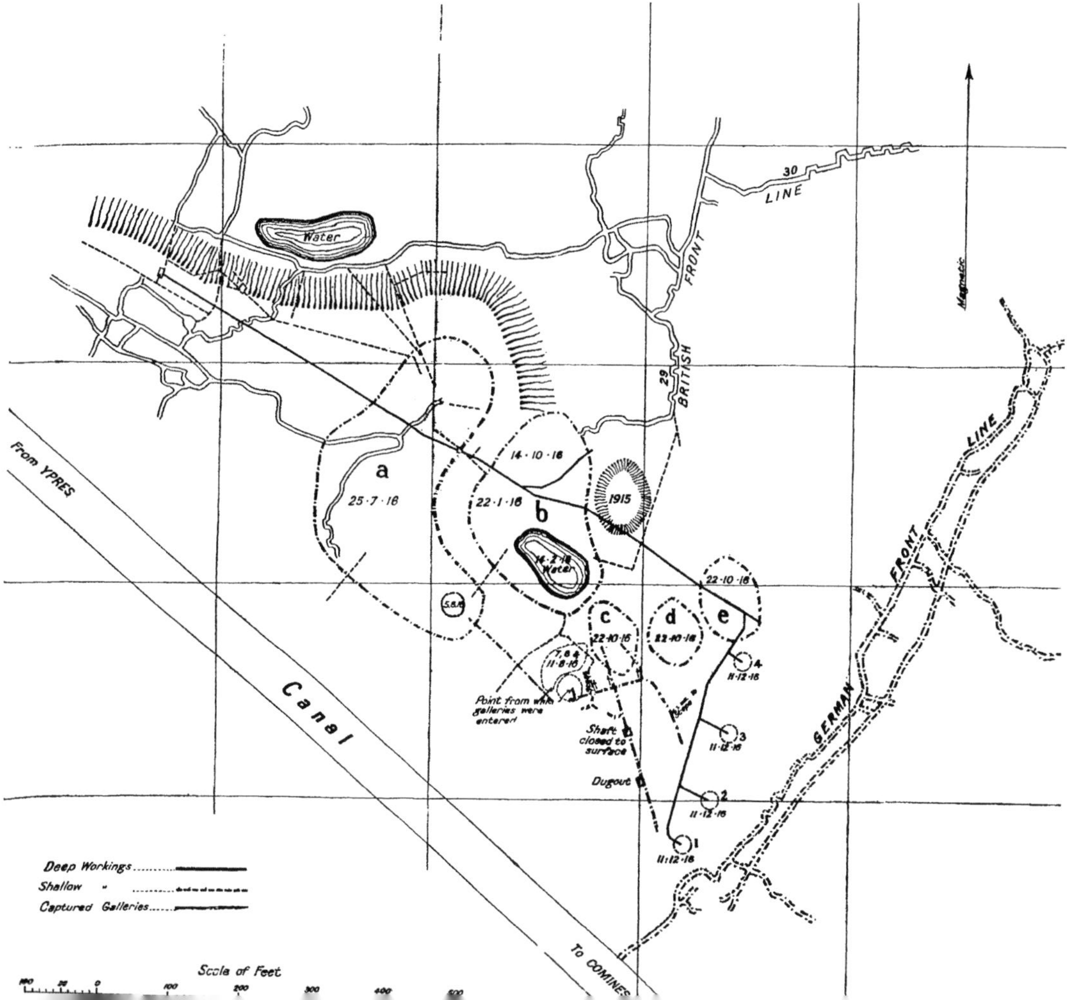

Deep Workings ....
Shallow   "   ....
Captured Galleries ....

Scale of Feet

To COMINES

Canal

From YPRES

PLATE XII.

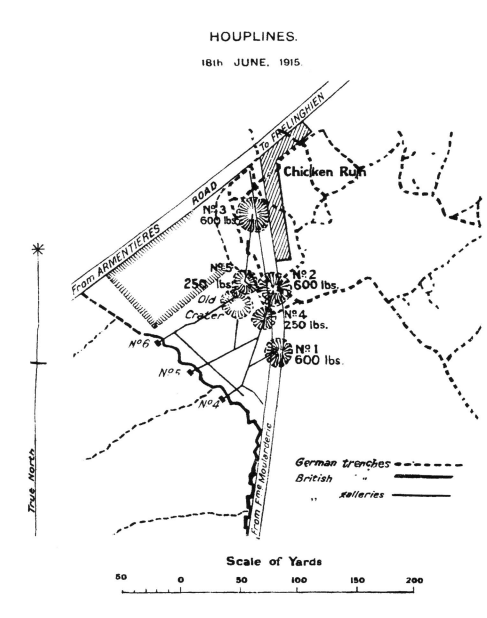

HOUPLINES.

18th JUNE, 1915.

To FRELINGHIEN

Chicken Run

From ARMENTIERES ROAD

Nº 3
600 lbs.

Nº 5
250 lbs.

Nº 2
600 lbs.

Old Crater

Nº 4
250 lbs.

Nº 6

Nº 1
600 lbs.

Nº 5

Nº 4

From Fme. Moulanderie

True North

German trenches ‑ ‑ ‑ ‑ ‑
British „   ━━━━━
  „   galleries ━━━━━

Scale of Yards

50   0   50   100   150   200

PLATE XIII.

SKETCH ILLUSTRATING ENEMY ENTRANCE
INTO CLOSE TIMBERED GALLERY.

11th FEBRUARY, 1916.

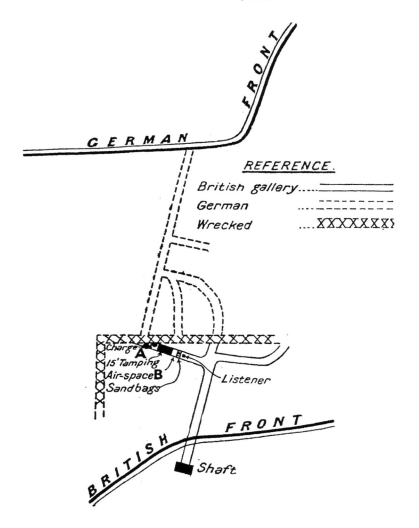

Not drawn to scale.

PLATE XIV.

SKETCH PLAN ILLUSTRATING ENTRY AND DESTRUCTION
OF ENEMY MINES IN CHALK, 2-3-1916.

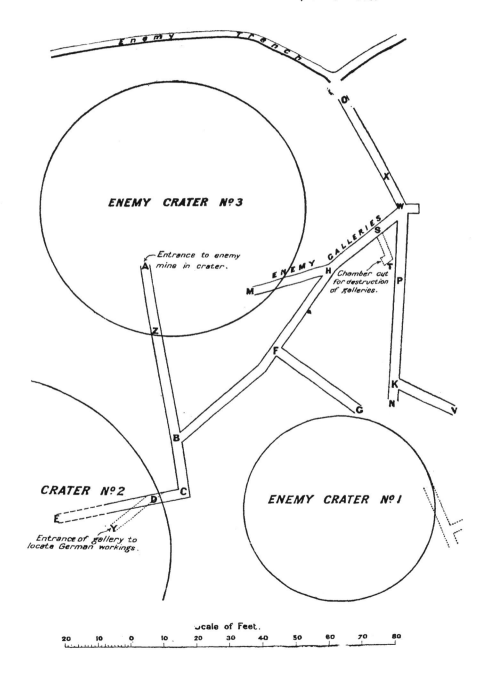

ENEMY CRATER Nº 3

Entrance to enemy mine in crater.

ENEMY GALLERIES

Chamber cut for destruction of galleries.

CRATER Nº 2

ENEMY CRATER Nº 1

Entrance of gallery to locate German workings.

Scale of Feet.

20 10 0 10 20 30 40 50 60 70 80

PLATE XV.

Fig. i.

HAWTHORN RIDGE REDOUBT.

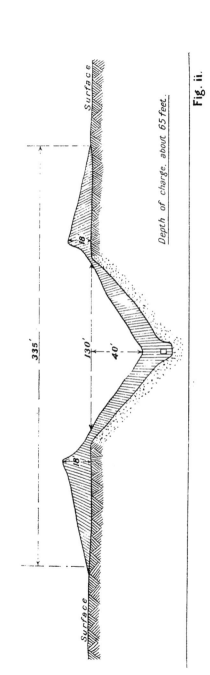

Depth of charge, about 65 feet.

Fig. ii.

LA BOISSELLE.

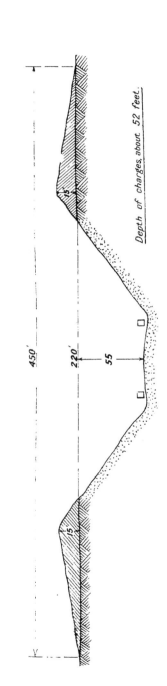

Depth of charges, about 52 feet.

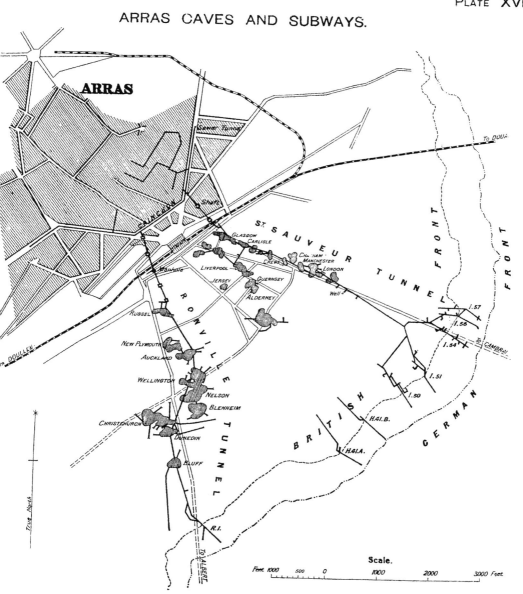

PLATE XVI.

ARRAS CAVES AND SUBWAYS.

Plate XVII.

THE BERLIN TUNNEL.

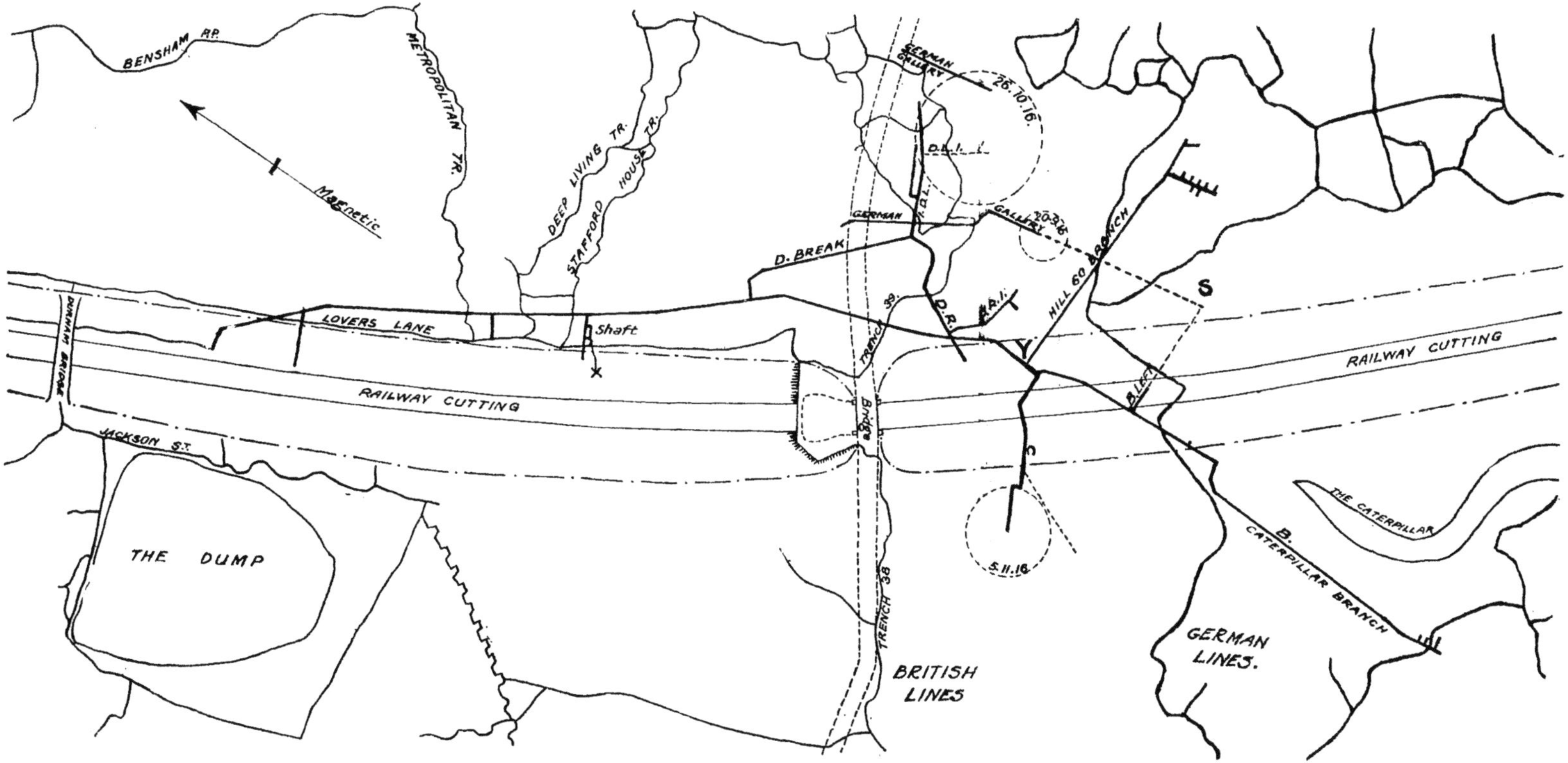

SCALE 1" = 100 FEET.

Feet 100 50 0 100 200 300 400 500 600 700 Feet

SUMMARY OF OFFENSIVE MINES, 7.6.17.   PLATE XVIII.

Name of Mine.	Date of Commencement.	Date of Completion of Charging.	Depth of Charge.	Charge in Lbs.	Method of Firing.	Diameter at Ground Level.	Width of Rim.	Depth Below Ground Level.	Height of Rim.	Diameter of Complete Obliteration.	Length of Gallery in Feet.	Diagram of Mines.
Hill 60	22. 8.15											
"A" Left		1. 8.16	90'	{ 45,700 Am. / 7,800 G.C. / 53,500 }	Power	191'	47'	33'	11'	285'	Branch 240'	
"B" Caterpillar		18.10.16	100'	Ammonal 70,000	Power	260'	60'	51'	17'	380'	1386'	
St. Eloi	10. 8.16	28. 5.17	125'	Ammonal 95,600	Exploder	176'	77'	17'	8'	330'	1340' / 300'	
Hollandscheschuur	18.12.15											
No. 1		20. 6.16	60'	{ 30,000 Am. / 4,200 Blas / 34,200 }	Exploder	183'	80'	29'	9'	343'	825'	
No. 2		11. 7.16	55'	{ 12,500 Am. / 2,400 Blas / 14,900 }	Exploder	105'	55'	14'	7'	215'	Branch 45'	
No. 3		20. 8.16	55'	{ 15,000 Am. / 2,500 Blas / 17,500 }	Exploder	141'	30'	25'	5'	201'	Branch 395'	
Petit Bois	16.12.15											
No. 2 Left		15. 8.16	57'	{ 21,000 Am. / 9,000 Blas / 30,000 }	Power	217'	100'	46'	4'	417'	Branch 210'	
No. 1 Right		30. 7.16	70'	{ 21,000 Am. / 9,000 Blas / 30,000 }	Power	175'	100'	49'	5'	375'	2070'	
Maedelstede Fm.	3. 9.16	2. 6.17	100'	{ 90,000 Am. / 4,000 G.C. }	Power					285'	1650'	

Mine	Date	Depth	Charge (lbs.)	Firing						
Peckham	20.12.15	70'	15,000 blas. / 7,000 G.C. / 87,000	Exploder	240'	45'	46'	9'	330'	1145'
Spanbroekmolen	19.7.16 / 28.6.16 (recovd. 6.6.17)	88'	Ammonal 91,000	Power	250'	90'	40'	13'	430'	1710'
Kruisstraat	1.1.16 / 2.1.16		30,000 Am.							
Nos. 1 and 4	No. 1 5.7.16 / No. 4 11.4.17	57' / 57'	18,500 Am. / 1,000 G.C. / 19,500	Power	235'	80'	34'	9'	395'	—
No. 2	12.7.16	62'	Ammonal 30,000	Power	217'	75'	40'	10'	367'	Branch 170'
No. 3	23.8.16	50'	Ammonal 30,000	Power	202'	65'	30'	7'	332'	2160'
Ontario Fm.	28.1.17 / 5.6.17	103'	Ammonal 60,000	Exploder	200'	10'	Practically nil	4'	220'	1290'
Trench 127	28.12.15									
No. 7 Left	20.4.16	75'	Ammonal 36,000	Exploder	182'	25'	10'	2'	232'	Branch 250'
No. 8 Right	9.5.16	76'	Ammonal 50,000	Exploder	210'	66'	16'	1'	342'	1355'
Trench 122	15.2.16									
No. 5 Left	14.5.16	60'	Ammonal 20,000	Exploder	195'	64'	22'	3'	323'	Branch 440'
No. 6 Right	11.6.16	75'	Ammonal 40,000	Exploder	228'	64'	28'	4'	356'	970'

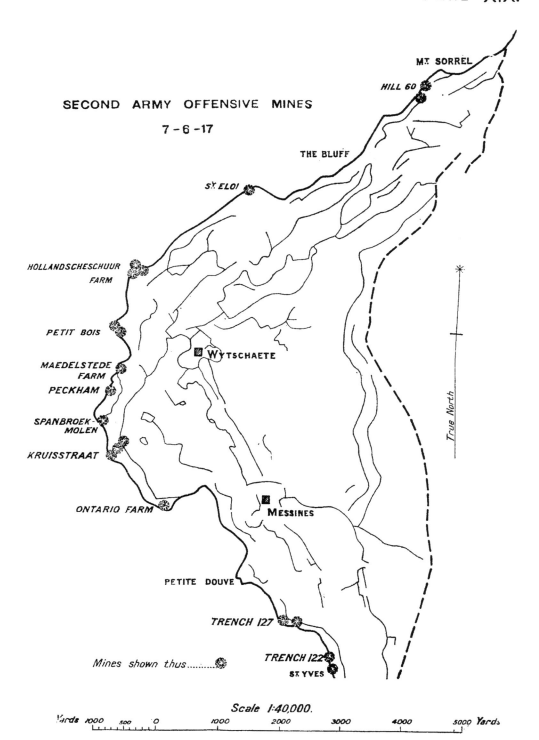

PLATE XIX.

SECOND ARMY OFFENSIVE MINES
7 – 6 –17

MT SORREL

HILL 60

THE BLUFF

ST ELOI

HOLLANDSCHESCHUUR
FARM

PETIT BOIS

MAEDELSTEDE
FARM

PECKHAM

SPANBROEK-
MOLEN

KRUISSTRAAT

WYTSCHAETE

ONTARIO FARM

MESSINES

True North

PETITE DOUVE

TRENCH 127

Mines shown thus...........

TRENCH 122

ST YVES

Scale 1:40,000.

Yards 1000   500   0   1000   2000   3000   4000   5000 Yards

CRATERS BLOWN AT HILL 60

3.10. A.M. 7th JUNE, 1917.

PLATE XX.

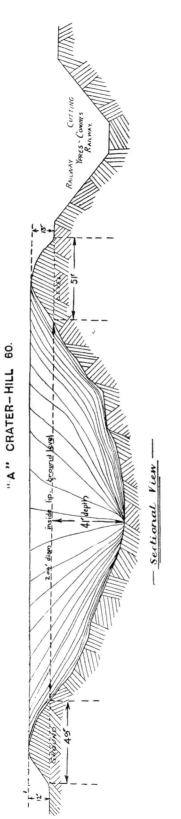

"A" CRATER—HILL 60.

— *Sectional View* —

"B" CRATER—CATERPILLAR

— *Sectional View* —

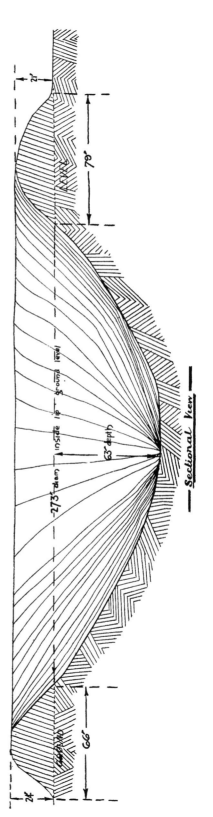

PLATE XXI

CHAMBER OF ST. ELOI MINE
BLOWN JUNE 7th, 1917.

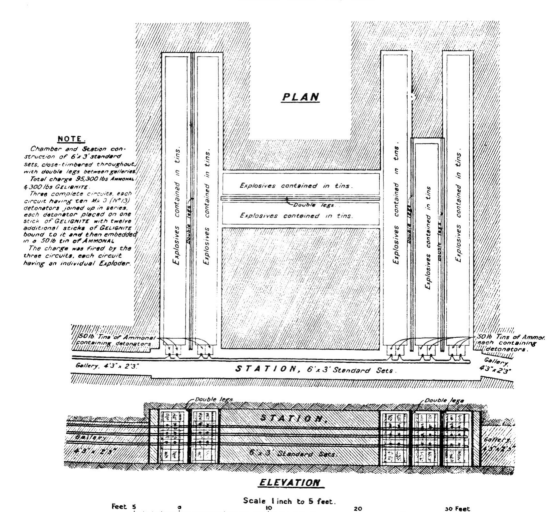

SWITCH BOARD: HILL 60. PLATE XXII.

7th JUNE, 1917.

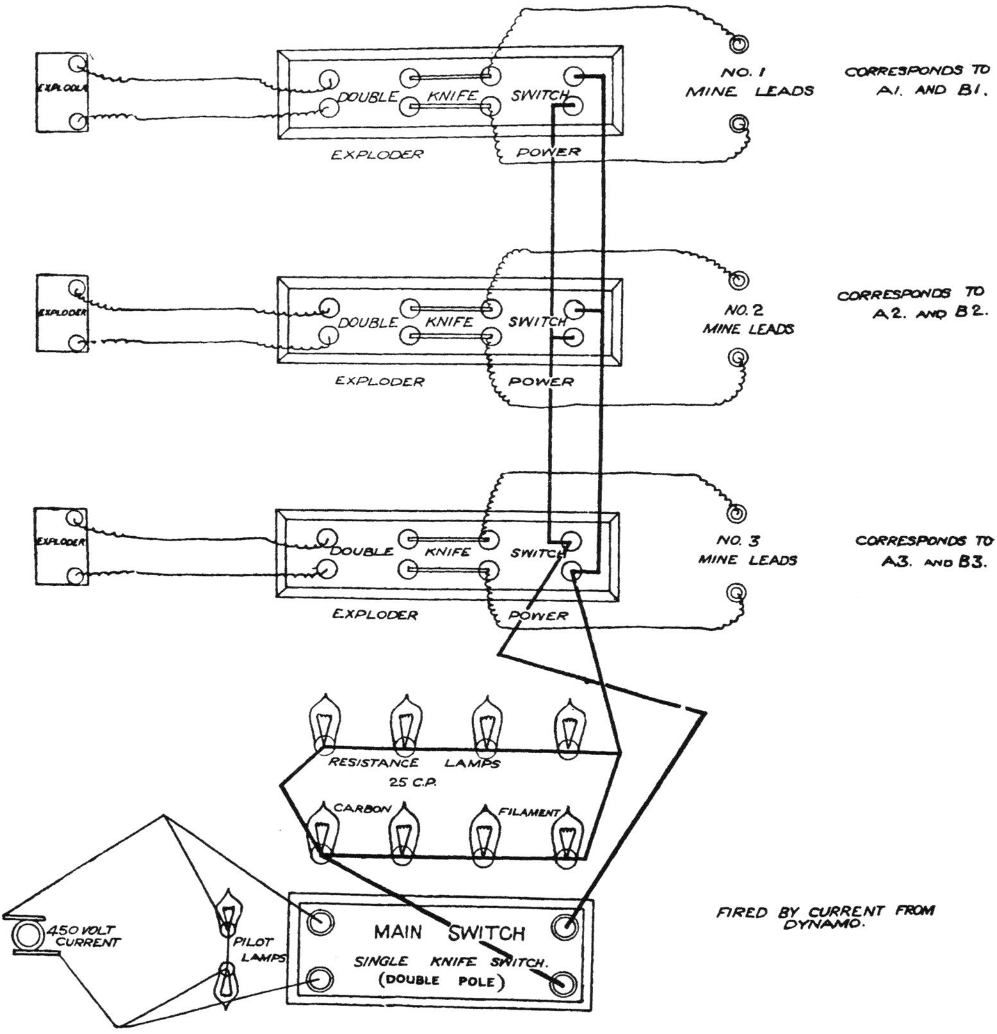

EXPLODER

DOUBLE KNIFE SWITCH

EXPLODER   POWER

NO. 1
MINE LEADS

CORRESPONDS TO
A1. AND B1.

EXPLODER

DOUBLE KNIFE SWITCH

EXPLODER   POWER

NO. 2
MINE LEADS

CORRESPONDS TO
A.2. AND B2.

EXPLODER

DOUBLE KNIFE SWITCH

EXPLODER   POWER

NO. 3
MINE LEADS

CORRESPONDS TO
A3. AND B3.

RESISTANCE   LAMPS
25 C.P.

CARBON   FILAMENT

450 VOLT
CURRENT

PILOT
LAMPS

MAIN SWITCH
SINGLE KNIFE SWITCH.
(DOUBLE POLE)

FIRED BY CURRENT FROM
DYNAMO.

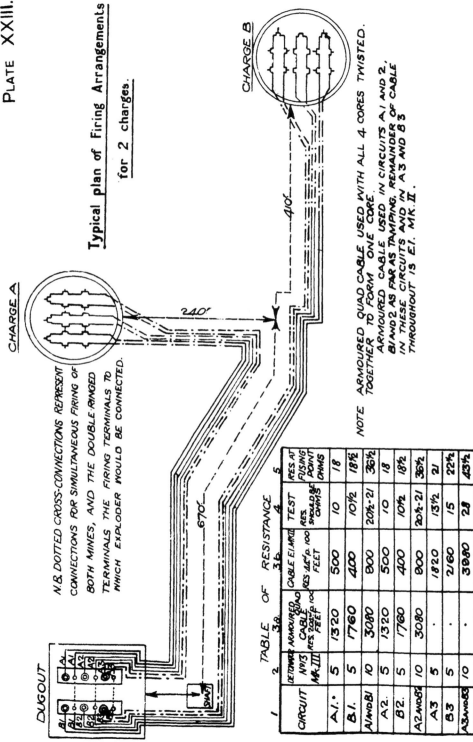

PLATE XXIII.

Typical plan of Firing Arrangements

for 2 charges.

CHARGE A

CHARGE B

DUGOUT

SHAFT

N.B. DOTTED CROSS-CONNECTIONS REPRESENT
CONNECTIONS FOR SIMULTANEOUS FIRING OF
BOTH MINES, AND THE DOUBLE-RINGED
TERMINALS THE FIRING TERMINALS TO
WHICH EXPLODER WOULD BE CONNECTED.

NOTE ARMOURED QUAD CABLE USED WITH ALL 4 CORES TWISTED.
TOGETHER TO FORM ONE CORE.
ARMOURED CABLE USED IN CIRCUITS A1 AND 2,
B1 AND 2 AS FAR AS TAMPING, REMAINDER OF CABLE
IN THESE CIRCUITS AND IN A3 AND B3
THROUGHOUT IS E.I. MK.II.

TABLE OF RESISTANCE

1	2	3a	3b	4	5
CIRCUIT	DETONATOR Nº13 MK.III	ARMOURED QUAD CABLE RES 20ᵂ P. 100 FEET	CABLE E.I.MK.II RES 4ᵂ P. 100 FEET	TEST RES. SHOULD BE OHMS	RES AT FUSING POINT OHMS
A.1.	5	1320	500	10	18
B.1.	5	1760	400	10½	18½
A1 AND B1	10	3080	900	20½-21	36½
A.2.	5	1320	500	10	18
B.2.	5	1760	400	10½	18½
A2 AND B2	10	3080	900	20½-21	36½
A3	5	·	1820	13½	21
B3	5	·	2160	15	22½
A3 AND B3	10	·	3980	28	43½

240'

410'

670'

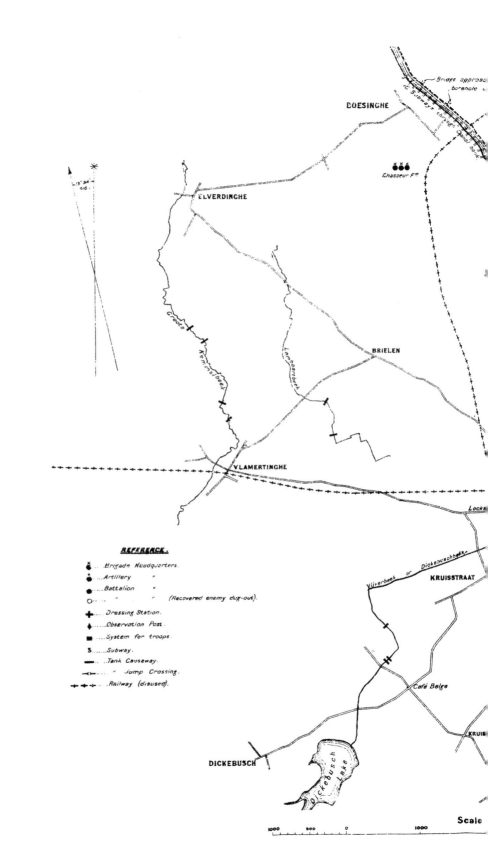

REFERENCE.

- ⚇ ... Brigade Headquarters.
- ⚉ ... Artillery   "
- ● ... Battalion   "
- ○ ...   "   "   (Recovered enemy dug-out).
- ✚ ... Dressing Station.
- ♦ ... Observation Post.
- ■ ... System for troops.
- S ... Subway.
- ▬ ... Tank Causeway.
- ◁▷ ... " Jump Crossing.
- ✛✛✛ ... Railway (disused).

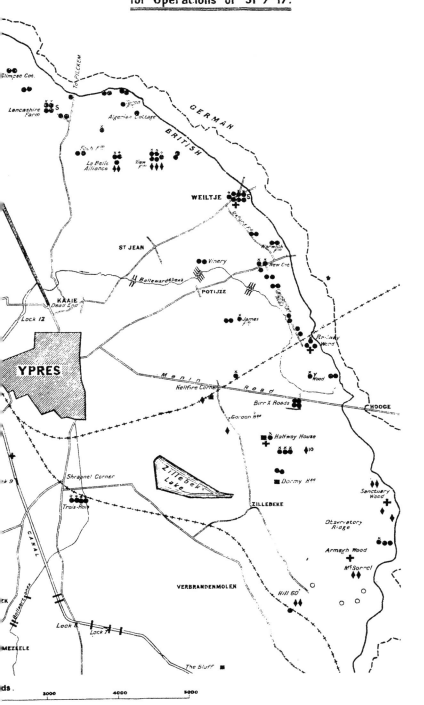

PLATE XXIV^A

Map to illustrate

WORK of TUNNELLING COYS in FIFTH ARMY AREA

for Operations of 31-7-17.

PART II.—MINE RESCUE WORK.

FOREWORD.

This part is a condensed version of a very full report by Lieut.-Colonel D. DALE LOGAN, D.S.O., M.D., R.A.M.C., who was responsible, under the Engineer-in-Chief, for the whole of the Rescue Organization throughout the War.

CHAPTER I.

INVESTIGATION AND SELECTION OF APPARATUS.

1. INTRODUCTION.

In the autumn of 1915 it was evident that for some time the conditions on the Western Front would be those of trench warfare accompanied by military mining on a large scale.

With the gradual increase in the size of explosive charges used in craters and in camouflets following upon the increased depth of mines, the more extensive mine systems, and the consequent increased personnel employed, the casualties from gas poisoning assumed serious proportions.

A diagram of trenches and mine galleries, showing the effect of camouflet and mine gas on galleries and ventilation, is given on *Plate* I.

In six weeks one Tunnelling Company had 16 killed, 48 sent to hospital, and 86 minor cases treated at the shaft head and returned to the company billets. Another company had, in a month, 12 killed by gas, 28 sent to hospital and 60 minor cases retained with the unit. As many of these were skilled miners, whose place it was almost impossible to fill at the time, the wastage was affecting in a very marked way the efficiency of the company.

In response to urgent demands from some of the companies for rescue apparatus, a qualified instructor of " Proto " apparatus had been sent from England in June, 1915 ; and shortly afterwards the first schools for the teaching of rescue work were started. (For further details of schools, see Part III., Chapter V.).

In September, 1915, Lieut.-Colonel D. Dale Logan, D.S.O., R.A.M.C., was attached to the Staff of the Engineer-in-Chief to organize a system of rescue work and of protection against gas in mining.

2. Nature of Gas Poisoning.

Before fixing upon the best type of apparatus and proceeding with the organization of rescue work, it was necessary first of all to be certain of the poisonous factor at work in gas poisoning cases, more especially as all sorts of rumours were spreading throughout Tunnelling Companies that the Germans were employing a new kind of gas, and forcing it through into our galleries. Such rumours were encouraged by the insidious nature of the poisoning, and the serious number of casualties caused.

New companies with little experience of mining conditions at the front, when they first encountered gas, were naturally inclined to believe that it was being forced through from German galleries for the following reasons :—

(a). On several occasions it was found that men who were in the galleries at the time of an explosion suffered from irritant gas poisoning. It was not generally understood at this period that nitrous fumes, under certain conditions, might be formed from explosives.

(b). Sometimes the gas came out in distinct puffs, accompanied by a whistling sound, showing that the gas was escaping under pressure.

(c). Hostile attacks by drift gas were very common at that time.

Extensive series of investigations were carried out of the conditions underground after a blow, the manner in which casualties occurred, and the symptoms of the men who had been exposed to the gas ; as well as post-mortem examination of a number of men, of canaries, and of white mice killed by gas, and analysis of various samples of gas. The results proved conclusively that carbon monoxide from the detonation of high explosives was the poisonous factor in mine fighting. The opportunities for the enemy to force carbon monoxide gas successfully into our galleries were so rare, that this source of poisoning could be ignored.

3. Choice of Apparatus.

Types Available.—Various types of apparatus had been procured by Tunnelling Companies at different times.

In deciding on a standard type the choice lay between the " Draeger," the " Meco," and the " Proto."

"Draeger."—The " Draeger " was rejected on the following grounds :—

(a). The injector was liable to become choked, and there was also the possibility of negative pressure being developed behind it, when, if there was the slightest leak in certain parts of the apparatus, poisonous air would be drawn into the breathing circuit.

(b). The objection to helmets and face masks. (See para. 6).

(c). The many connections and joints in the apparatus, and its construction, which rendered it liable to be damaged against the roof, etc.

(d). Want of flexibility and bad distribution of weight, which made it uncomfortable to wear.

(e). It did not give sufficient scope for movement.

The objections to this apparatus were confirmed by subsequent experiments with captured sets, and by accidents in collieries in England, which were reported from time to time.

" Meco."—The " Meco " resembled the " Draeger " in many ways, especially as regards points (b), (c), and (d). There was the same grave objection to it that the circulation was induced by an injector.

" Proto."—The " Proto " was selected for the following reasons :—

(a). It was already in use and had given good results.

(b). It is simple, has fewer joints and connections than the " Draeger " and " Meco," and consequently does not get out of order readily.

(c). It is entirely under positive pressure ; small leaks in the apparatus are consequently not so dangerous as in such types as the " Draeger."

Unlike the " Draeger " and " Meco," the circulation of air is entirely dependent on the lungs of the wearer.

(d). It is better balanced, and consequently more comfortable to wear than the " Draeger " or " Meco."

(e). It permits freedom of movement to the head and arms ; it is much more flexible, and, as only the cylinders are carried behind, and no parts of the apparatus project at points liable to be knocked during use, it is less liable to be injured.

(f). The mouthpiece is more comfortable.

Disadvantages.—

(a). Absorption of CO_2 is not so efficient as in the " Draeger."

(b). After the apparatus has been worn some time the inspiratory air becomes very hot owing to chemical action in the bag, the heavy rubber and stout canvas covering preventing proper dissipation of the heat.

As the result of the hard work carried out in the schools and in the trenches, several defects came to light and were remedied. Various suggestions for improving the apparatus were forwarded from time to time from the schools, a large number of which were incorporated in future orders.

4. DESCRIPTION OF " PROTO " APPARATUS.

(See *Plate* II.). Twin cylinders of compressed oxygen (BB), containing 5 c. ft., or 280 litres of oxygen under a pressure of 120 atmospheres, are slung over the back, fitting comfortably. These are fitted with a wheeled valve (H), the main valve, which is supplied with a device which makes it impossible to turn off accidentally. A reducing valve (C) is screwed to the delivery nipple, and can be adjusted to pass from $1\frac{1}{2}$ to 3 litres of oxygen per minute. The reducing valve is provided with a bye-pass which short-circuits it, so that, should the reducing valve fail to act, or should the wearer require a larger supply of oxygen than can be delivered by the reducing valve, as in very strenuous work, he can get a special supply direct from the cylinders. The reducing valve delivers the oxygen through a flexible tube (F) to the breathing bag (D), which is carried on the wearer's chest. Here it mixes with the air to be drawn into the lungs. There is another connection at (V), to which is connected a flexible high pressure tube (W), at the opposite end of which is fitted a pressure-gauge (P), which is carried in a pocket and ready for inspection.

The breathing bag (D) is of vulcanized rubber contained in an outer bag of strong tanned canvas. It is divided into two compartments by a partition running from the top to within a short distance of the bottom. In this bag are placed the sticks of caustic soda. Light mica valves are placed at the junction of the tubes and the bag at (M) and (L), so that the wearer inhales from the bag on one side of the partition and exhales into the other side, where the air passes over the caustic soda and CO_2 is absorbed. A saliva trap (Z) is fitted under the exhaling tube ; it prevents the saliva from entering the breathing bag. (K) is a relief valve for the relief of any excess pressure in the bag. The mouthpiece is of soft vulcanized rubber fitted to a German silver connecting piece (R). To the connecting piece are fitted strong corrugated tubes (X) which connect the mouthpiece with the upper corners of the bag. A noseclip compresses the nostrils. *Photos* I. and II. illustrate the " Proto " apparatus as worn by a mine rescue man.

5. THE " SALVUS."

The oxygen in the " Proto " is sufficient to last two hours. In certain work it was found that such a large supply of oxygen was not necessary, and that it was better to sacrifice a considerable percentage of the oxygen to obtain a lighter and less bulky apparatus.

The " Salvus " apparatus, which is designed on similar principles to the " Proto," and by the same manufacturers, satisfied these requirements.

The manufacturers were asked to modify the existing type of " Salvus " to comply with the following conditions :—

(a). A supply of oxygen sufficient to last one hour.

(b). A sufficiently large cartridge of caustic soda to outlast the oxygen (this is absolutely necessary in all apparatus. No amount of oxygen will neutralize the breathing of a high percentage of CO_2).

(c). A reducing valve to do away with the necessity of the wearer constantly looking after the supply of oxygen, as was the case in the original apparatus.

(d). A relief valve.

It was found that if the bag became over-distended with oxygen there was difficulty in breathing, and men have been overcome in this way. When there was less demand for oxygen, as could be the case after finishing severe muscular exertion, the oxygen collected and the pressure in the bag and tube leading to the mouth became so great that the lungs were not able to exhale properly.

(e). Pressure gauge with a cap which acts as a mirror to show the reading, and at the same time prevents the gauge from being broken.

Description of Apparatus.—(See *Photo* III.).

(A). Steel cylinder containing about 3 c. ft. oxygen

(B). Main valve.

(C). CO_2 absorbent cartridge.

(D). Breathing bag.

(E). Reducing valve.

(F). Pressure gauge.

(K). Bye-pass.

(L). Relief valve.

(M). Mirror.

(P). Mask of box respirator.

Disadvantages.—This modified " Salvus " was very popular in Flanders, and in the earlier days of mining, when galleries were small, it was largely used all along the line. Later on, when mine systems became more extensive and galleries were increased in size, it fell into disfavour, and in most places, especially in chalk areas, the men had much more confidence in the " Proto," only using the " Salvus " for reconnaissance work.

The complaint was general that, after wearing the apparatus for more than thirty or thirty-five minutes, the air became too hot for comfortable working. If work was persisted in after that time the pulse-rate became greatly accelerated.

Another complaint was that breathing was sometimes interfered with, owing to the bag doubling under the wearer while at work.

Generally speaking, for the purposes for which the " Salvus " was intended, *viz.*, reconnaissance work which did not entail a long stay in the mine or great exertion, the " Salvus " gave excellent results ; but for all-round efficiency it cannot be compared to the " Proto."

6. HELMETS, MASKS, ETC., USED WITH RESCUE APPARATUS.

These were never used in France with the exception of sponge rubber goggles and the box respirator mask. There are grave objections to their use, *e.g.*, risk of CO_2 collecting in helmets, risk of leakage owing to difficulty of proper fitting, and interference with vision.

When rescue work had to be carried out in the presence of lachrymatory gas, sponge goggles were used with " Proto " and " Salvus " sets, and afforded complete protection until early in 1917, when it was discovered that, in certain heavy concentrations of the new lachrymatory gases employed by the enemy, the gas came through.

To overcome this difficulty, a method of fitting the mask of a box respirator to the mouthpiece of the " Salvus " apparatus was designed in March, 1917, at one of the schools.

The mask was fitted into the mouthpiece of the " Salvus " and " Proto " in exactly the same way as it is fitted to the mouthpiece of the box respirator, all mouthpiece straps being done away with. (*Photo* IV.).

The arrangement has the following advantages :—

(*a*). Goggles, mouthpiece and noseclip are all in one part, and are therefore fitted at one time to the face, and cannot get lost.

(*b*). In the event of the noseclip slipping off, the wearer cannot inhale impure air through the nose before he has time to readjust the clip.

(*c*). The same is the case with the mouthpiece, which can be partly removed for talking.

(*d*). Goggles can be cleaned without taking them off.

(*e*). In the event of a man becoming unconscious he cannot breathe foul air.

The question of a perfectly fitting mask is solved by each rescue man having his own mask and adapter.

Fire Fighting Apparatus.—For fires a special asbestos hood and apron were worn with the " Proto " apparatus (*Photo* V.).

The work of rescue is made very difficult owing to the reduced vision and consequent loss of sense of direction, and it was found necessary to connect members of a rescue party by means of a white rope. Electric lamps and torches give only a poor light in smoke, but were found better than oil lamps.

7. OXYGEN RESUSCITATING APPARATUS.

In selecting a standard type automatic apparatus, the *Pulmotor,* which is the best known, was rejected on the following grounds :—

(*a*). It was too heavy and complicated for use by mine rescue men when in the trenches.

(*b*). The great danger of inducing expiration by mechanical suction.

(*c*). Prolonged use may cause injury to the lungs. In many cases of CO poisoning it is necessary to administer oxygen for long periods—this apparatus wasted oxygen.

(*d*). Even in the hands of a medical officer the apparatus might cause damage—used by a rescue man it might be fatal.

The Novita Pattern Oxygen Reviving Apparatus was fixed upon as the simplest and most efficient. It was considerably modified to meet the conditions in the trenches, being coupled in the box ready for immediate use.

The box and handle were arranged in such a way that it was easily carried down the shafts. (See *Photos* X. and XI., XII., and XIII.).

The *Novita* consisted of :—

Oxygen cylinder, 6 c. ft. capacity, fitted with a main valve.
A pressure gauge.
A fine adjustment valve.
A flexible bag ; and
A mask.

Instructions for Use.—See that the oxygen cylinder is fully charged and that all joints and connections are quite tight.

Place patient in the prone position, turn on main valve, and then carefully and gradually open the fine adjustment valve. Then apply the mask to the patient's face. The fine adjustment valve should be set so as to keep the bag about half full of oxygen. Over-inflation of the bag should be avoided.

8. THE MINE STRETCHER.

(See *Photos* VI., VII., and VIII.).

This was designed at one of the Mine Rescue Schools. It proved of the greatest value in dragging a man along the galleries with the least possible exertion for the rescue man ; the skids on the bottom of the stretcher facilitating this, and bringing him safely to the surface.

It was also very useful for carrying a wounded or gassed man along a trench when the ordinary stretcher could not be used.

Rescue men became so expert in the use of this stretcher that a man could be securely fixed to it in a few seconds.

As will be seen from the photographs, when a man was brought up shaft, the weight of the body rested on the loop underneath the feet. The attachment of the chains across the breast was an objection, but this did not actually interfere with breathing ; as it was rare for shafts to be deeper than 90 ft., the time passed on the stretcher was very short.

Directions for Use.—Place the man on the stretcher and pass his arms through the arm loops, bringing the arms close to the sides.

Connect the snap hooks with the rings on the arm loops so that the chains cross the breast just below the nipple line, and the swivels of the hooks are on the centre line of the chest. Pull the ropes tight and bring to the front over the arms, crossing them in front over the thighs underneath the stretcher, and again to the front.

The ends of the rope are then passed through the opposite side of the loops, pulled tight across the front of the legs above the ankle, and finished off with two complete turns round the ankles and secured with a reef-knot.

9. Mine Gas Testing Set.

(See *Photo* IX.).

This was designed at the Central Laboratory, G.H.Q., and proved very effective in detecting small quantities of CO.

It consisted of a small wooden box, $3\frac{1}{2}$ ins. $\times 5\frac{1}{4}$ ins. $\times 4\frac{1}{2}$ ins., with leather handle for ease in carrying, and was marked "Mine Gas Testing Set Carbon Monoxide." It contained a small drop bottle of palladium chloride solution and a number of test papers. These were circular and framed with white cardboard, and were suspended by a piece of tape from waterproof cases, which protected them against drops of water falling from the roof in wet galleries. Attached to the protective frame was another piece of tape with pin for attachment to the roof, etc.

The following instructions were issued with each set :—

(a). Drop *one drop only* of the liquid in the bottle on to the *middle* of one of the white test papers.

(b). Hang up the paper by the attached pin and tape so that it hangs freely and is protected from dropping water by the waterproof paper.

(*c*). A yellow ring will appear round the edge of the paper, *and will remain unchanged if no gas is present.*

(*d*). *If the ring darkens rapidly and becomes black in two minutes and a half or less there is a dangerous amount of gas present.*

(*e*). If the ring becomes slowly grey, and blackens in five to ten minutes, gas is present, but may be breathed safely for a short time.

(*f*). Do not put back used papers in the box.

Special Instructions.—The following orders regarding the use of the sets were also issued :—

(*a*). This apparatus is for the purpose of detecting the presence of CO by means of chemical reaction.

(*b*). It is to be used in testing galleries after a blow, or when galleries are known to contain a dangerous amount of gas, *before work is resumed.* In this way a considerable reduction in the wastage of canaries will be effected.

(*c*). *Canaries or mice are to be used* for testing galleries for gas *after work has been resumed in them.*

(*d*). One testing set is to be kept at each mine rescue station and a spare set at company headquarters.

The results showed that the paper was more sensitive than either canaries or mice, detecting percentages that left them unaffected.

With 0·1 per cent. the ring will become quite distinct in one minute and black in two and a half minutes ; with 0·2 per cent. the ring will become distinct within half a minute and black in 55 seconds.

The presence of H_2S affects the paper, but high explosives used in mining do not give rise to this gas.

The changes on the test paper were different from those produced by CO, the spot becoming evenly blackened and the discoloration less dark.

10. USE OF CANARIES AND MICE.

General Remarks.—Small birds and mice are of value as guides to the presence of CO, because they absorb the poisonous gas so much more quickly than man, owing to their rate of breathing and circulation being so much more rapid.

In an atmosphere containing a percentage of CO which would begin to affect a man in half an hour, a canary or a mouse would be affected in two minutes.

Canaries are more sensitive to CO than are mice. The latter are sluggish in their movements, and should be prodded from time to time, as some of them have a tendency to be quiet.

When affected, a mouse becomes restless, pants, and, after staggering about, rolls over.

Mice, if properly trained, are not so easily frightened as canaries, and some consider them easier to test with.

The Officer in charge of one of the Mine Rescue Schools preferred them. When descending a shaft he carried one in his pocket, holding it in his hand while inspecting galleries, and he believed that, if they are properly tamed by frequent handling, and if the rescue men understand them properly, they are more easily observed than a bird in a cage. This method of testing for CO was adopted by a number of officers and men.

Tests with Canaries.—Lieut. McCormack, Officer in Charge of another Mine Rescue School, carried out a series of tests with canaries.

In an atmosphere containing 0·25 per cent. CO it was found that there were three distinct stages in the development of poisoning—

(i). The first indication of poisoning ; the bird rubs its beak on the wires of its cage or against its perch, shakes its head vigorously and very often brings up seed as though slightly sick.

(ii). The second stage is very clearly defined ; the bird pants, with its beak invariably kept open. The legs are more widely separated to maintain the balance of its body, and the body being near the perch gives it a characteristic crouching position.

(iii). Just before collapsing the bird sways backwards and forwards on its perch trying to maintain its balance, till it suddenly makes a wild flight from the perch and falls into the bottom of the cage.

It is important to see that the canary's claws do not get fixed round the perch, as may happen when the perch is of small diameter ; otherwise the bird might remain fixed there without showing any further movement after the first signs of poisoning have appeared. If the bird is uncared for, and allowed to have long claws, the same difficulty might perhaps arise ; the claws should be gently cut from time to time.

From experiments, which were spread over a period of three months, it seems a debatable point whether toleration is established in a canary, as the same canary was used for 33 tests and it did not deteriorate as an indicator. Orders were issued that birds and mice should always be kept in good air.

If they are kept in a tainted atmosphere a certain tolerance to CO may become established, and they become less efficient detectors.

Reported Failures of Canaries and Mice.—Occasionally reports were received from companies which appeared to throw doubt on the value of canaries as detectors of CO, but in every case the fact of the canary showing little sign of gas poisoning, while men were more or less seriously affected, was explainable after careful examination of the facts.

In some cases incorrect or imperfect information from witnesses, when reports were being compiled, led to wrong deductions being made. In other cases the fact that gas may have a purely local action if it issues from a crevice was not appreciated. In such a case poisoning of man or canary would only take place in the immediate vicinity, and a number of yards away the gas would be so diluted as to become harmless. The greater the mine system, the more extensive the galleries, the more perfect the ventilation, the more rapidly will dilution of the gas take place, and the more strictly localized will be its action.

In one case in which the reliability of the canary was questioned, the canary was brought down and left with a man at the bottom of the shaft, while an officer engaged in certain duties went 30 ft. along the shaft and became affected by gas. Enquiry showed that the officer was in the vicinity of gas issuing from a strictly localized area (the gallery had been driven through disturbed ground), and was affected after a certain exposure to it.

A canary at the shaft bottom or in another part of the mine system would not show signs of poisoning, simply because the gas was so diluted by the time it reached the canary as to be harmless.

The length of exposure too must not be forgotten. For example, it has happened that men passing to and from the face of a gallery which was being driven through disturbed ground, after being at work for a couple of hours, developed headache and other signs of gas poisoning. A canary would then be brought into the mine, taken up to the face, and left there. The air in that part of the mine might be quite good, and the gas which had affected the men might be issuing from some spot further along the gallery. In such a case, if the air were delivered to the face, it is not difficult to realize that the canary would be unaffected.

The fact that the canary was unaffected at the face only conveys the information that the air is good at that particular spot. An actual case that happened can be explained in much the same way.

During rescue operations after an enemy blow a canary collapsed almost immediately on being brought into a lateral, and a rescue man who lost his noseclip became unconscious ; but a sapper who was at the face, and seriously injured by the blow, lay there for an hour and showed no signs of gas poisoning.

One case is on record where, owing to repeated testing after blows, a rescue station had only one canary left. This bird had been for a number of months in the " Proto " dug-out with the mine rescue men, and had been made a pet of. When a blow occurred and they were ordered to take the canary down and test for gas they did so, but hung the cage near an opening of the armoured hose supplying air to the working face, so that whatever happened the canary would get good air !

The obvious lesson is that, in order to examine a gallery and detect where gas is issuing, mice or canaries should be taken into every part of it.

It should be added that, owing to the fact that CO is a cumulative poison, the same mouse or canary must not be used in several successive tests on the same day.

In any atmosphere which may cause serious symptoms of poisoning the canary will give ample warning long before the gas has any effect on a man.

Small Birds—Suitable Kinds.—Experience during the war with small birds has shown that only the hardiest strains should be used. When it was necessary in France to depend on local supplies it was found that in the trenches they quickly died. Many of these, as well as some obtained from London, were tuberculous. Redpolls did extremely well in the trenches ; they were very hardy and, if anything, more delicate indicators than canaries.

Small birds and mice do not seem to suffer after-effects from CO and, when placed in good air, generally recover completely in a few minutes.

Use of Canaries and Mice to detect Deficiency of Oxygen in the Air of Disused Caves, etc.—Some officers and men, after their experience of the value of canaries and mice as detectors of CO, thought they would be useful in exploring disused caves or underground quarries, but they found they were useless.

The following example is illustrative of the behaviour of man and of small animals when exposed to small percentages of CO and decreased percentage of oxygen :—

In the Flanders area the enemy blew a heavy charge. The gas cleared very quickly, as it usually did in the clay, and very shortly afterwards no gas could be detected. Seventeen hours afterwards three men, who had been working for three hours in the gallery which was affected by the blow, had to be assisted out of the mine, as they were suffering from headache, giddiness, loss of power in the legs, and sickness. A mouse taken into the place where these men had been working was quite unaffected. The ventilation of the mine had been interfered with by a heavy minenwerfer shell, which had nearly closed the upcast shaft, with the result that it was impossible to get lights to burn in the gallery. The oxygen content of the air had dropped very considerably, and it is quite possible there was a small percentage of CO present. This had affected the men after prolonged exposure, the action of the CO being intensified no doubt by the decreased percentage of oxygen. Such an atmosphere would have no effect on small animals.

This chapter will be concluded with a canary story in lighter vein :

An officer, issuing from a shaft on a front where the utmost secrecy was essential in the mining work, had the misfortune to let his canary escape. The bird flew to a bush in " No Man's Land," and heralded its freedom in cheerful song. The local sniper, who was at once summoned, only succeeded after several shots in making it move to another tree, nearer the German lines. The problem was finally solved by the arrival of a trench mortar officer, who grasped the situation at once, and at the first attempt bodily removed bird and tree.

CHAPTER II

ORGANIZATION OF MINE RESCUE WORK.

11. FIRST PRECAUTIONS.

Earliest investigations showed the necessity for the issuing of such orders as might avoid the more obviously preventable sources of accidents.

Some of these naturally resulted from ignorance of the action of CO. For example, a number of fatal accidents had occurred owing to men who had been slightly gassed making their way out by climbing the vertical ladder in the shaft or walking up a steep incline, thus greatly increasing the demand on the already impoverished oxygen content of the blood ; this resulted in loss of consciousness and the men falling to the bottom. Orders that no man, however slightly gassed he might seem, should ascend the shaft without being roped and hoisted, and that life-lines should be kept at each shaft-head were at once circulated. Until a suitable mine stretcher was available this method of bringing up an unconscious man was unavoidably attended by dangers and difficulties—the constriction of the chest wall, attended by possibilities of a rope slipping, as also the great exertion entailed in hauling a man along the galleries.

The danger of entering an atmosphere which permitted walking a certain distance in it before perceptible symptoms of poisoning developed was not appreciated.

A considerable percentage of the casualties were among men who rushed in without apparatus to rescue their comrades. Certainly the restricted length of galleries as compared with colliery workings in England was a great temptation to the men to attempt rescue without apparatus. The order, "No man is to descend the shaft without rescue apparatus till the mine is reported clear of gas," which was circulated, resulted in a noticeable decrease in the number of casualties.

In some mines braziers were used to assist ventilation, and in one case there was definite proof that this had led to seven casualties. The use of braziers in mines to assist ventilation was forbidden.

The great value of warmth and rest after gas poisoning was not appreciated at first. In some cases men who had just recovered consciousness were walked about in the trenches, under the impression that this was the quickest way to clear the gas from the system. Several men died on the way to, or on reaching, the dressing station owing to the exertion of walking.

Various methods of artificial respiration were employed, but there was no oxygen reviving set. Oxygen was employed, but the method used—holding a tube connected to a cylinder to the patient's nose—made it valueless.

Distribution of Available Apparatus.—There was great difficulty at first in obtaining all apparatus, and the small supplies available were distributed according to the mining activity and number of gas casualties in each sector. For example, very little was allotted to the companies in Flanders, as gas poisoning in clay is not nearly so frequently met with as in chalk areas.

A number of " Salvus " sets of an old type were available ; these were originally issued to machine gunners as protection against drift gas, and were discarded immediately " Proto " and new " Salvus " sets began to arrive in greater quantities.

At first there were no mine rescue dug-outs, and apparatus had to be stored in any convenient quarter, such as officers' or other dug-outs, or at the shaft-head.

Under these conditions it was impossible to keep the apparatus in good order, and it was frequently rendered useless by being tampered with.

Collection of Reports.—In order to gain all information possible regarding mine explosions, companies were instructed to send reports of all cases of gas poisoning occurring in their mines as early as possible after the explosions, accompanied by a sample of the gas.

The following particulars were asked for :—

(*a*). Cause of gas poisoning ; whether due to our own or enemy's explosion, or working through ground impregnated with gas.

(*b*). Nature of workings where accident took place, depth of shaft, length of gallery, nature of stratum, etc.

(*c*). The number of men in the mine at the time, the casualties, number affected by gas.

(*d*). The rescue apparatus used, number available, if in working order, work done by these, and whether they proved of value.

These reports enabled measures to be devised, and orders drawn up, which prevented a certain percentage of the cases occurring again ; exposed inefficient rescue operations due to defective organization or inefficient rescue men ; and discovered defects in apparatus, which led to modifications and improvements.

A " Memorandum on Gas Poisoning in Mines " was issued as a guide to companies and to medical officers who had to deal with CO poisoning cases. Two revisions of this pamphlet were made subsequently.

12. SELECTION OF RESCUE MEN.

This is a most important question, as upon it depends the whole efficiency of rescue organization.

Experience proved the absolute necessity of ensuring that only the proper type of man was selected. Rescue work is most arduous and trying, requiring both coolness and initiative, and careless selection of men may result in serious accidents when danger is encountered, whilst the uselessness of one single member may involve a whole party in danger and seriously retard rescue operations.

The men should have the following individual characteristics :—

(a). Coolness of nerve under all circumstances. This may be called for at any moment should an apparatus fail, or local dangers, such as fire, falls of ground, running sand, failure of another member of the rescue squad, suddenly arise.

(b). Appreciation of the necessity of attending to details, either in the adjustment of apparatus, or in the general routine of entry to and examination of the mine.

(c). *Amenability to discipline at all times. Undoubtedly much of the success in rescue work as well as actual mining operations, with men wearing apparatus under the most trying conditions, was due to the fact that there was the strictest discipline. Obedience to orders means smooth and rapid work, which in rescue work is of vital importance.*

Disobedience may involve a whole rescue party in disaster, or may delay rescue.

In addition the leader of a squad should have :

(d). Prudence in avoiding any unnecessary risks.

(e). Power of command, and quick decision in dealing with an emergency.

(f). Ability to allay excitement, and tact in handling men who have lost nerve, whether members of the rescue party who have broken down, or personnel whose rescue is being attempted.

Qualifications for Admission to Schools.—Before any officer or man was admitted to a mine rescue school he had to produce a certificate from the company medical officer showing that he was in good health.

The following physical requirements were insisted on :—

(a). Good physical development—miners as a class are sturdy, stocky men, with well developed arms and chests.

(b). Men inclined to stoutness are not suitable. It is well known that obesity predisposes to CO poisoning.

(c). Men who faint readily should be rejected—the candidates should be very closely questioned regarding this disability.

(d). Men over 40 years of age should be rejected—the best men were from 26 to 38 years of age.

(e). All men suffering from recurrent colds, chronic nasal catarrh, bronchitis or asthma should be rejected. No man suffering from cold was admitted to a school.

(f). Men suffering from any organic disease or functional derangement of the heart should be rejected. The functional power of the heart is the decisive factor in a man's ability to withstand fatigue.

(g). Men with low blood pressure should be rejected, as fainting is easily produced.

(h). Men suffering from any organic or functional disease of the nervous system should be rejected.

(j). All men suffering from nystagmus should be rejected.

(k). Some men are temperamentally unsuited to wear apparatus. This may not be disclosed till some days after training is commenced.

A considerable number of men passed by the company medical officers were rejected at the schools. In many of these cases functional disturbance of the heart and nerves was discovered immediately hard work was commenced. A small number of such cases were not eliminated until near completion of the course. During the early days of training there was a tendency to persevere with these men, more especially as the men themselves were anxious to go on ; but later on they were rigidly rejected.

Elimination of Unsuitable Men.—Only by frequent practices under the most trying conditions can some men be eliminated.

At the beginning the same importance was not placed upon weeding out doubtful men, with the result that some broke down while actual rescue operations were being carried out.

It was also very important to get rid of men who showed signs of " oxygen deficiency," that is, anyone who became seriously affected when the oxygen percentage dropped even a little.

Some men collapse often without the slightest warning.

In the trenches it was frequently found that very good men became useless for rescue work owing to the strain which continuous work in the trenches had on the nervous system. Silent work, and the trying nature of very active mining, often affected the temperament of rescue men adversely, and it is a great mistake to think " Once a rescue man, always a rescue man." A man who for any cause became questionable, as far as rescue work was concerned, was struck off the list.

F

13. FINAL ORGANIZATION OF MINE RESCUE WORK: G.H.Q., ARMY, COMPANY.

Date of Completion.—By the end of the year 1915 the rescue organization was practically complete, and systematic training at army schools in full swing. The general organization and duties were as follows :—

Duties of the Adviser to I. of M. at G.H.Q.—These included general supervision of mine rescue organization in the armies, the periodic inspection of the army mine rescue schools, circulation of orders and all information regarding rescue work, and general control of rescue apparatus and stores.

All mine explosions, gas explosions, gas casualties, etc., were reported to the Inspector of Mines.

A considerable part of the Adviser's time was occupied visiting companies and the mines in which these accidents occurred, seeing the actual conditions, and reporting the results of the enquiries to the Inspector of Mines. From the company reports and from these enquiries into all casualties much valuable information was gained regarding the causation and prevention of accidents.

The work at G.H.Q. involved investigations being made from time to time into the following conditions :—

Ventilation of mines, dug-outs and caves.
Secondary gas explosions.
Dangers to infantry occupying freshly made craters.
Fumes from various high explosives, ammonal, blastine, etc.
Gas poisoning in blasting operations.
Action of CO and deficiency of oxygen on canaries and mice.
Value of gas doors in localizing gas after explosions.
Gas poisoning in connection with the working of compressor
   plants for ventilation of mines.
Dangers of using low flash-point oils for lubrication.
Gas poisoning and fumes from use of petrol engines in dug-outs.
Dangers in using inferior quality of oxygen in rescue apparatus.
Protection of dug-outs from shell gas.
Use of liquid oxygen as an explosive in mining.
Use of liquid oxygen in rescue and resuscitating apparatus.
Fires in dug-outs—orders—and methods of prevention.
Pumps for use in underground fires.
Dangers of opening up old caves (underground quarries).
Use of lachrymatory gas by the enemy in French colliery system.
Suggested improvements in mine rescue apparatus.
German and French mine rescue and oxygen reviving apparatus.

Information regarding a number of these investigations was circulated to companies by means of " The Mining Notes," which were periodically issued to keep all companies informed of the latest developments in mining.

Other miscellaneous duties of the Adviser were :—

The training of medical officers of tunnelling companies in mine gas poisoning.

Lectures on the causation, symptoms, treatment, and after effects of CO poisoning, to medical officers in Corps, Divisions, etc., and in hospitals.

The writing and revision of the " Memorandum on Gas Poisoning in Mines," which was issued as the manual of training.

Duties of the Officer in Charge of Army Mine Rescue School.—He was responsible for the general management and training of the school, supervision of training generally, and the control and distribution of all rescue apparatus and stores in his army. He was the technical adviser to the army in all rescue work and organization. One of his most important duties was to inspect from time to time the rescue organization of each company, and to submit any recommendations he had to make for its improvement to the C.O., who was responsible that the arrangements for mine rescue in his sector of the line were adequate and efficient.

These reports were forwarded to G.H.Q. Every case of accident at the schools was also carefully enquired into. The rarity of accidents, in spite of the extensive scale on which training was conducted, is testimony to the efficiency with which the work was done, and the closeness of the personal supervision given to each man.

In any big mining operation involving the use of rescue apparatus, the aid of the officer in charge of the school was always asked.

Company Mine Rescue Organization.—The Commanding Officer of each Tunnelling Company was responsible that the arrangements for mine rescue for the front on which his company was working were adequate and efficient.

It was his duty to ensure that all ranks were aware of the rescue arrangements that had been made for the mines in which they were working, and the location of the mine rescue station for that part of the line.

He was also responsible that the rescue organization was kept efficient by weekly practices, reports of which were forwarded to the army.

Since arrangements for mine-rescue for any system of mines vary according to the local conditions, no hard-and-fast rules could be laid down as applicable to all companies, and each particular case had to be treated on its own merits.

The O.C. Company was also responsible that detailed reports of all cases of gas poisoning and secondary explosions were made to the

Controller of Mines of the Army, who forwarded them to the Inspector of Mines, G.H.Q.

Duties of " Proto " Officer.—In each company one officer, known as the " Proto " officer, was detailed to superintend the rescue organization, and to see that all apparatus and material was kept in thorough order and in constant readiness, and that this was distributed according to the scheme drawn up in consultation with the officer in charge of the school.

The " Proto " officer was responsible for the return of all defective apparatus to the school ; weekly reports regarding the distribution of stock in the trenches and in reserve ; and the personnel in the company available for rescue work ; and the work done in the weekly practices. If available he personally supervised all rescue operations.

Company N.C.O. Instructor.—In each company in addition a N.C.O. Instructor, who had attended the special instructors' course of training at the school, was appointed.

His duties were to examine and test all rescue apparatus in use at company headquarters and mine rescue stations twice weekly, to re-charge apparatus where necessary, and to return at once all defective stock in the school.

He was also required to take part in all rescue operations.

14. SPECIAL MEDICAL SERVICE.

A few months after the mine rescue organization was completed—in early 1916—a special medical service for Tunnelling Companies was instituted under the general supervision of the Adviser at G.H.Q. This special medical service was urgently required on account of the serious wastage in companies, the difficulty in obtaining recruits, and the vitally important work tunnellers were engaged in. The fact that the average age of the specially enlisted tunnellers was very high, and that so many of them suffered from various disabilities, contributed to the high incidence of disease. Not only so, but the evacuations to hospital were often unnecessarily high, owing to the fact that so many of the ordinary medical officers, who looked after the sick of the companies, had not the necessary experience of miners and their special ailments.

The main object was to provide medical officers who were expert in the treatment of miners as a class and the diseases peculiar to their calling, and with a knowledge of gas poisoning in mines.

All the medical officers chosen had been for years in mining practices ; several had done special work in industrial diseases ; three had previously had considerable experience in connection with rescue work at colliery explosions and fires ; and one had gained the Albert Medal for gallantry at the Darran Colliery explosion.

Before proceeding to their companies each medical officer went through a special course of instruction in mine gas poisoning and mine rescue work at the Army Mine Rescue Schools.

The great advantage of having close and systematic co-ordination of the medical work in Tunnelling Companies, and the expert character of the special medical services, were quickly shown by the surprisingly small sick rate and number of evacuations to hospital.

There is no doubt that by this means many hundreds of skilled men were saved to the Army.

The training of the company rescue personnel in first aid, more especially of gas poisoning (artificial respiration and the administration of oxygen), was also included in the duties of the medical officers.

CHAPTER III

RESCUE ORGANIZATION IN THE TRENCHES.

15. MINE RESCUE STATIONS.

These were chosen after examination of the mine system by the O.C. Mine Rescue School in consultation with the Company Commander. Where convenient one station served a group of mines, but when possible they were never placed more than 200 yards away from any mine shaft.

Signboards, " To Rescue Station," were placed at various points in the trenches as a guide to the infantry.

Plate III. shows the Mine Rescue Stations in the First Army (September, 1917).

Plate IV. illustrates the relation of mine rescue stations to a mine system, and *Plate* V. is a detailed plan of a typical mine rescue station (Second Army).

When placing apparatus, consideration had to be given to difficulty in moving along the fire-trench owing to the condition of the trench. In certain cases it was found necessary, owing to the dangerous character of the work and the gassy condition of the mine, to keep apparatus ready for immediate use at the shaft-head ; when this was done it was kept in the cupboards specially designed for that purpose.

Unless in these exceptional circumstances, no rescue material other than life-lines was stored in any other place than the rescue stations.

In estimating the amount of apparatus required for each company the following points were taken into consideration :—

(i). Number and position of shafts ;
(ii). Length of galleries ;
(iii). Condition of trenches ;
(iv). Character of stratum, *e.g.*, chalk, clay, etc. ;
(v). Frequency of gas poisoning in the workings ; and
(vi). Whether the ground had been much disturbed by camouflets.

There should never be less than two-thirds of the total apparatus available for immediate use in the trenches.

In certain cases, where company headquarters was at a considerable distance from the trenches, the reserve stock was kept at advanced stores or advanced headquarters under the charge of a N.C.O.

The rescue dug-out should always be isolated from the mine system.

Accidents have happened by gas penetrating from a blow where the dug-out opened into the shaft chamber or incline to shaft-head. In one case the mine rescue men on duty were all overcome, and rescue men from another station had to be called up.

Stations should be made as damp-proof as possible. Some were situated in a dug-out breaking off from the engine and drying rooms. They should not contain any other material than rescue apparatus and stores. Where it was impossible, owing to trench conditions, to provide separate accommodation, the apparatus was stored in cupboards specially designed for the purpose, and placed in the officers' or other dug-out.

" Proto " sets were always kept coupled up ready for immediate use, and never kept in the boxes.

At each rescue station two trained men were constantly on duty, or working within easy reach.

Many of the rescue stations were lit by electricity, and were in telephonic communication with the company headquarters and the officers' dug-out. Bunks for the accommodation of gassed men were generally provided.

16. APPARATUS AND STORES.

The following was the minimum amount of apparatus, spare parts, and rescue material kept at each rescue station :—

Apparatus.	*Stores.*
4 " Proto " sets.	4 twin cylinders.
4 " Salvus " sets (of which 2 were fitted with mask of box respirator).	8 " Novita " 5 c. ft. cylinders.
	4 tins caustic soda.
	4 " Salvus " cartridges.
4 " Novita " oxygen reviving apparatus.	6 noseclips.
	12 spanners.
6 sponge rubber goggles.	6 check chains.
2 asbestos hoods and aprons.	Washers.

(In the Armies in the Southern Areas, where " Proto " was preferred to " Salvus," six " Proto " were kept instead of four, and only the " Salvus " sets fitted with the mask of the box respirator.)

Other Rescue Stores.

6 blankets.	10 miners' electric lamps, with 10 spare accumulators.
1 Primus stove.	
6 hot-water bottles.	1 trench stretcher.
2 tins café-au-lait.	2 mine stretchers.
4 small testing cages.	1 saw (hand).
2 large cages for mice and canaries.	3 life-lines.
	1 axe (hand).

There should be at least three canaries and three mice at the rescue station or officers' dug-out.

A complete inventory of apparatus and rescue material was hung up in each station and copies kept at company headquarters.

Gas doors frequently proved of the greatest value in isolating sections of a level, or for cutting off upper-level attack galleries from deep-level " backing up " galleries from the same shaft. The location of these doors required careful consideration.

The following illustrates the manner in which they prevented a mine system from being flooded by gas from an enemy camouflet :—

" The enemy fired a camouf.et, but, as it was stand-to time in the trenches, no men were underground and the gas door leading to the gallery involved in the blow was closed.

"About half an hour later a rescue man went down with a canary ; the latter was quite unaffected until the door was opened—when it immediately collapsed, and the ' Proto ' man returned to the surface. He and another rescue man were then sent down to take the air line into the face, and leave the door open to clear the affected gallery of gas, a man being kept on the blower at the surface. After about two hours the man on the blower was affected by the gas, but without serious result. In this case the door, when kept closed, confined the gas to the one gallery, and would have enabled men in other parts of the mine system to make their escape."

17. Standing Orders.

General Instructions.—The following orders will give some idea of the rescue organization in the trenches and the measures adopted to prevent casualties :—

After a mine explosion—

    (i). *When a blow occurs, even if this appears to be a long way off, all men working below must come up at once.*

    (ii). The officer in charge must be notified at once, and information sent to the nearest rescue station for the trained rescue men and apparatus. Where possible all the rescue apparatus and material should be carried by fatigue men, in order that the rescue men may arrive at the mine perfectly fresh.

    (iii). Whenever a blow occurs, all the trained mine rescue men are to proceed to the nearest rescue station.

    (iv). The officer in charge is to superintend rescue operations, and is responsible that all orders are obeyed.

        He should see that everything is done to improve the ventilation. A gallery should be cleared of gas by exhausting the foul air and not by delivering fresh air to the face.

(v). *No man is to descend the shaft without rescue apparatus till the mine is reported clear of gas.*

(vi). A sentry must be posted at once at the shaft-head to enforce that order.

(vii). Men who have had no previous training in the use of rescue apparatus are forbidden to use it.

(viii). *Infantry are prohibited from taking part in rescue operations.*

Where this order has been disobeyed the would-be rescuers have often been seriously affected, necessitating attention from the trained rescue party to the prejudice of the men in the mine, valuable time and lives thus being lost.

(ix). Rescue men should always work in pairs, never singly, unless in very exceptional circumstances.

(x). *No naked lights are to be used in the mine till it is clear of gas.* Electric lights only are to be used, as the gas in the mine may be present in explosive amount.

When men are in a mine when a blow occurs and their lights are extinguished, they should make their way out without re-lighting these ; and, where the force of the blow has not been sufficient to put out the candles, they must be immediately extinguished.

A sufficient supply of miners' electric lamps should be brought to the mine from the rescue station, as work is more rapidly carried out in a well lighted shaft and gallery.

(xi). The life-line (which is to be used for no other purpose than rescue work) at the shaft-head should be unwound ready for immediate use, and spare lines brought from the rescue station and kept in readiness.

(xii). A strong canvas belt with a hook should be kept with the life ropes at the shaft-head for use where mine stretchers are unavailable or cannot be used.

(xiii). Mine stretchers should be sent down the mine. *No man who has been gassed is to ascend the shaft without being roped.* Serious cases are to be brought up on the mine stretcher.

(xiv). Great care must be taken with all men, however slightly gassed, when they reach the shaft-head, as exposure to cold often leads to loss of consciousness.

(xv). *Before any apparatus is worn it must be carefully examined by the man who is actually going to wear it, special attention being paid to the valves and gauge.*

Cases have frequently occurred where men have had to leave rescue work owing to some small defect in the apparatus, which should have been adjusted before descending the mine. A spanner and spare noseclips should always be carried in the pockets.

When a number of men are involved in a blow, a relief squad with apparatus ready should be in readiness to assist at a moment's notice.

Whenever any defect is discovered—punctured bag, leaking valve, diminished supply of oxygen, overheating of caustic cartridge owing to exhaustion of caustic soda, etc.—the squad should immediately come out of the mine.

(xvi). Blankets, trench stretchers, hot-water bottles, and café-au-lait must be brought from the mine rescue station and kept in readiness.

(xvii). Oxygen reviving apparatus ("Novita") is to be taken into the mine by the rescue men whenever possible.

Where there are a number of men poisoned, and it is difficult to move them until further assistance arrives, oxygen may be administered ; and in desperate cases it should always be given, as it will drive sufficient CO from the blood to permit the removal of the men with safety.

(xviii). If any difficulty is experienced in getting down the small and medium circular steel shafts while wearing apparatus, a straight-down emergency ladder in the hoisting compartment should be installed at once.

(xix). In very cold weather it is found that the caustic soda does not absorb CO_2 with sufficient rapidity for the first few minutes the apparatus is worn, with the result that difficulty in breathing is experienced. This difficulty is readily overcome by wearing the apparatus for a few minutes without putting on the noseclip, when the warm breath will quickly raise the soda to the temperature necessary for efficient absorption of CO_2.

(xx). *Men should be warned that the gas helmet and box respirator issued to the armies for protection against hostile gas (chlorine, etc.) afford no protection against mine gas, as CO is not acted on by the chemicals in the helmet or box.*

Precautions to be taken where gas is known to be present in the galleries in such small quantity that work can be carried out, and minor symptoms of gas poisoning, *e.g.*, headache, etc., only develop after long exposure :—

(i). Canaries or mice must be kept constantly in the mine, and changed every two hours.

(ii). Should the canary or mouse show any signs of being affected, all the men must come up at once.

(iii). When it is urgently required to carry out work in a gallery where exposure causes headache, etc., to develop in two hours, work should be carried out in relays, the men working 10–15 minutes with 30 minutes out.

(iv). Two " Proto " and two " Novita " sets, ready for instant use, should be kept at a place convenient to the shaft-head ; and two rescue men engaged in such surface work as will permit of them being in instant readiness should their services be required.

Photo X. shows a mine rescue squad · carrying mine stretcher, " Novita " oxygen reviving apparatus, and miners' electric lamps, entering a mine after explosion.

Photo XI. shows mine rescue squad carrying gassed man on mine stretcher in the trenches.

On returning from rescue work it was the duty of the company instructor to see that all apparatus was thoroughly cleaned and overhauled. The empty cylinders of oxygen were replaced, and the caustic soda renewed. All damaged or defective apparatus was immediately sent to company headquarters and exchanged for fresh, and all defective apparatus sent back to the school, where it was replaced.

It was the duty of the officer in charge of the section, when the explosion took place, to see that these orders were carried out immediately rescue work was over, as the apparatus might be needed again almost immediately. It sometimes happened that a series of mines was blown at short intervals.

18. Maintenance of Efficiency in Rescue Work.

In order to test the efficiency of the company mine rescue organization, periodical practices were carried out by the " Proto " officer, assisted by the company instructor.

Later, when all the officers and a large number of men had been through re-training courses at the school, these weekly practices were carried out under the supervision of the O.C. School, who visited the companies in his army in rotation.

The practices were conducted under conditions approximating as closely as possible to those met on service. In this way the men became familiarized with the apparatus in their own galleries and gained greater efficiency.

A very important part of the training was the reassembling of " Proto " sets which had been taken to pieces. Men who had finished their course of school training some months before were apt to forget the different parts of the apparatus.

An air of reality was given to the work, and the practice generally commenced with an emergency call, and was controlled from the mine rescue stations, which were used in rotation.

Apparatus which had been longest in the trenches was used for these practices, and was afterwards returned to the mine rescue school for exchange.

A report of the practice was sent through the Controller of Mines to the school, and then to the Inspector of Mines, G.H.Q.

The weekly practices occasionally discovered men who were no longer suitable for rescue work owing to change of temperament or development of some functional disturbance of the heart or nervous system. Whenever a rescue man failed in rescue operations and reported defective apparatus, the company concerned were obliged to forward the apparatus at once to the school with a note explaining the circumstances. When, on examination, it was found that the apparatus was in proper working order the certificate of that man was cancelled, and he was prohibited from taking part in any future rescue work.

Other steps that were taken to maintain efficiency in the company were :—

Periodical lectures by the " Proto " officer on —

(a). Mine gases and how gas poisoning cases arise in mining operations, and how they may be prevented.

(b). Rescue work and its organization in the trenches ; and the design, construction, assembling and care of apparatus.

Lectures by the special medical officers on the dangers and more common symptoms of gas poisoning, the disposal of gas poisoning cases and first aid work in the trenches, with practical demonstrations including administration of oxygen by the " Novita," and artificial respiration.

Control of apparatus, with which object the following instructions were laid down :—

(i). All rescue apparatus must be numbered, and a record of each set kept.

(ii). All apparatus for distribution to companies must pass through the schools.

(iii). All apparatus must be kept in the box except that immediately in use at the rescue station.

(iv). All apparatus must be stored in a proper place and a N.C.O. be made responsible for its condition.

(v). In each box a small slip is to be pasted showing number of set ; date of examination at school ; date returnable to school for re-examination ; signature of the instructor of the school.

19. Treatment of Gas Poisoning in Mines.

The following instructions regarding treatment of gas poisoning were drawn up and printed on cardboard, and placed in all mine rescue stations and Tunnelling Company headquarters. There was also a copy in every " Novita " box.

Experience of first aid work in the trenches proved the necessity for having rigid rules as regards treatment.

Everything must be stereotyped. It was essential that all rescue men should be thoroughly conversant with Schaefer's method of artificial respiration, and the administration of oxygen by the " Novita." The importance of persevering with treatment for a considerable time, even although the case appeared hopeless, was always insisted on.

Gas Poisoning in Mines.—Directions for restoring the breathing and circulation of those seriously affected by gas poisoning :—

Send at once to mine rescue station for blankets, hot-water bottles and hot strong coffee. Where cases are serious send for medical officer.

Proceed to treat the patient immediately. The points to be aimed at are : first and immediately, the restoration of breathing ; and secondly, after breathing is restored, the promotion of warmth and circulation.

The efforts to restore life must be persevered in for a considerable time. A number of cases have occurred where life was supposed to be extinct, and yet energetic treatment was successful in restoring animation.

To restore breathing, artificial respiration and administration of oxygen. The administration of oxygen is of the utmost value in gas poisoning in mines. It drives out the carbon monoxide in the blood five times more quickly than air. Oxygen is administered by means of the " Novita."

In all cases where breathing has stopped or become shallow, the giving of oxygen should be combined with artificial respiration until the breathing becomes sufficiently deep to enable the blood to be cleared of carbon monoxide and replaced by oxygen.

Schaefer's method is the one adopted in mine rescue work. (See *Photos* XII. and XIII.).

Treatment after Natural Breathing has been Restored.—Stop artificial respiration, but still continue for some time giving oxygen by the " Novita." This will have the effect of lessening the severity of the after effects of gas poisoning—headache, giddiness, sickness, and pain in the pit of the stomach, palpitation of the heart and oppression about the chest—and the patient will more rapidly recover the use of his legs.

To Induce Circulation and Warmth.—Warmth is essential in treatment of all gas poisoning cases. It is frequently found that those who have been seriously gassed collapse when exposed to the cold air, and men, who have apparently recovered when below, suddenly become unconscious when they reach the shaft-head. Wrap the patient in dry blankets, and promote warmth of body by hot-water bottle, heated bricks, etc., applied to the pit of the stomach, the arm-pits, and the soles of the feet. Energetic friction of the skin of the chest, and of the limbs in an upward direction, will not only increase body heat, but stimulate the circulation.

Rest is absolutely necessary. Under no circumstances must the patient be walked about after he has come to. This is frequently done in those cases where the patient gets into a drowsy state. Men who have been unconscious should be kept in a dug-out near the shaft-head for at least two hours, if possible, before being taken to the dressing station.

Stimulants.—When the patient is able to swallow, hot strong coffee may be given. No other stimulant is to be given.

In serious cases a hypodermic injection of strychnine or pituitary extracts will be found of great value. Where this appears necessary, no time should be lost in sending for the medical officer.

Warning.—In all serious cases of gas poisoning the patient must be carefully watched, as relapses are frequent. If the breathing again becomes shallow, very slow, or threatens to cease, artificial respiration with administration of oxygen should immediately be resorted to.

Phenacetin, aspirin, etc., should never be given to relieve headaches ; serious attacks of heart failure have followed the administration of such drugs in gas poisoning.

CHAPTER IV.

DIFFICULTIES AND DANGERS OF RESCUE WORK IN THE TRENCHES.

20. GENERAL RESCUE WORK.

The following is a good example of rescue work and mine recovery work, such as removal of obstacles caused by explosion, clearing of air pipes and the re-installation of ventilation, and the dispersal of gas from the galleries—a combination of rescue work and mining operations which was so frequently carried out along the whole front.

Six men were at work in a mine when the enemy blew a mine, and two men working at the face were killed.

On hearing the sound of the explosion, the rescue men from the rescue station made their way along the trenches to the shaft under the heavy shelling which at that time generally accompanied mine explosions, entering the mine a few minutes after getting the alarm and rescuing four men, all of whom were unconscious, one being wounded as well by a piece of flying timber. On being brought to the surface on the mine stretcher the gassed men were treated by two other rescue men, artificial respiration and the administration of oxygen being required by two of the men who were seriously gassed ; the other two quickly regained consciousness on exposure to the fresh air.

After waiting for a quarter of an hour the same " Proto " men, who had rescued these men, descended the mine to discover the amount of damage, and to find whether the mine was clearing of gas. A mouse which they carried with them died after they had penetrated a short way into the galleries.

Having cleared obstacles from the galleries, they proceeded to instal ventilation, and made it possible to resume work that evening.

The following day gas again came through into the gallery, probably as a result of settling of the ground disturbed by the blow. Three men who were rendered unconscious were rescued and brought to the surface, where oxygen was administered and the men wrapped in blankets with hot-water bottles, and kept in the rescue station for a few hours before being sent down to the aid post.

21. VALUE OF OBEDIENCE TO STANDING ORDERS.

The following is an example of how prompt obedience to standing orders, and orderly and efficient supervision of rescue work by the officer in charge, prevented more casualties, and permitted work to be carried out smoothly and rapidly.

Eight men were underground in one of our mine systems at the time of an enemy blow. Of these, two were working at the face near which the blow occurred. Immediately, the men made their way out after extinguishing their lights.

One reported to the N.C.O. in charge that the man who was working with him at the face was partly buried by débris, and that in attempting to rescue him he felt himself being overcome by the gas and thought it advisable to go back for help. The N.C.O. ordered all to the surface. The exertion of making his way out rendered the man who had been gassed unconscious.

On hearing the blow, the officer in charge immediately ordered the mine rescue men to stand to, and they arrived at the shaft-head ready to descend a couple of minutes after the men emerged from the shaft. They descended the shaft and found the man half covered with débris and unconscious. He was liberated, dragged to the bottom of the incline, placed on a trolley and sent to the surface. Notwithstanding everything that was done (artificial respiration and administration of oxygen were persevered with for two hours) this man died.

Had the men who were down the mine remained to rescue their comrade, as was so frequently done in the early days of mining, instead of obeying standing orders and immediately coming to the surface, it is certain that more serious results would have occurred, and the work of the rescue men would have been complicated and delayed.

22. Value of Prolonged Treatment with Oxygen, etc., in Bad Cases.

The wonderful effect of oxygen, combined with artificial respiration, in reviving men who have been seriously—apparently even hopelessly—affected by CO poisoning, and the necessity of persevering for a considerable time in efforts to resuscitate men, even though to all appearance life is extinct, was demonstrated in the following rescue work.

After an intense bombardment the enemy raided our trenches, and with a large mobile charge blew the entrance to the shaft leading to a tunnel in which 36 infantry were sheltering. Of these, 25 lost their lives from the effects of the explosion and from CO poisoning before they could be rescued.

Australian mine rescue men with apparatus were quickly on the scene, and succeeded in rescuing and resuscitating 11 men, and recovering the bodies of the others. All the men who were rescued were in an unconscious condition and seriously affected by CO poisoning. Two appeared lifeless, and a medical officer who was present thought it hopeless to persevere. The rescue men, however, have orders to persevere in all such cases, which they did, and had the satisfaction of saving both men after ten hours' work, for a good part of which oxygen was administered. All the men required oxygen, and most of them artificial respiration.

23. DIFFICULTIES.

(i). *Difficulties Caused by Enemy Bombardment.*—The difficulties of rescue work under trench conditions and enemy bombardment are illustrated in the following cases. During an enemy bombardment a heavy minenwerfer bomb or shell pierced an officers' dug-out quarters and exploded, killing three officers. Five other officers were more or less gassed. " Proto " men from the rescue station, who had to pass through heavy shelling, were quickly on the scene, and succeeded in rescuing and resuscitating these officers. Further investigation showed that the explosion had almost closed the batmen's quarters, communication being only possible through an opening which was only just large enough to let one " Proto " man through. This part of the system was heavily charged with CO.

A " Proto " man entered and found six men all apparently dead. Part of the roof was destroyed, and the ground overhead being running sand made the place very dangerous, particularly near the entrance.

When coming out to report, the " Proto " man got into difficulties on account of his feet and apparatus becoming entangled in some electric wire, and it was with great difficulty that he was dragged to safety. Another " Proto " man entered to make a further inspection, but near the entrance was buried by a fall of earth. An officer who was directing operations at once freed the head and shoulders of this man, and applied the mask of a " Novita " apparatus to his face. "The man was breathing for a period of nearly two hours in this position, the mask being kept constantly applied, the cylinders of oxygen being quickly changed when fresh ones were required. Time after time we got the earth off his head and shoulders, but another fall would bury him again. On some occasions he was completely buried for over a minute, but breathing was resumed with the administration of oxygen. There was only room for one 'Proto' man to work at a time, and they were constantly relieved." (Official Report). A heavy fall at length occurred which completely buried him, and partially buried the " Proto " man, who was dragged out. When the man's body was recovered it was found that his feet had become entangled in electric wire, and that wire had caught round his waist.

(ii). *Difficulties Caused by Enemy's Active Mining.*—Two men were cut off by a blow and separated by 70 ft. of wrecked gallery from

F1

the rescue party. Fortunately, the two armoured air hoses were not quite flattened, and this not only prevented the men from being asphyxiated, but permitted communication being kept up with them.

The rescuers worked in double parties, one pushing ahead as fast as possible, and the other following up their work with temporary sets and struts to make the gallery safe.

Work was still in progress 12 hours later, when the enemy blew a camouflet against another part of the mine. The workings had to be cleared to test for gas, which, however, was found to be absent. Work was resumed after being suspended for an hour, and five hours afterwards the men were released.

(iii). *Difficulties Caused by Bad Trenches.*—A few days after the French part of the line at Arras was taken over by the British, the enemy sprang a mine.

The trenches were very deep and narrow, overlooked by the enemy, and in bad repair.

On the morning of the blow they were so badly damaged by heavy shells as to be almost impassable; 12 ft. to the left of the shaft the parapet had been completely destroyed the night before.

The very small dimensions of the old French incline rendered all work with " Proto " extremely difficult, the great exertion entailed exhausting the men very quickly. The galleries were very low and narrow (3 ft. × 3 ft.), and the head-room was further diminished by a 6-in. air-pipe attached to the roof.

As the cylinders of the " Proto " apparatus protrude three inches from the wearer's back, the difficulty of passing down this gallery will be understood. Immediately following the explosion of the mine there was a violent inrush of gas, which not only flooded the mine, but passed up the shaft and flowed along the trenches, where it rendered unconscious a number of infantry men, and a mine rescue man who was coming along the trench from the rescue station was also overcome before he could apply the mouthpiece and noseclips of his apparatus—the custom being to apply these only on arrival at the shaft. The experience of gas flowing along the trenches was an unusual one, and is explained by the narrow, deep character of the trench, and by the atmospheric conditions, which did not favour rapid dispersal of the gas.

As the trench was so congested it was necessary to clear it before any rescue operations in the mine could proceed; the men who had been overcome were treated with oxygen and removed.

In the circumstances it is not to be wondered at that rescue operations in the mine were considerably delayed. Fortunately, such trench conditions were not often encountered, the galleries of our own mines and all approaches being very much larger.

24. Rescue Work at Fires in Mines and Dug-outs.

There is no more dangerous or terrifying accident than a fire underground. It is not difficult to realize that in such confined places, where the galleries are comparatively narrow, the slightest confusion may lead to the most serious consequences.

Owing to the way in which mines and dug-outs are ventilated with upcast and downcast shafts or inclines, the fumes are quickly carried through the workings, and gas poisoning may quickly occur at points a considerable distance from the fire.

The mine rescue men were frequently called upon to deal with fires in dug-outs, and by their work were the means of saving a considerable number of lives, and much valuable material.

The Tunnellers were soon recognized as experts in this work, and in the great fires at Arras and Béthune, which threatened to destroy these towns, it was the Tunnellers who were called upon to deal with the situation, which they did successfully.

In the rescue stations, asbestos hoods and coverings for the " Proto " to give protection against heat were stored.

Fires in mines were rarely encountered, though there was one most unusual case after an enemy blow as the result of three heavy explosions of gas, the gas being ignited by naked lights. Four men working in the mine at the time lost their lives from gas poisoning.

25. Accidents due to Defects in or Damage to Apparatus.

Control of Apparatus.—Proper control over workmanship is essential, as well as arrangements for the most careful storing and supervision of all apparatus after issue. The vast majority of accidents due to faults in apparatus are caused by improper storing and want of supervision.

The careful testing, control and supervision of apparatus in army schools, tunnelling companies, and trenches contributed greatly to the immunity from accidents both during training and actual mining operations.

Accidents from actual defects of apparatus were remarkably few, which is a testimonial to the careful workmanship of the makers.

Examples of Accidents with Apparatus.—A few accidents that actually occurred may be briefly described :—

(a). *Fracture of the brass end of oxygen tube, due to defective casting.*—This happened several times, and on one occasion caused the death of a rescue man, while important rescue operations were in progress.

The use of some of the modern high tensile alloys would probably eliminate such troubles.

(b). *Main valve.*—In order to prevent the main valve of the oxygen cylinders of the " Proto " becoming accidentally turned off by knocking against anything, check chains with hook springs were used to lock the valve. In the early days of rescue work many of these were removed by men to suspend their knives on, and several accidents occurred from the want of them.

The hook spring may also break while the apparatus is in use, and the valve become closed accidentally.

The design of the " Proto " valves—main, bye-pass and pressure gauge—was poor, the main valve being a special cause of trouble.

A new " Proto " valve has now been designed which is a great advance on the old.

(c). *Reducing valve.*—This joint is occasionally loosened by a blow during operations. It should be screwed up as tightly as possible.

(d). *Bye-pass.*—It occasionally happened during training that the bye-pass was open when the main valve was turned on ; occasionally it was opened by repeated rubbing during use. The sudden rush of oxygen may—

Burst the rubber oxygen supply pipe ;

Burst the breathing bag ;

Blow the mouthpiece out of the wearer's mouth: in every case waste a considerable amount of oxygen.

(e). *Punctured bag.*—The rubber bag is protected by a stout canvas bag, and no accident due to the bag being punctured during operations was reported. Bags have frequently been punctured by the sharp end of stick caustic, owing to careless handling while being cleaned. Collapse of the bag, which frequently happens with other apparatus, never occurred with the " Proto " owing to its design. In any case it would have been prevented by the fact that the rescue men made such frequent use of the bye-pass.

(f). *Obstruction in reducing valve.*—This may be caused by a particle of the ebonite facing disc becoming detached and choking the jet orifice ; very occasionally by rust from the oxygen cylinder getting into the orifice.

The supply of oxygen may become irregular owing to—

The jet orifice becoming partially obstructed ;

The carriage sticking ;

The diaphragm becoming punctured.

This may take place unobserved by the wearer ; the only guide is the cessation of the sound made by the oxygen escaping from the supply tube into the bag.

(g). *Caustic soda.*—The quality supplied was generally good, but occasionally some of inferior quality was found. This had a dirty yellowish or creamy appearance, and only absorbed CO_2 sufficiently for 45-60 minutes. The wearers complained afterwards of headache, and in several cases sickness. Sticky bags were frequent when the absorbent was defective. If kept in stock some time the tins were apt to get punctured. If this occurred, or if the lids were insecurely fastened, it was found that the sticks of caustic were coated over. A considerable part of such soda will appear satisfactory, but after being used for about an hour it ceases to absorb CO_2. There was the same trouble with the " Salvus " absorbent cartridges.

Accidents due to Cold Weather.—During the winter of 1916 it was found necessary to draw the attention of companies to the dangers which may be experienced with rescue apparatus in very cold weather. A good deal of trouble was caused with " Proto " sets, owing to the intense cold interfering with the absorption of CO_2 by caustic soda, and rendering the mica valves immovable.

The trouble disappeared after the apparatus had been in use for a short time, but until this occurred the men had great difficulty in breathing and were almost overcome.

Doubtful Purity of Oxygen.—In the autumn of 1916 the question of purity of oxygen was taken up with the French firm who were supplying it. Analyses had shown that the average purity supplied was 95·5 per cent., but that some cylinders showed as low as 91 per cent. It was pointed out that, whatever percentage of purity was supplied, we should be informed what it was, in order that measures might be taken at the schools to protect against accidents due to rapid fall of oxygen percentage in the bag of the rescue apparatus. Oxygen of 99 per cent. purity was asked for, but the firm declared that this was not a commercially possible proposition. This firm declined to give any guarantee of purity.

Doubtful Purity of Oxygen : Protective Orders.—In order to prevent accidents the following order was circulated, in framing which the possibility of getting oxygen as low as 90 per cent. purity was taken into consideration :—

" The quality of oxygen available for use in rescue apparatus has fallen off, and the manufacturers are unable to guarantee a definite percentage of purity.

It is possible that the percentage may drop below 92 per cent.

In view of this, in order to guard against accidents arising from accumulation of nitrogen in the bags, the following precautions must be adopted :

For training in schools, all—

Reducing valves to be set at $1\frac{3}{4}$-2 litres per minute ;

Bags to be flushed out with oxygen as soon as noseclips are adjusted ;

Bags to be emptied through the relief valve and filled with oxygen every 30 minutes ;

Reducing valves sent to trenches to be set at 2 litres per minute."

This washing out of the bag with oxygen at the start, with the use of the bye-pass should extra oxygen be demanded, and regularly every half-hour, prevented accidents.

Experience also proved that when the bag is washed out occasionally, the men can work harder, and that no fatigue is afterwards felt. Waste of oxygen was not such a pressing problem in military mining as it is in colliery rescue work, where, on account of the lengths of the roads to be traversed, it is necessary to conserve the supply with the greatest care.

Rusting of Oxygen Cylinders.—A number of " Proto " twin cylinders had to be discarded owing to rust developing inside. The presence of rust leads to a slowing down of the delivery of oxygen, or the connection between the two cylinders becomes occluded. If particles of rust get carried into the reducing valve from the cylinder, the orifices of the valve may be choked and the flow of oxygen interrupted.

Noseclip of Apparatus slipping or becoming detached.—An efficient noseclip for the " Proto " is urgently needed. A large number of different patterns were tried in the schools—spring, screw, ratchet, and one attached to a frame like spectacles. All were liable to slip off, and most of them were uncomfortable to wear. The screw pattern was abandoned, and trials generally concluded with a return to the original spring pattern, which was found the most satisfactory.

26. Improvements in " Proto " Apparatus.

The principal points in which mine rescue apparatus is still capable of improvement appear from experience gained in the war to be :

(*a*). Decrease in weight by using light pattern oxygen cylinders.

(*b*). Methods for the prevention of overheating of the absorbent.

(*c*). Control of oxygen supply ; manipulation of reducing valves.

(*d*). Adoption of new type of valves (see *Plate* VI.).

(*e*). Design and attachment of noseclip.

There is little doubt that the above modifications should result in a much improved apparatus.

The " Proto " is decidedly the simplest apparatus that has yet been invented, and the most foolproof. These are the most valuable qualities for work in the trenches.

APPENDIX.

GERMAN MINE RESCUE ORGANIZATION.

1. INFORMATION FROM CAPTURED SYSTEMS.

Information regarding the nature and extent of the enemy mine rescue organization was obtained from a careful examination of the captured mine system after the Battles of the Somme, Ancre, Vimy, and Messines.

At the Somme the only rescue stations at all comparable with the British were found at the Tambour and La Boiselle.

One was found in each of these sectors, and served a very extensive front. They were in direct communication with the officers' dug-out and the main mine system, being separated from them by a heavy gas door. The telephone was established in both stations. These dug-outs appear to have been intended more as trench rescue reserve stores and repair shops than rescue stations, as they served much too large a frontage to be of any immediate use after a blow, some of the mines being several thousand yards away. Both were probably used as dressing stations as well, as they contained considerable quantities of dressings, splints, etc., and also a number of bunks for the wounded or gassed.

A number of sets of rescue apparatus were hung on pegs at various points along the walls of the dug-out. According to German Orders (1916), 25 " Draeger " sets were issued to each Pioneer Company, but afterwards this number was reduced considerably. Only one oxygen reviving apparatus was found in each station.

Minor repairs to apparatus were carried out in these stations, each of which contained a small compartment with a work bench. Spare cylinders, potash cartridges and material for repairing apparatus were also stored.

In these stations, and in some of the mines, wooden stretchers shaped like toboggans were found. (See *Photos* XIV. and XV.).

These were obviously used for assisting gassed men along the galleries to the shaft bottom. A number of canvas belts of very simple design for hoisting gassed men up the shaft were also found at the top of the deep shafts. (See *Plate* VII.). Both of these were inferior to the British mine stretcher as regards general utility.

On the Vimy–Arras front, only two places were found which contained apparatus, and which at all resembled rescue stations. In one company a small recess had been made off an infantry subway about 800 yards from the nearest mine, and in this several " Draeger " sets were stored. At another company there was a large dug-out near a mine entrance, in which several sets of apparatus were kept. It was fitted with cupboard and sleeping bunks. No oxygen reviving sets, stretchers, etc., were found in either dug-out, and the " Draegers " were

97

kept in their boxes uncoupled, instead of being ready for immediate use.

In the Messines area there was no evidence at all of anything approaching a mine rescue station ; nor was there any sign of mine gas doors or curtains, nor of drift gas curtains, in any of the mine systems explored. .

At Arras and Messines a few belts for bringing to the surface men who had been gassed were found, but no stretchers of any kind. The belts were very similar to those found on the Somme front.

In some of the dug-outs not in connection with mines " Draeger " sets were found, and along the whole German front, sets have been found scattered about. These were used by units other than miners, *e.g.*, machine gunners.

The " Draeger " sets were very liable to be tampered with owing to the arrangement of distribution, and captured orders show that the Germans had considerable trouble owing to apparatus getting out of order. The keeping of apparatus constantly exposed to the atmosphere of damp shafts and galleries would also lead to rapid deterioration.

To sum up, it may be said that, with small exceptions at Arras and on the Somme, there appeared to be a total absence of any regular mine rescue organization along the whole German front.

2. TYPES OF GERMAN APPARATUS.

Three types of " Draeger " were found—large, small and " Tubben," the latter being a modification of the small type.

The disadvantages of the " Draeger " have been explained previously (see Part II., Chapter I., para. 3). The small type is illustrated on *Plate* VIII. and the " Tubben " as worn is shown on *Photo* XVI.

Heeres-Sauerstoffschutzgerät (Army oxygen defence apparatus).— Somewhat similar to the small " Draeger." (See *Photo* XVII.).

This might have been for use for reconnaissance or work such as the " Salvus " is used for, but would be quite useless for hard work.

Flottenatmer K. III. 1917. A few of these were found after the Arras Battle. (See *Photo* XVIII.).

It has the following *advantages* :—

(i). Extremely light compared with the "Salvus" (10 lbs. against 17 lbs.).

(ii). Circulation of air in the apparatus due to the presence of inhaling and exhaling valves ensures cool breathing.

(iii). Well balanced and permits freedom of movement for working.

(iv). Mechanical construction is much better than that of the small " Draeger."

Disadvantages are :—

(i). Doubtful if sufficiently strong to stand rough usage.

(ii). Cartridge and breathing bag being carried on the back are liable to damage when travelling along a low gallery or amongst broken timber.

(iii). No automatic feed for oxygen.

(iv). No pressure gauge.

(v). The generator is too small for proper absorption of CO_2, and work becomes most uncomfortable after half an hour.

(vi). Mouthpiece is uncomfortable and insecure.

(vii). Small size of the breathing tubes makes breathing difficult and laboured during hard work.

Magirus Rescue Apparatus.—The poorest type of apparatus found. An unusual feature was the presence of an exhale valve at the bottom of the air bag. The apparatus was physiologically unsound, and, under certain conditions, might prove a regular death trap to the wearer.

Oxygen Reviving Apparatus.—Nothing corresponding to the " Novita " was found. Three sets of an efficient type were found at the Somme, two at Vimy, but none at Messines.

In this apparatus oxygen is wasted owing to the fact that the mask cannot fit closely to the face on account of the absence of pneumatic rubber round the rim. (See *Photos* XIX. and XX.).

Carbon Monoxide Detector.—Cardboard boxes containing half a dozen tubes of CO testing papers were found in many of the boxes containing mine rescue apparatus.

Owing to the rapid deterioration of the test papers, these cannot be regarded as reliable guides to the presence of CO.

They are much less reliable than mice or canaries, and inferior to the testing sets used by the British Service.

The modifications in German mine rescue apparatus carried out during the last two years were all prompted by the necessity of economy, owing to the scarcity of rubber, etc. As a result all their apparatus became less and less efficient and reliable.

The Germans had nothing at all approaching the " Proto " in comfort, safety and efficiency, nor any method of giving oxygen equal to the " Novita."

Photo I.   Photo II.

"Proto" Mine Rescue Apparatus.

Photo III.—"Salvus" Apparatus.   Photo IV.—"Proto" Apparatus with mask

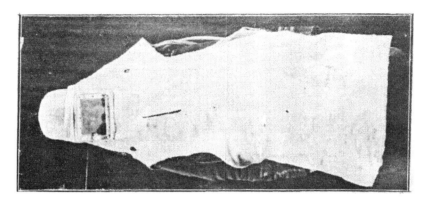

Photo V.—Fire Fighting Apparatus.

Photo VI. Mine Stretcher.
Showing Skids.

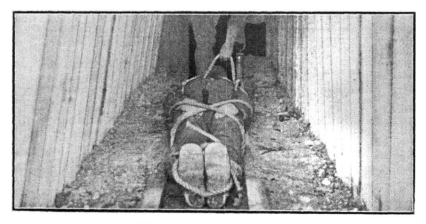

Photo VII. Mine Stretcher.
Use in galleries.

Photo VIII. Mine Stretcher.
At shaft bottom before being hoisted.

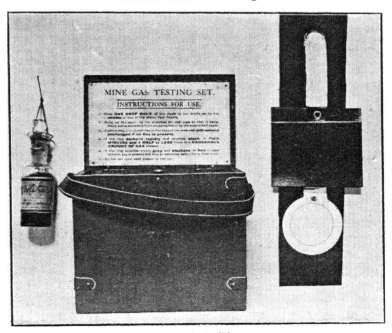

Photo IX.

Photo X.

Photo XI.
Mine Rescue Squads.

Photo XII.

Photo XIII.
Oxygen combined with Artificial Respiration.

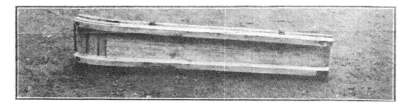

Photo XIV.

Photo XV.
German Toboggan Stretcher.

Photo XVI. Draeger Tübben.   Photo XVII. Army Oxygen Apparatus.

Photo XVIII. Flottenatmer.

Photo XIX.   Photo XX.
German Oxygen Reviving Apparatus.

PLATE I.

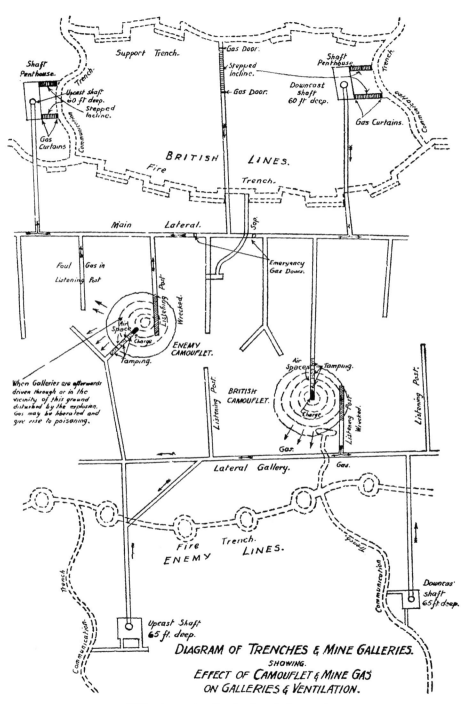

DIAGRAM OF TRENCHES & MINE GALLERIES.
SHOWING.
EFFECT OF CAMOUFLET & MINE GAS
ON GALLERIES & VENTILATION.

NOTE:- Arrows show the direction of air currents.
To assist in making clear the mine is shown charged
and tamped, and not destroyed.
A Camouflet is a mine which explodes but does not crater.

PLATE II.

DIAGRAMMATIC VIEW OF THE
"PROTO" PATENT RESCUE APPARATUS

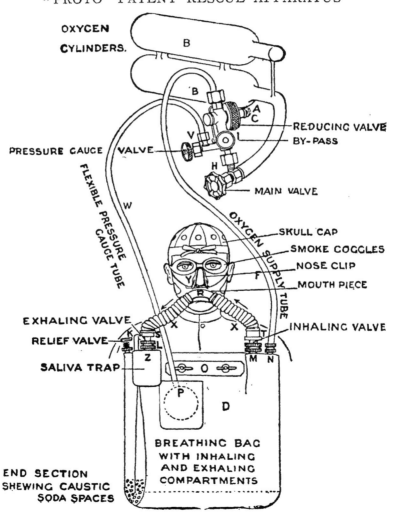

OXYGEN CYLINDERS.

REDUCING VALVE

BY-PASS

PRESSURE GAUGE VALVE

MAIN VALVE

FLEXIBLE PRESSURE GAUGE TUBE

OXYGEN SUPPLY TUBE

SKULL CAP

SMOKE GOGGLES

NOSE CLIP

MOUTH PIECE

EXHALING VALVE

RELIEF VALVE

SALIVA TRAP

INHALING VALVE

BREATHING BAG
WITH INHALING
AND EXHALING
COMPARTMENTS

END SECTION
SHEWING CAUSTIC
SODA SPACES

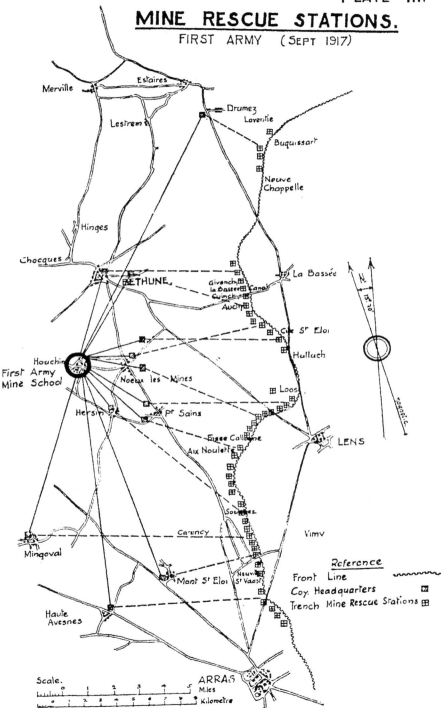

PLATE III.

MINE RESCUE STATIONS.

FIRST ARMY (SEPT 1917)

PLATE IV.

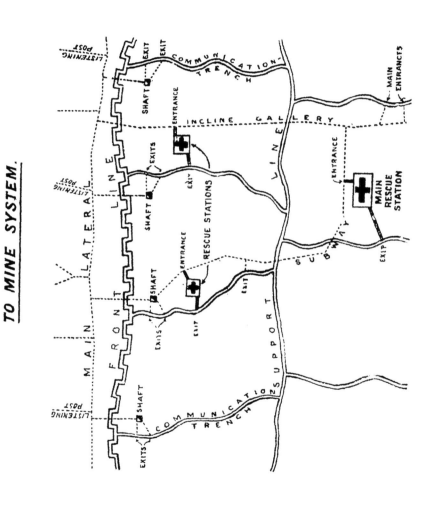

PLAN SHOWING RELATION OF MINE RESCUE STATIONS

TO MINE SYSTEM.

PLATE V.

PLAN OF MINE RESCUE STATION.
2nd ARMY.

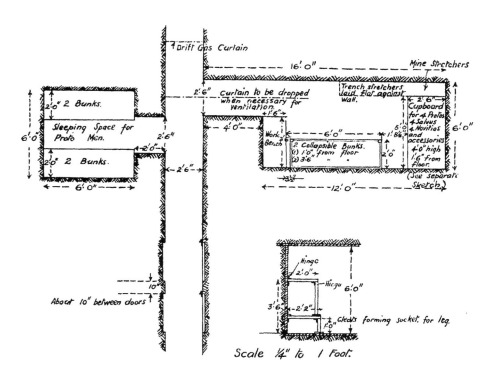

Drift Gas Curtain

Mine Stretchers

16' 0"

Trench stretchers laid flat against wall.

2' 6" Curtain to be dropped when necessary for ventilation.

2' 0" 2 Bunks.

Sleeping Space for Proto Men.

6' 0"

2' 0" 2 Bunks.

2' 6"

2' 6"

6' 0"

4' 0"

1' 6"

Work Bench

6' 0"

2 Collapsible Bunks. (1) 1' 0" from floor (2) 3' 6"

2' 0"

3½'

12' 0"

2' 6" Cupboard for 4 Protos 4 Salvus 4 Novitas and accessories 4' 0" high 1' 6" from floor.

5' 0"

1' 8½"

6' 0"

(See separate Sketch.)

About 10" between doors

10"

Hinge

2' 0"

Hinge

3' 6"

2' 2"

1' 0"

6' 0"

Cleats forming socket for leg.

Scale ¼" to 1 Foot.

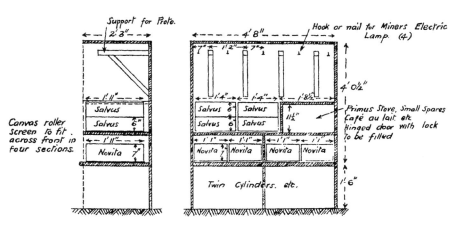

Support for Proto.

2' 3"

Hook or nail for Miners Electric Lamp. (4)

4' 8"

7"

1' 2"

7"

4' 0½"

Canvas roller screen to fit across front in four sections.

1' 11"

Salvus

Salvus 6"

1' 4"

1' 4"

1' 8½"

Salvus 6"

Salvus

Salvus 6

Salvus

11½"

Primus Stove, Small Spares Café au lait etc.
Hinged door with lock to be fitted

1' 11"

Novita 7"

1' 1"

1' 1"

1' 1"

Novita 7

Novita

Novita

Novita

1' 6"

Twin Cylinders. etc.

DESIGN FOR CUPBOARD FOR RESCUE STATION.
Scale ½" to 1 Foot.

PLATE VI.

SPECIAL MAIN VALVE (PROTO)

Siebe, Gorman & Co., Ltd.

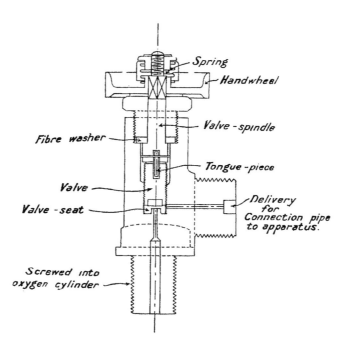

Spring
Handwheel
Valve-spindle
Fibre washer
Tongue-piece
Valve
Delivery for Connection pipe to apparatus.
Valve-seat
Screwed into oxygen cylinder

Description.

There is no stuffing box, the valve spindle revolving, not working vertically up and down, which effectually holds the pressure when the valve is open.

The valve itself is threaded on the outside, and screws into the body of the valve above the seat, as shown, and it is operated by a steel-tongue piece, pivoted in the bottom of the spindle, which engages in a slot in the top of the valve.

By revolving the hand-wheel the valve is caused to rise and fall from its seat. When fully opened, the valve causes the spindle to jamb up tightly on the fibre washer, thus making an effective joint.

Advantages.

(1.) Easy operation

(2.) No stuffing box for spindle with usual attendant leakages

(3.) Positive closing and positive opening without leakage.

PLATE VII.

GERMAN BODY BELT FOR USE IN MINES
FOR BRINGING UP THE SHAFT MEN GASSED
OR INJURED IN MINE EXPLOSIONS.

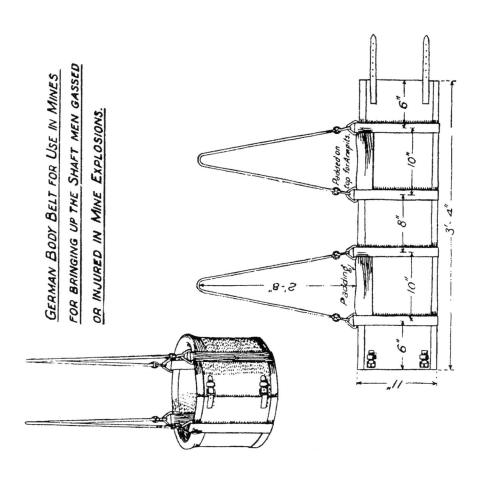

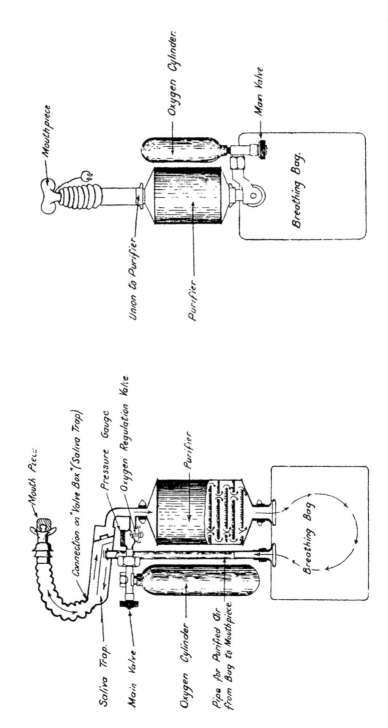

PLATE VIII.

GERMAN MINE RESCUE APPARATUS.

DRAEGER APPARATUS (SMALL).

Mouthpiece

Oxygen Cylinder.

Main Valve

Breathing Bag.

Union to Purifier

Purifier

ARMY OXYGEN APPARATUS.

Mouth Piece.

Connection on "Valve Box" (Saliva Trap)

Pressure Gauge

Oxygen Regulation Valve.

Purifier

Breathing Bag

Saliva Trap.

Main Valve

Oxygen Cylinder

Pipe for Purified Air from Bag to Mouthpiece.

PART III.—TECHNICAL.

CHAPTER I.

GENERAL PROCEDURE IN LAYING OUT A MINE SYSTEM.

1. INTRODUCTION.

Any attempt to describe in detail the methods employed in underground warfare is fraught with difficulties. Certain broad principles gradually emerged, and met with general acceptance, most of which will already be apparent to the reader. But in the application of practical details there was, and no doubt still is, a wide diversity of opinion. There are many schools of Miners, each accustomed to employ the methods that best suit their particular place and nature of work. All of these methods had their uses and applications to Military Mining; but to describe them all is impossible, whilst to select some and omit others would be invidious. In the following pages many points of both historical and technical interest will be found; but for detailed description of most actual methods of work reference should be made to the textbook of *Military Engineering*.

2. FIRST PRINCIPLES.

From Part I. a general impression will have been obtained of the way in which mine-fighting first started, and of the disjointed or individual nature of the earliest efforts. The original mine systems —if they can be termed systems—appeared in plan like a number of trees :—

The tree was probably abandoned after a few blows, and a new one started. This was, of course, encouraged by the frequency of alarmist reports from troops in the front line (See Part I., para. 8).

Such reports are inevitable in similar circumstances, and it may be useful to record the instructions that were issued early in 1915 on this question :—

" *Instructions to Infantry when Hostile Mining is Suspected.*

(1). The ground should be cleared of all men for at least 60 yds. radius from the spot where sounds are heard, and the men should be posted on the flanks and in a retrenchment in rear, ready to charge up to the crater should the trench be blown up. Machine-guns and bombers should be posted on the flanks. If it is essential to post sentries within 40 yds. of the spot, they should be ordered to keep absolutely quiet.

(2). If suspicious sounds are heard during this period, a hole should be sunk to water-level, if possible, and 4 ft. square at the suspected point, and further listening carried out there. Every care should be taken to ensure absolute quiet while listening is being done.

(4). Patrols at night should be instructed to listen for sounds of pumping, pulleys, tackles, trucks or other special work.

(5). An observation officer should, during the day, be detailed to examine the enemy's trenches with periscope and field-glass for signs of work, movement of materials, accumulations of sandbags, appearance of blue clay or white chalk. He should observe from the front trenches and from convenient artillery or other observation stations.

(6). If there are suspicions after these investigations, a mining officer should be sent for, who should report at Brigade and Battalion Headquarters before going into the trenches.

(7). The evidence of persons reporting the sounds, and of the listeners, also any evidence bearing on the subject from patrols and Observation Officers should be collected, together with information as to distance of trenches apart, and handed to Mining Officer on his arrival at Battalion Headquarters.

(8). It should be borne in mind that suspicious sounds can sometimes be traced to wind, telephone wires, filling and hammering sandbags, noise of feet on planks, rats, frogs, etc. Further, it is more difficult to hear sounds when above them ; and though shallow mining might be heard from the surface, deep mining probably would not, and it is essential to get into the same strata, and if possible to the same depth, to hear countermining distinctly."

This phase of mining only lasted a short time, and, as underground warfare developed, certain main principles became evident ; these may be summarized as follows :—

(i).   The best form of defence is attack.

(ii).   Surface and underground fighting must go together ; underground defence must be subject to surface defensive requirements, and underground attack must be co-ordinated with surface attack.

(iii). The surface effects of mine explosions must be studied, so that they can be accurately foretold and used to the best advantage.

(iv).   The advantage underground is to the lower man.

(v). No two galleries should be driven within destructive distance (*i.e.*, within the radius of rupture of blows) of one another.

(vi). In order to detect and stop enemy progress, galleries must be sufficiently close together to prevent an enemy gallery being driven between them without being heard by one of them ; and the explosion of mines in two adjacent galleries will wreck all the ground between those galleries.

(vii). Natural ventilation is of great advantage.

(viii). Rapid work immediately after a blow, close to that blow gains ground without risk.

(ix). Rise of permanent water-level must be studied to prevent flooding of workings.

(x). Well-secured entrances and approaches facilitate rapid work.

The normal system for defence or attack that was gradually adopted therefore consisted of two or more shafts or inclines situated well back ; the main galleries driven from these were connected by a lateral to give ventilation and safety ; and from this lateral the fighting galleries (*rameaux de combat*) were driven out ; the lateral therefore was as far forward as possible, to avoid unnecessary lengths of fighting galleries ; but it was sufficiently far back to secure it from the effects of mine* explosions from our own or enemy fighting galleries.

It was now realized that advantage must be taken of explosions to gain ground by working quickly round or under the blow from galleries lying just outside the radius of rupture of the blow, and for this reason attack galleries were usually driven in pairs for mutual protection ; so that if one was destroyed or forced to fight, the other might push on under cover of the blow of the first. *Plates* I and II illustrate these principles of mine-fighting tactics.

It was recognized by both sides that " purely defensive mining is the weakest form of mine-fighting " ; in other words, to be successful in mining, the general policy must be as offensive as possible in character. This axiom is illustrated in *Plate* II.

C–D denotes a gallery blown on account of the approach of hostile working W–X.

Immediately the gallery is pronounced free of gas, work is commenced from galleries A–B and E–F to positions B^1 and F^1 respectively, to meet any attempt of the enemy to gain ground.

On his recovering his gallery as far as possible, and driving to X^1 he is blown again, gallery A–B being advanced to B^{11} ; similarly. on the enemy blowing a mine at Z, and destroying our gallery L–M, N–O and G–H are immediately driven to O^1 and H^1 respectively. In this way advantage is taken of blows on either side, and the enemy is gradually forced back to his own line. An example of this form of mining took place in the Hohenzollern Redoubt during the early part of 1916. At the commencement of operations in this salient, it was found that the enemy had already driven a gallery under our line, which caused us to sink a shaft hurriedly and blow up our own line in order to destroy his gallery.

In a space of $2\frac{1}{2}$ months after the explosion of this mine we had forced him back to his line and blown it up in three places by a successful application of this policy.

3.   RECONNAISSANCE.

Upon taking up a new position a general reconnaissance was normally made of our own defences and those of the enemy. The information gained from all sources was co-ordinated by the General Staff and became available for the Mining Officer, who carried out further detailed investigations on the surface, and, when considered necessary, constructed shafts or inclines for listening underground.

It will be easily understood how important it was for a thorough reconnaissance to be made before mining obligations were undertaken on any portion of the front, and it was just as essential that the Mining Officers should continue their observations and study of surface indications after underground work was started.

The first necessity was a reliable plan showing the enemy positions and our own. In 1915 this was obtained by detailed survey of our front line trenches, and the German trenches were surveyed by intersections of bearings sighted through a periscope. This method was laborious and slow, but sufficiently accurate. The detail on the plan could be obtained from aeroplane photos, but as these were distorted, care had to be exercised in using them. Later on, when air photos reached a high degree of accuracy, a reliable trench plan could be made without taking sights on the German lines. Base lines and triangles were accurately surveyed in our own lines, and, using these as a framework, the photos could be enlarged to make accurate trench maps of both our own and the German trenches.

The observation and study of the enemy position made by the Mining Officers and N.C.O.'s to detect signs of enemy mining activity were supplemented by the results of the study of aero photos, and information received from Infantry Patrols with whom the Mining Officer on duty was in personal touch.

The reconnaissance would include a study of the local geology to determine the nature of the ground and the depth of the underground water-level. In chalk country it was especially important to determine the seasonal variation in the water-level ; in some sectors of the Western Front it was found that the difference between the winter and summer water level was as large as 30 ft. (See Part I, para. 5).

4. PRELIMINARY SCHEME.

The Company Commander, having made his reconnaissance and drawings, worked out the details of the scheme, taking into account the time, labour, material and plant required to carry out the work desired by the General Staff.

In selecting entrances to shafts and inclines the following points had to be borne in mind :—

The question of siting entrances is governed by the military situation in the sector, and the urgency of the work to be carried out. Entrances should be :—

(i).   Hidden from enemy ground and aerial observation.
(ii).   Easy of access.
(iii).   Near a good dumping ground for spoil, and
(iv).   As far as possible sited so as not to interfere with the Infantry Garrison of the line.

The front line or sap heads were not good places to site entrances, owing to the possibility of their being destroyed by enemy raiding parties, and were used only in cases of extreme emergency, when galleries would be driven back to give an entrance in the support or reserve line as soon as possible, and front line entrances then closed.

The close support trench from 20 to 30 yds. behind the front line was found to be a suitable place, owing to its being little used for traffic, and more or less immune from raids.

As soon as the positions for entrances were fixed on the ground they were plotted on the plans, so that the survey could be carried underground when the shafts and inclines were down.

The success of mining operations depends to a great extent on getting below the enemy, for the reason that it is easier to damage workings which are above than it is those which are below ; the latter can rarely be destroyed without cratering, and so upsetting the overground defences.

The earliest galleries were driven at a depth of only 12 ft. to 20 ft. ; later on the depth was limited mainly by the water-level, and could only be decided on after the geological reconnaissance was complete.

In considering whether to sink shafts or inclines the possibility of enemy blows had to be remembered. If a long incline was blown, both depth and length of gallery were lost ; but with a vertical shaft the depth would usually remain available for starting new work. The principal advantage of the incline was rapidity of advance.

5. NORMAL COURSE OF WORK.

Two shafts or inclines would be sunk simultaneously, and, when they reached the depth required, galleries known as main galleries were driven from 3 to 4 ft. above the bottom of the shaft. They would rise slightly from the shaft so that the workings drained into the shaft bottom, and would also be as far as possible parallel to one another.

When the main galleries reached a point sufficiently far to ventilate our attack galleries, but not within range of the enemy's mines, a gallery (R1–L1 on *Plate* III) would be driven to connect them. This gallery was called a lateral, and would normally be about under our wire. As the lateral advanced, galleries A, B, C and D would be driven at intervals of not more than 60 ft. along the lateral, so as to protect it and the flanks of the main galleries ; these were pushed out to such a distance that, if they had to be blown, no damage would be done to the lateral. Directly the lateral was connected a current of air would circulate through the workings, one of the shafts becoming the upcast and the other the downcast shaft.

Speed in connecting shafts was very important because, if the shaft-head were blown in by hostile artillery fire before this was done, the men working in the faces were cut off ; also there was no natural ventilation, and air had to be pumped into the workings. The flanks of the main galleries also needed protection from hostile attack. This could be done by driving galleries out to the flanks (See G and H, *Plate* III).

Either of the main galleries or any of A, B, C and D could be used as " fighting galleries " or galleries of attack.

In chalk, or where depth of water-level was over 40 ft., galleries have been driven at two or three levels ; the intermediate levels being used for listening, the shallow and deep levels for attack.

The shallow level was usually driven with 5 or 6 ft. of head-cover in the soft loam or clay above the hard chalk. Silent work could be carried out here, and mines laid under the enemy's wire and front line without his knowledge. Two galleries of this nature were driven for an attack on the Triangle, South of Loos, on the 30th June, 1916 (See *Plate* IV), but were a failure, as the defensive system had not been sufficiently advanced.

The deep level could be pushed ahead for attack well below the enemy's workings, and without being seriously damaged by his blows. When economy in explosives and carrying party were necessary, it could rise when once inside the enemy's mining defences. Speed and silence were generally essentials to success in attack.

There was, of course, a practical limit to the depth at which a charge could be fired so as to break the surface, under service conditions of size of chamber, etc. In a concentrated charge this depth was generally taken as 180 ft.

In the earlier days of mining at two levels connections were made between the shallow and deep workings (*e.g.*, St. Eloi), but this practice was definitely given up early in 1916.

CHAPTER II.

DISPOSAL OF SPOIL AND OTHER DETAILS.

6. HAULAGE IN GALLERY.

In the forward workings which were in close contact with the enemy the spoil was bagged in sandbags.

Two methods were commonly used to transport the bags to the main lateral :—

(i).   By dragging.

(ii).   By carting them on a truck with rubber-tyred wheels.

One Company used a wheelbarrow with a rubber-tyred wheel, but this was not universally used.   (See *Plate* V).

All these methods caused little noise, which is the most important factor to be considered in arranging haulage to fighting-heads.

The German miners often loaded their spoil into trucks at the face and trammed them down the gallery.   This method caused a great deal of noise which was easily heard by our listeners.

In the main lateral two methods were generally used for transporting spoil to the bottom of shafts and inclines and sometimes up inclines to surface dumps :—

(*a*).   On trucks fitted with rubber-tyred wheels running on wooden track.

These trucks and track were made by Company carpenters and could be easily repaired.   They were fairly quiet when in motion and carried from 10 to 12 bags.

(*b*).   On trucks fitted with flanged wheels running on steel track. (See *Plate* VI.)

These trucks made more noise than those with rubber tyres, but there was not much friction, consequently greater loads could be trammed with less exertion.   The steel track was often carried on up the inclines and out to surface spoil dumps.

7. COMPARISON OF SHAFTS AND INCLINES WITH REGARD TO HOISTING.

Shafts were more used in mining systems than inclines, owing to the advantages gained by getting down quickly.   Towards the end of the mine fighting, when our miners had gained control over the German miners, more carefully laid-out systems replaced the emergency front-line shafts, in which it was possible to arrange shafts and equipment for maximum efficiency and convenience.

Economy in man-power was always the chief factor to be studied in arranging the hoisting scheme. Vertical hoisting (*i.e.*, in shafts) is the most economical, owing to the reduction of friction and the high ratio of nett to gross load.

Convenience of access, and the benefit of the haul from an advanced point, make easy inclines the most serviceable form (in chalk) for permanent conditions. (It is rarely possible to sink inclines in clay owing to trouble of surface water—the Berlin Tunnel taught a never-to-be-forgotten lesson in this respect.) A slope between 1 in 2 and 1 in 3 was found to be most suitable.

In an incline the truck which has been trammed from the fighting galleries along the lateral can be hitched on to a rope and hauled up the incline without being unloaded, which cannot be done in a shaft. This saves time and labour.

8. HAULING UP INCLINES.

For short steep inclines, constructed chiefly for mined dug-outs, a chute and windlass were found to be the most economical method of haulage. The chute was made of 1-in. planking, 12 in. wide, with guides nailed to the sides (See *Plate* VII.). The windlass was fixed at the top of the incline—its drum was 9 in. to 12 in. diameter of varying length, and the handle 1 ft. 2 in. to 1 ft. 6 in. long, giving a mechanical advantage of about $2\frac{1}{2}$ to 1. (See *Plates* VIII and VIIIa.). An ordinary hemp rope double-ended was used with two hooks.

Two bags at a time could be hoisted. This method was greatly favoured and widely used by Companies for all short hauls.

Towards the end of active mine warfare, when defences were complete and the heavy fighting over, main inclines were widely and effectively used in the chalk, the slope being from 15° to 30°.

Steeper slopes for long inclines were not found to be so satisfactory for " permanent " schemes. The usual gradients were 1 in 2 and 1 in 3, and the methods of hoisting were :—

(i). Geared winches ; single purchase and geared about 4 or 5 to 1. (See *Plate* IX.)

The winch was constructed as follows :—

Gear	5 to 1.
Drum	10-in. diameter.
Handle	14-in. radius.
Mechanical advantage ...	14 to 1.
Load hauled per trip ...	24 sandbags.
Load hauled up per 24 hours	1,450 sandbags.

This is equivalent to 35 ft. progress in average galleries per 24 hours.

Two men are required for hoists and two men unloading and clearing the top of inclines.

If the trucks are run straight on to the incline from the lateral below, the trammer does the hooking on.

If this method is employed, two trucks are required below : one to be loaded whilst the other is being hoisted to surface.

If the bags have to be trans-shipped at the foot of the incline, two men, other than the trammer, will be required.

The figures given above denote the maximum output.

Steel track and long trucks with flanged wheels (18-in. or 24-in. gauge) were used to carry maximum loads with minimum of friction.

(ii). Ordinary Windlass. (*Plates* VIII. and VIIIa.)

Windlasses were made by company carpenters and could be easily modified and repaired.

A ¼-in. wire rope was used on a small drum for all lengths of hoist. Trucks with flanged wheels running on steel track were used in preference to rubber wheels on wooden track because of there being less friction.

The windlass was constructed as follows :—

Drum	6 in. diameter.
Handles	14 in.
Mechanical advantage ...	4½ to 1.
Load hoisted per trip ...	8 bags.
Load hoisted per 24 hours ...	1,200 bags.

Two other methods were experimented with for steeper inclines, but were not universally adopted.

(*a*). Mono rail. (See *Plate* X.)

The rail is carried on wood or steel brackets fixed to the gallery setts. The rope lies on the brackets, rollers being placed between the rail and the setts where necessary. A small hand windlass is used, with 14-in. handle and 7-in. conical drum.

This method hoists from 4 to 5 bags per trip and 1,150 bags per day, with 2 or 3 men on the windlass, which would clear from 2 to 3 works' faces.

(*b*). Differential drum. (See *Plate* XI.)

Dimensions.

Large drum	12 in. diameter, 10 in. wide.
Small ,, ...	6 in. ,, 15 in. ,,
Crank radius ...	15 in.
Mechanical advantage	10 to 1.

Two men can haul 8 to 10 bags up an incline of 85 ft. at 45° in 3 minutes.

9. Hoisting Up Shafts.

Two methods were universally employed :—

(1). Windlass—(a) Direct over shaft.

     (b) Set back in hoisting chamber with small pulley or sheave while over shaft.

  (a). This method requires a smaller shaft top than (b).

The hoisting men can unhook the bags, which save a man, and can see what is going on in the shaft and give signals, which they cannot do if the winch is set back from the shaft.

For shallow or medium shafts a windlass with 14-in. handle and 6-in. diameter drum was found to be the most useful. Two bags are a good one-man load, and are hauled up a 35-ft. shaft in 30 seconds.

For deep shafts drums were made of 10 in. to 12 in. diameter with 14-in. handles, giving a mechanical advantage of $2\frac{1}{2}$ to 1.

Two men will hoist two bags up an 80 to 100 ft. shaft in 1 minute, which gives about 1,200 bags a day, i.e., equivalent to about 30 ft. of driving per day.

(2). Single pulley wheel direct over shaft.

A double-headed hook was used for short hauls, and kept two faces clear of bags.

Two men are employed hauling and stacking bags in entrance to shaft top.

For long hauls the load should be limited to one bag, which will be hauled up a shaft from 60 to 70 ft. deep in between 25 and 30 seconds.

If one bag is hauled up every three minutes, it will keep one face clear per working day.

This method of haulage was almost universally used in the early days of mining, and found successful for all depths of shaft.

10. Methods of Disposal of Spoil.

Disposal of spoil was always a difficult problem owing to the enemy usually being able to overlook our position by ground observation, and also to the enormous amount of spoil produced by large mining operations.

In various parts of the line different methods were employed. In the flat country north of La Bassée Canal camouflage was rigged up on poles behind the parados and the spoil dump underneath. A popular method was to build the spoil bags into actual lines of dummy breastwork. Another method adopted was to form craters. Holes of 10 in. diameter were bored to a depth of 6 to 8 ft. and 9 ft. apart. Two to four holes were put down at each site and charged with 25 lbs. of ammonal each (representing small over-charged mines). The result of exploding these charges was a crater shown in *Plate* XII.

Poles were laid horizontally across the top, supported in the centre by vertical props. The whole was then covered with camouflage material of the same colour as the surrounding ground.

Saps were dug into these craters and camouflaged, the spoil being dumped under the camouflaged crater.

Disused trenches, shell craters, and dead ground which were covered with camouflage were good places for dumping spoil. If spoil is not hidden, it discloses the position of the shafts and inclines to the enemy, and invites bombardment with heavy trench-mortars.

Sites for spoil dumps should always be carefully camouflaged before any spoil is dumped in them.

It has been already explained in Part I. that the importance of these points was not always realized by the Tunnelling Companies.

II. SURVEY

The best time for surface survey of the trenches to connect up shaft tops and mine systems was found to be just after dawn, as there was generally little shelling or movement at that time. (*See* Part I., para. 22.) *The Theodolite* was used when extreme accuracy was necessary, especially for above-ground survey. It was used for connecting up systems, but often the conditions made accurate work very difficult. The 3-in. theodolite was the most suitable, but was difficult to obtain. Specially shortened legs had to be provided, the service pattern being too long for trench-work.

The Germans had a useful little trench theodolite, a copy of which is illustrated in *Photos* I and II. The legs, which were telescopic, were 5 ft. long extended, but could be shortened to 3 ft.

The Miners' Dial was the favourite instrument in use by Companies. It was far more reliable than the prismatic compass, and much handier than the theodolite for underground work. It was fitted with a vertical arc and telescope which enabled bearings to be taken underground down inclines of all grades. It was useful because both fast and loose needle survey could be made.

The Prismatic Compass was not very suitable for accurate survey work owing to the amount of local attraction in the shape of iron in the trenches, but this instrument was very handy underground for checking bearings and laying off angles in small headings where the dial could not be used with comfort.

Levelling.—The Dumpy Level was universally used for surface levels and also in large galleries underground.

For work in small galleries the *Abney Level* was used more often than the Dumpy. Being very much smaller it was more easily handled in a confined space, and as extremely accurate levelling was not necessary, the Abney did all that was required, except where exact drainage levels were required.

Survey Lines.—The face-men were kept straight by weighted lines hung from the roof of the galleries. Two lines were hung about 10 to 15 ft. apart on the bearing required. To test the face for being on the line, the face-man held a light at the centre of his face, and if this was in line with the survey lines, the face was going straight to bearing. The average face-man requires a great deal of supervision in order to keep him on the line. Straight driving is essential for quick work and good ventilation underground.

12. VENTILATION.

Good ventilation is indispensable for quick and efficient work, especially in workings which are in close proximity to the enemy or are close to or in blown ground.

When working in blown ground pockets of gas are encountered, and it is essential to have a good current of air circulating in the gallery in order to clear this gas out. Men work very much better and faster when there is good ventilation, and it also keeps the sick rate of the Company down. In order to help natural ventilation, galleries should be driven as straight as possible. Doors were used to shut off one part of a system from another (See *Plates* XIII. and XIV.) to regulate the air currents into parts of the workings which required most air, and also to shut off gassy parts of the workings.

Precautions against surface gas have to be taken in all underground workings (*i.e.*, mine systems, dug-outs and subways). This was done by hanging gas-curtains (blankets soaked in anti-gas mixture) at the top and bottom of inclines to shaft tops, and in inclines themselves.

For long headings (galleries), where there is little natural ventilation, air has to be pumped in. The first method adopted for giving air to the faces was by means of bellows, the air being carried underground by a tin pipe, 6-in. to 9-in. diameter with canvas joints This method was extremely quiet, gave a volume of air, was easy to work, and fool-proof, but was very cumbersome to instal, and required a big chamber off the shaft penthouse. It was eventually dropped in favour of the Holman pump, Keith Blackman, and several other types of air pumps and rotary blowers, which were more portable. In these the air is carried to the faces by armoured rubber-hose of smaller section ($2\frac{1}{2}$ in.) which, being flexible, is easier to manipulate and connect up.

The objection to the pumps and blowers was that they all made a noise, and had a habit of breaking down when most air was required.

In the summer of 1916 electrically-driven fans were installed, which proved very satisfactory. The air was carried underground by a tin pipe about 6 in. to 9 in. in diameter. This pipe was carried along the gallery by means of brackets in the roof, connections being made of rubber and canvas. These pipes were fitted into the fighting heads, and joints were made with the main pipe. If the enemy blew a mine and filled part of the workings with gas, the pipe was connected up and air pumped in, which drove the gas out in a very short time. The fan made little noise and delivered a large volume of air to the face. Air compressors were also used by one or two Companies, and proved successful.

13. PUMPING.

In the flat clay area north of the La Bassée Canal, and in the Ypres Salient, a great deal of trouble was caused by surface water. Each shaft had to be fitted with one or more pumps to deal with the water. These pumps were fixed on a platform half-way down the shaft. The water from the working was collected in a sump at the bottom of the shaft and pumped up to the surface. This sump required constant cleaning, as a great deal of spoil fell into it when hoisted, etc.

Three types of pumps were used :—

  (i).   The Service Lift and Force Pump.
  (ii). The Dando Diaphram Pump.
  (iii). Beck Trench Pump.

These pumps worked well with clear water, but with the dirty water, mud, and sand which collected in a sump, the only pump which was of value was the " Beck," which pumped sludge and gave very little trouble.

At the end of 1916 electrically-driven pumps were installed and proved a great success. The mine system was kept clear of water with an hour or two's pumping per day.

14. EXPLOSIVES AND CHARGES.

The explosives most commonly used for charging mines were ammonal, blastine and guncotton. Gunpowder was the first explosive used, but each of those just mentioned was found to be about three and a half times more powerful than theoretical gunpowder, and the use of powder was discontinued.

Ammonal, and to a lesser extent blastine, are hydroscopic, and had to be packed in waterproof covers when laid in a charge in order to ensure complete detonation.

If a charge had to remain in a mine for several days before being exploded, it was found that the tins in which ammonal was packed, and the waterproof covers to blastine cartridges, were not absolutely watertight.

Guncotton bags were used to a great extent for keeping charges dry when the charge had to remain a few days before being blown. When the supply of these was short, 4-gallon petrol tins, which are very portable, were used ; each tin carrying about 40 lbs. of ammonal, the mouth of the tin being sealed with pitch. It is an interesting fact that ammonal has practically the same density as water—a tin of 4/10 cub. ft. capacity carries 25 lbs. of water, and a little more than 25 lbs. of ammonal.

The charges were exploded by inserting guncotton primers and detonators into the charge.

CHAPTER III.

MISCELLANEOUS NOTES.

15. SUBWAYS.

The use and development of infantry subways has been described in Part I. *Plate* XV gives the details of one of the most elaborate systems that was constructed. The dimensions varied a good deal — 6 ft. × 3 ft., 6 ft. 2in. × 3 ft., 6 ft. × 3 ft. 6 in., 7 ft. × 3 ft., 7 ft. × 3 ft. 6 in. were all used at different times. Perhaps the most suitable size was 7 ft. × 3 ft., which would just allow one man carrying full equipment and stretchers to pass along comfortably. Passing places were often constructed by widening the subway at every 100 ft. or so. The average speed of driving in chalk reckoned over a long period may be given at about 80 ft. per week. This figure makes due allowance for common delays caused by shelling, irregularities of working parties, cutting recesses, and interruptions affecting progress under practical conditions. On several occasions remarkable records of speed were obtained when working against time. Single day runs of 30–50 ft. were made by several companies. The following are good examples :—

(*a*) A subway was being driven in chalk at a depth of 21 ft. with dimensions of 2 ft. 6 in. at top and 3 ft. at bottom, height 6 ft. 4 in. A normal speed of 13 ft. per day was being attained when the company received orders to push the speed to a maximum, regardless of economy in labour, etc. During the next seven days no less than 241 ft. 9 in. of progress was made, and thereafter an average of 25–30 ft. per day was maintained until the subway was completed. Eight-hour shifts were adhered to, but three miners were employed at the face—one constantly picking, one shovelling into bags, and a third resting. Infantry carrying parties averaged 30 per shift, a large number being necessary owing to limitations placed on trolleying by need for silence at a certain point. The bags were passed from man to man from the face to the head of the tramline, and from the end of the line up a 1 in 2 incline of 64 ft. Timbering was kept up to the face, about 50 sets being used in the week's run. Good air was maintained by one Holman pump.

(*b*) Another subway in chalk driven from the side of a quarry— size of subway, 6 ft. 2 in. × 3 ft. inside timber ; total length driven from main face, 437 ft. ; average rate per 24 hours, 20 ft. ; maximum length driven in 24 hours, 52 ft. During the first fifteen days the work was done by blasting, giving an average rate of progress per 24 hours of 16 ft. Hand work, which was employed subsequently, resulted in an average rate per 24 hours of 27 ft.—for this a party of six men was employed. These were distributed as follows :—

Relieving each other every ten minutes
{
1 tunneller at the face.
1 ,, shovelling from face to iron sheet.
1 ,, loading truck.
1 ,, resting.
}

1 tunneller's mate running truck.

1 ,, ,, working blower, and getting timber ready for the men at the face.

Spoil was evacuated in steel side-tipping trucks of 12 cub. ft. capacity, and was dumped directly behind in the quarry.

(c) The following is a record of progress made in a 6 ft. × 3 ft. 6 in. close-timbered gallery in shallow sandy clay :—

May.			Progress.
22nd	...	...	... 20 ft.
23rd	...	...	... 20 ft. 4 in.
24th	...	...	... 33 ft. 2 in.
25th	...	...	... 36 ft. 2 in.
26th	...	...	... 40 ft.
27th	...	...	... 20 ft. 4 in.
28th	...	...	... 42 ft.

212 ft.

or 30 ft. per day.

The comparatively low footages on May 22nd, 23rd, and 27th were due to long interruptions for " Stand-to " on these days. An average of five sappers (two at the face) and seven infantry were employed in six-hour shifts.

(d) During a ten-day run, also in clay, a 6 ft. × 3 ft. gallery was advanced 331 ft. 3 in. ; the best seven days' run was as under :—

June			Progress.
3rd	...	...	... 31 ft.
4th	...	...	... 45 ft.
5th	...	...	... 46 ft.
6th	...	...	... 29 ft. 3 in. (with push-pick)
7th	...	...	... 30 ft. ,, ,,
8th	...	...	... 30 ft. ,, ,,
9th	...	...	... 30 ft. ,, ,,

241 ft. 3 in.

or 34½ ft. per day.

This total is six inches below the week's record for chalk [See (a)].

The influence of push-pick work required for silence is very marked, and seems to prove that 30 ft. per day is the limit of practical possibility by this means of working.

16. TRENCH MORTAR BOMBARDMENTS AND SHALLOW MINING.

The enemy frequently showed great enterprise in attempting to damage our mine workings and impede operations by destructive raids and trench-mortar bombardments.

He systematically bombarded our shallow galleries in the clay at five sectors on the First and Second Army fronts at the beginning of 1917. The damage done shows that good results may be obtained by well-directed trench-mortar activity in sectors where the conditions are favourable.

Plate XVI. illustrates the damage done at two sectors, where either round timber sets and lagging, or close-casing of light timber were used. In other workings, close-cased with 9 in. × 3 in., the effects were not so extensive as where, in similar ground, frames and lagging or lighter casing were employed.

The conditions and results recorded may be summarized as under :—

SECTOR A (*Plate* XVI.) (Head-cover about 16 ft.).

Refer-ence.	Dimensions of Gallery.	Timbering Methods.	Damage.
1.	4 ft. 3 in. × 2 ft. 3 in.	Close-casing. Legs, 1½ in. Sills, 2 in.	Cases broken for about 24 ft. (legs only).
2.	4 ft. 3 in. × 2 ft. 3 in.	Legs, 1½ in. Sills, 2 in.	Slight damage for 80 ft.
3.	—	Round timber, sets and lagging	22 ft. damaged, 16 ft. caved in.
4.	—	Ditto	30 ft. damaged, 16 ft. caved in.

"SECTOR B. (*Plate* XVI.) (Head-cover about 15 ft.)

1.	4 ft. 3 in. × 2 ft. 3 in.	Legs, 1½ in. Caps, 2 in.	Legs and caps broken—clay driven 2 ft. through roof (11 ft. damaged).
2.	4 ft. 3 in. × 2 ft. 3 in.	Legs, 1½ in. Caps, 2 in.	All caps broken and 8 legs. Gallery half closed in from top and E. side (16 ft. damaged).
3.	4 ft. 3 in. × 2 ft. 3 in.	Legs, 3 in. Caps, 3 in.	All caps broken and 11 legs on E. side. Very little clay brought down (22 ft. damaged).
4.	—	—	Pent-house destroyed.
5.	4 ft. 3 in. × 2 ft. 3 in.	Legs, 3 in. Caps, 3 in.	Remaining gallery completely crushed in (10 ft. damaged).
6.	—	—	Badly crushed (20 ft. damaged).
7.	—	—	Badly crushed (10 ft. damaged).
8.	4 ft. 3 in. × 2 ft. 3 in.	Legs, 3 in. Caps, 3 in.	Caps only broken (5 ft. damaged).

H

Refer-ence.	Dimensions of Gallery	Timbering Methods.	Damage.
9.	—	—	Completely crushed in 30 ft. owing to direct hits (2) by H. T. M., repaired and again crushed in.
10.	4 ft. 6 in. × 2 ft. 6 in.	Legs, 3 in. Caps, 3 in.	Caps only broken (5 ft. damaged).
11.	—	—	Badly crushed.
12.	—	—	Badly crushed.
13.	—	—	Pent-house badly damaged.
14.	4 ft. 3 in. × 2 ft. 3 in.	Legs, 3 in. Caps, 3 in.	Ten legs broken (10 on N. side), $1\frac{1}{2}$ caps broken (10 ft. damaged).
15.	4 ft. 3 in. × 2 ft. 3 in.	Legs, $1\frac{1}{2}$ in. Caps, 2 in.	All caps broken, 7 legs broken, 1 ft. roof crushed in (10 ft. damaged).
16.	4 ft. 3 in. × 2 ft. 3 in.	Legs, 3 in. Caps, 3 in.	Five legs broken, 11 caps broken (11 ft. damaged).
17.	—	Skeleton frames and lagging.	Badly damaged.
18.	4 ft. 3 in. × 2 ft. 3 in.	Legs, $1\frac{1}{2}$ in. Caps, 2 in.	Three sets broken (3 ft. damaged).
19.	—	—	Five frames and lagging almost completely crushed in (15 ft. damaged).
20.	—	—	Shaft completely destroyed.

17. RECORDS AND REPORTS.

The importance of accurate records of all mining work is obvious. One of the first acts of the Inspector of Mines, on his appointment at the beginning of 1916, was to draw up and issue regular forms for use by Tunnelling companies. By means of this a full record was obtained of all work in progress, British and enemy blows, and other items of technical interest. In the Inspector of Mines' Office these reports were collated, and any points of general interest were issued in the form of classified Mining Notes to all concerned. The Inspector of Mines also sent regular periodical reports on the whole mining situation to the C.G.S. Copies of three forms are given on *Plates* XVII., XVIII., and XIX. *Plate* XVII. is the form on which every tunnelling company sent in its weekly progress report. *Plate* XVIII. was used in the case of all blows, either British or enemy, and was sent in as soon as possible after the necessary data could be collected. Every blow had also to be reported by telegram without waiting for details. *Plate* XIX. gives the list of the special mining tools and instruments, the issue of which was controlled by the Inspector of Mines, and which were not obtainable through the ordinary stores channels.

18. COMPARISON OF BRITISH AND ENEMY REPORTS ON THE SAME BLOWS.

Amongst the enemy mining records captured in the advance on the Somme, there was found a " Sprengbuch " or Blow Book, giving tabulated conditions and results of mine explosions in the mining sector of the Tambour du Clos, termed by the enemy Fricourt West. The data are compiled on similar lines to the classification in our own printed reports (*Plate* XVIII).

The reports on six mine explosions—three enemy and three British—are given below, in parallel column with our own reports on the same occurrences.

The general accuracy of the reports, even when unfavourable to the enemy, and the detailed nature of the report, deserve attention :—

Enemy Reports.

No. 1. Date—30. 4. 16.
Place—D.2.
Time—3.30 a.m.
Nature.—Crater.
Effects.—Mine exploded with strong clouds of smoke and powerful flames. Crater diameter about 30 metres.
Result.—In our own position only the middle crater saps destroyed. Effect on the enemy's mine system apparently none, as the charge was not at effective depth.
Crater Number.—XXXXIV.
Losses.—None.
Charge.—6000kg.   W = 15 m.
C = 1˙5. D = 1. (L = 5062).
Tamping.—About 20–25 m. with sandbags and cross beams.
Method of Firing.—Two electric leads, 1 safety fuse. Fired electrically.
Remarks.—The blow took place to distract attention of the enemy from a raid of the —— on the S.E. corner of the main work. It was ascertained later that an English post was blown in by the blow.

Our Own Reports.

(1). At 2.15 a.m. on 30. 4. 16 enemy exploded a mine between G.3.F. and G.19.A. and in the same direction, another at 7.30 p.m. on the same day. The latter mine has not been exactly located as it did no damage. The former threw up a column of flame and debris, and formed a crater in front of our galleries, which were undamaged. These explosions caused an increase of water in the neighbouring galleries.

(*Second Report*).—Enemy exploded two mines on 30. 4. 16, but no damage was caused either above or underground. Incessant bombardment of our trenches destroyed several of our shaft entrances and hindered underground work considerably. Enemy activity underground also diminished, probably for similar reasons. There was an unsuccessful attempt by enemy to raid our trenches with evident intention to blow in our shaft-heads.

Enemy Reports.   *Our Own Reports.*

No. 2.   Date.—30. 4. 16.
Place.—E.
Time.—8.45 p.m.
Nature.—Crater.
Effects.—The mine exploded with great quantity of smoke and made a crater of some 20 m. diameter.
Result.—Some damage in our own position.   Effect on enemy's system middling.   The charge was only 12 m. deep.
Crater Number.—XXXXV.
Losses.—None.
Charge.—2000 kg.   W = 10 m.
   C = 1·5.   D = 1.   (L = 1500).
Tamping.—About 20 m. sandbags and cross beams.
Method of Firing.—Two divided electric circuits and 1 safety fuse. Fired electrically.
Remarks.—The blow took place to divert enemy's attention from a great raid against the group of houses at Fricourt Station.
   Raid did not take place.

No. 3.   Date.—10. 5. 16.
Place.—(a) ½-left from R.
Time.—6 a.m.
Nature.—Camouflet.
Effects.—H.5. head-cover driven in, H.4. crushed in to 5 m. from the fork to H.5.   R. crushed in to a depth of 20 m.   W. head slightly damaged.   Our position slightly damaged.
Losses.—None.
Charge.—About 1500–2000 kg.
Remarks.—Enemy's trenches damaged.

We fired three mines simultaneously at 4 a.m. 10. 5. 16 with the object of destroying certain enemy workings, which were in close proximity.   Craters were formed and slight damage was caused to some of our trenches.

The enemy ceased work for two days, but has now resumed as usual, almost entirely blasting.

Charge.—12,000 lbs. guncotton and ammonal.

No. 4.   Date.—10. 5. 16.
Place.—(b) ½-left from P.
Time.—6 a.m.
Nature.—Crater.
Effects.—P. crushed in at 18 m. depth.   L. crushed in at 15 m. depth.
Crater Number.—XXXXVI.
Losses.—None.
Charge.—About 1,500 kg.
Remarks.—Probably damaged by being crushed in.

Charge.—11,000 lbs. ammonal.

Enemy Reports.

No. 5.　*Date.*—10. 5. 16.

Place.—(c) ½-right from enemy's crater saps.

Time.—6 a.m.

Nature.—Crater.

Effects.—L. crushed in at 15 m.

Remarks.—Crater quite small between V. and XIX.

Result (regarding above three blows).—The heads of R. and W. which are little damaged can be pushed forward under protection of the enemy's blows. Similarly L. 1 and new P.1. between W. and L.1.　L. and P. remain abandoned for the present as too weak.

No. 6.　*Date.*—1. 6. 16.

Place.—Gallery R.

Time.—11.15 a.m.

Nature.—Camouflet.

Effects.—The charge worked well, as the two opponents were so close.　At the moment of explosion, the gas appeared in form of smoke clouds behind the English first line.

Result.—Our trenches slightly damaged for 150 metres.　Our mine system, except H.5., not affected.　Work will be continued in galleries R., W. and V.

Charge.—6,000 kg.

Tamping.—Sandbags and wooden beams as far as the mine barricade.

Method of Firing.—Electric.

Our Own Reports.

Charge.—9,500 lbs. ammonal.

At 9.30 a.m. on 1. 6. 16 enemy exploded two mines.　Explosion was followed at 9.40 a.m. by a short bombardment which did no damage.　The shock of the explosion was distinctly felt in Meaulte.　Explosion caused the death of ten men, crushed or entombed.

It is almost impossible to say if a crater was formed ; some fresh earth is thrown up and the absence of gas would also denote surface action.

There is no indication from listening reports to show position of enemy charges.　On the left of G.20.A. enemy were closest, estimated 40 ft. away 10 o'clock.

It is reported, but unconfirmed, that our men in G.23 were using two picks to finish off chamber, contrary to orders.

CHAPTER IV.

MINE-LISTENING INSTRUMENTS AND THEIR USE.

19. INTRODUCTION.

Of the many branches of Military Mining, Mine-Listening is one of the most important.

To be able to detect and locate accurately the hostile workings is of the utmost value in mining operations, and a great deal of attention was accordingly paid to bring this science to as high a standard as possible.

Efforts were most successful in this respect, and on the capture of the various hostile systems it was found that the actual position of their galleries corresponded exceedingly well with the position they had already been accorded on our listening plans.

In the early days of mining many types of instruments were tried, e.g., Stethoscope, French Water-Bottle and Water Electric, but the Geophone and Seismomicrophone were the two that were ultimately used practically exclusively. With the aid of the former, it was possible by listening in the posts themselves accurately to determine the position of the hostile working; by the aid of the latter all listening-posts were linked up to a Central Listening Exchange, and on the detection of mining sounds, the final investigation was made with the Geophone.

This system of " Central Listening " was brought to such a high degree of perfection that it was possible to listen from 50 posts extending over three miles of front from one Listening Chamber, thus affording a great saving in man-power and greatly increasing the safety of the men engaged in listening. It was, however, quite a late development, and only really came in after active mine-fighting had ceased.

Many theoretical ideas and delicate scientific instruments can be successfully applied in laboratories and experimental galleries, but are useless in the trenches ; it is only severely practical methods and instruments which are of value in mining warfare.

After careful investigation and testing, the following instruments were approved as the three standard types :—

Instrument.	Use.
Geophone	Determination of Direction.
Western Electric Detector ...	Determination of Distance.
Seismomicrophone	Central Listening Stations. Listening in gassy galleries. Tamping in with charges.

(*The notes that follow were written immediately after the war (December, 1918), by* CAPT. H. STANDISH BALL, R.E. (T), *and must be read with due regard to that fact*).

20. THE GEOPHONE.

The Geophone (*Plate* XX. and *Photo* III.) is undoubtedly the best instrument yet devised for determining direction.

One of the chief factors which determined its universal use is the true reproduction of sound obtained by its means.

Constructed on the principles of the ordinary stethoscope, the sound waves are transmitted from the ground through the instrument to the listener at an intensity approximately two and a half times greater than would be obtained when listening with the ear alone.

Several different types of instrument have been made, all based on the same principle ; a description of the Geophone and its use will suffice for all.

Plate XXI. shows its method of use. Its construction is simple, consisting of a mass of mercury enclosed on either side by a mica disc, the whole contained in a wooden frame. On the exterior of the pot are two small nipples to which are attached the rubber tubes and ear-piece—if two Geophones are to be used, one nipple is blocked up by means of a small rubber plug.

Single Geophone.—One Geophone only is used when it is desired to magnify the sound only, and no direction is required—it is used generally by listeners who have not been trained in double Geophone work, but at the same time can be relied on for their accurate knowledge of mining sounds. It is impossible to obtain direction by means of the single Geophone ; its use, however, is of the utmost value for sound magnification, and all mining sounds can be heard over a considerable distance by its means, as is seen later in the table of sounds.

Double Geophone.—For the successful use of two Geophones in the determination of direction, experience shows that the listener must be possessed of unimpaired hearing, and have been thoroughly trained at a School of Instruction and have obtained a creditable pass.

Working on the principle that the Geophones are two highly sensitive ears, the listener manipulates them to and fro on the ground until the sound is reproduced equally in both ears. When that condition is satisfied, the source of the sound will be in a direction at right angles to the line joining the centre of the two pots.

Plate XXII. shows the principle of working. Assume that the two Geophones are placed on the ground, about 1½ ft.–2 ft. apart, their position at starting being L1 and R1, L1 being the left Geophone and R1 the right one. If the source of sound is as shown by the arrow in the diagram, the sound will strike the left ear first, pointing to the fact that L1 is too far round and is nearer the source of sound than R1. The Geophones will now be shifted to position L2, R2 ; the first impact of sound is immediately transferred to the right ear, showing the fact that R has been brought too far round, and the fact is now established that the correct position for L is somewhere in the arc L1–L2, and that for R between R1–R2. After a little bracketing backwards and forwards, a position L3–R3 will be found, where the sound will be heard simultaneously in both ears.

On the Geophone Compass being placed between the pots, the direction of the arrow pointing to the source of the sound is read and booked. Thus it will be seen that in *Plate* XXII. the direction of the working place is 41° W. of N. If a direction determination has been made from the end of a listening-post, a further determination is made either from an adjacent post or from a point further back in the gallery ; on the two directions being plotted in the plan, the intersection should give to a close degree of accuracy the position of the working face. The Geophone may be used in a similar manner to ascertain the level of the working. The Geophone pots are placed against the side of the gallery, one above the other—if the sound is on a higher level, it will strike the upper pot first, if on a lower level, the bottom pot. When making a determination, great care must be taken that the pots are resting on a solid foundation, and are not on any foreign matter such as sandbags or straw. If the condition of the ground is such that it is difficult to find a suitable foundation, a ledge must be constructed in the side of the gallery large enough to allow of the free movement of the pots.

When listening, all leather equipment or articles liable to produce any creaking sound must be removed ; the slightest noise disturbs the listener and leads to the production of inaccurate results.

On moving the Geophones around, the body should be made to follow them as far as possible, the shoulders being kept close between the pots.

Silence is naturally an essential feature of a listening-post, and on no account should more than two listeners be allowed in together.

Standard listening forms should always be used for booking results, Army Form W.3379 being used for this purpose.

Mine Listening Report.   A.F. W. 3379.

Listener's Name—Sapper Evans.   *Date*—27/11/17.

Name of Gallery.	*Time.*	*Sounds heard.*	*Estimated distance in feet.*	*Estimated direction.*
" A "	2 p.m.–4 p.m.	Picking and Shovelling.	40	N.30°W.

Compass.—The compass should be mounted in a wooden frame about 18 in. long, into the ends of which the Geophone pots will fit. The compass is graduated in 36 segments, each segment representing 10°, and reads from 0 to 18 to the right and left of the arrow respectively. This arrow always points directly at the source of sound, and its position is recorded E. or W. of Magnetic North, *e.g.*, 30° W. of N. or 150° E. of N.

Care of the Geophone Set.—Great care must always be taken of the set, the listener being taught to regard his Geophone in the light that an infantry man should regard his rifle.

The following are practical points which should always be tested by the listener when examining his set :—

(i).   The rubber tubes must be of an equal length.

(ii).   The pots must be a pair, and must correspond with the numbers on the box.

(iii). The tubes, ear-piece, and Geophone nipples must be free from any obstruction.

(iv).   The compass must be in the box.

Each side of the Geophone must be tested, as it sometimes happens that one side may be rendered useless and not the other.

Geophones have lately been constructed containing lead in place of the mercury mass. This type is quite satisfactory, but gives a slightly different reproduction of the sound from the mercury type —hence care must be taken that only one or the other is used ; if one mercury and one lead were used in combination, difficulty would be experienced in determining the final point.

21. WESTERN ELECTRIC MINING DETECTOR.

This instrument consists of an earth-wave detecting apparatus which is capable of transforming the energy received from earth-waves originated by mining operations into electrical impulses, when supplied with current from a battery placed in circuit ; and of reproducing those noises in a telephone receiver. In circuit with this detector is an apparatus capable of reducing all received sound to one level, called the " Zero Sound," by the introduction of variable resistances into the circuit, thus altering the current. The amount by which the apparatus has to reduce the received sound to attain this zero limit can be measured ; and, by means of suitable calibration curves, such measurements can be expressed in feet.

Hence it follows that, if the apparatus is accurately calibrated in that type of ground in which it is desired to use it, any mining sound can be picked up and the distance determined by the application of the calibration curve for that particular sound and ground.

Further, if exact location of a point is required, both as regards direction and level, it is only necessary to take determinations from three points, one of which must be at a higher level than the others, the position of the working place being determined by triangulation, and if direction is required only two measurements in the same level are necessary.

Apparatus (See *Photo* IV.).—The apparatus provided comprises a case containing :—

> Double head-gear receiver
> Four detectors.
> A switch-box.

In this latter are :—

(*a*). Five keys associated with five pairs of terminals to which the detectors are connected, and numbered 1 to 5.

(*b*). One key marked C, with two positions marked L and H in addition to the normal position. When thrown to L, the low resistance shunt is across the receiver, and when thrown to H, the high resistance shunt is across. Revolving the knob on top of the instrument changes the value of these shunts.

(*c*). Two keys, A and B ; these serve to insert extra resistance in the circuit, a resistance of 450 ohms being obtained when using both together.

(*d*). Two dry batteries.

The following notes are practical, simplified instructions on the use of this instrument :—

Detectors.—These should lie in close contact with the ground. In the case of damp and wet galleries a niche should be cut in the side of the gallery and a waterproof cover placed over the terminals.

Calibration Curves.—Calibration must be done in ground similar to that in which the instrument is to be used. Two curves are generally necessary, being known as the long and short distance curves, ranging from the limit of the instrument down to 30 ft. for the long-distance one, and from 30 ft. to zero for the short distance one, when working in chalk.

Method of Calibration.

Long-Distance Curve.—Place the detector at maximum distance required from the source of the sound and connect to the instrument, the latter being placed in a secluded spot free from external noises.

Adjust the ear-piece to fit closely and comfortably.

Note that dial-pointer over switchboard reads a maximum.

Throw circuit switch in bottom row corresponding to number of terminal to which leads are connected.

Throw key C to H.

The instrument is now in a state of maximum sensitiveness and zero should be clearly heard.

Insert resistances by keys A and B until sounds can only just be detected ; finally reduce the current flowing through the receiver by rotating pointer over switchboard, counter-clockwise, till the sound is just cut out.

Book Reading ; Keys A, B and C are now constant for this curve and should not be altered.

Move the detectors to the next desired distance, throw circuit switch in again and cut out the sound by a further rotation of the pointer. Repeat this at 10 ft. intervals down to 30 ft., or whatever the limit of the circular control may be, and plot the results, taking distances as ordinates and dial-readings as abscissæ.

Short-Distance Curve.—To obtain a short-distance curve, start at, for example, 30 ft., and proceed as before, key C being thrown to L instead of H.

Application of Results.—To determine the distance of enemy working, place detector at a convenient point, throw keys A, B and C to positions used when calibrating, cut out sound by inserting the adjustable resistance, and note the dial-reading.

Reference to the curve previously obtained gives the distance of the enemy working from the detector.

It is essential that the sounds cut out to give the distance are of the same intensity as that obtained when calibrating. This is the one disadvantage of the instrument, for it is extremely difficult to gauge the intensity of the hostile work, as the nearer the enemy is to you the more carefully he will work. It is on this account that very little use was made of the Western Electric in the trenches for distance detecting.

Plate XXIII. shows calibration curves for chalk. A separate calibration should be made by each listener. In each calibration the conditions should be made as practical as possible.

In ground of a dense clayey nature one curve will probably be sufficient. The batteries must be rested as much as possible by releasing the detector key the moment the observation is completed.

If it is desired that the detector should be placed nearer the hostile working than our own gallery, a borehole can be made and the detector pushed in to the end.

The apparatus is sometimes used as a sound detector only, in which case keys A and B remain at neutral, and key C is thrown to H.

22. THE SEISMOMICROPHONE (*Plate* XXIV.).

The Seismomicrophone, or as it is more commonly called, the Seismophone, is the instrument most generally used for Central Listening Stations, and for tamping in with charges.

Fig. 1 shows a section of the instrument. A brass case, consisting of the bottom part (AB) and the cover (ECDF), contains a solid mass (M), isolated from AB by rubber rings (C1, C2, C3, C4). Two carbon pastilles (P1, P2), the first of which has six cells hollowed in it, are fixed to M and ECDF respectively. Each cell of P1 contains four carbon granules 1·5 mm. in diameter. CD carries two terminals, one of which is insulated from the cover and connected with M by a flexible insulated wire, in order that P1, P2 can be connected to the battery.

The instrument fits inside a wooden case containing two external terminals (H). When in use the detector is placed firmly on the ground with the handle uppermost, in a dry place at the end of the post, or preferably in a niche cut in the side of the gallery, and connected by leads to the receiver (*Fig.* 2).

A special water-tight box (*Fig.* 3) must be used in damp posts, care being taken that all joints are properly water-tight.

The Seismophone was found to be quite satisfactory in different types of ground, giving a true reproduction of sound and being much stronger and less likely to go out of order than other instruments manufactured for the same purpose.

Owing to its reliability, natural sound production, and simplicity of constructional detail, it was used in preference to any other type of electrical detector.

23. RANGE OF SOUNDS.

The distance over which sounds can be heard with different instruments naturally varies with the nature of the ground, and experiments must always be carried out to obtain a local sound range table as soon as listening is instituted.

The following tables give an idea of the distance sounds can be heard in average chalk and sandy clay :—

Average Chalk.

Nature of Sound.	Naked Ear.	Distances in feet. Seismophone.	Geophone.
Picking	150	200	300
Shovelling	70	70	120
Dirt falling	35	50	60
Walking	50	70	80
Talking	12	45	50

Sandy Clay.

Picking	...	...	50	...	70	...	100
Push-picking	...	...	15	...	25	...	35
Shovelling	...	...	8	...	15	...	30
Dirt falling	...	...	5	...	12	...	20
Walking	...	...	10	...	25	...	40
Talking	...	...	5	...	10	...	15

Tests were carried out to compare the relative audibility of mining noises in chalk, with the following results :—

Nature of Sound.				*Audibility Units.*
Wedging	...	...	...	...	90
Drilling	...	...	...	...	82
Timbering	...	...	...	...	65
Picking	...	...	...	...	62
" Wombat " Boring—Calyx Bit 6 in.				55
Walking	...	...	...	...	20
Shovelling	...	...	...	...	19
Boring—Auger Bit 2 in.	...	...		17
Falling chalk	...	...	...	16
Dragging bags	...	...	...	15
Trolleys	...	...	...	...	14
Shouting	...	...	...	...	8
Talking	...	...	...	...	6

Sounds sometimes carry an extraordinary distance, in one case pile-driving in a shaft in blue clay being heard in a second shaft 1,700 ft. away with the naked ear.

24. CENTRAL LISTENING STATIONS AND THEIR ORGANIZATION.

The results obtained from this system of listening can only be used as a general guide to enemy activity. They do not afford evidence as to direction or distance, nor do they necessarily give a definite interpretation of sounds heard. Its chief merit is the great saving in man-power that can be effected when a mining system is complete, or where our mining operations do not lead to a confusion of sounds.

While the advantages of Central Listening Stations are obvious, they were never intended to replace general routine listening at the face with Geophones. They must be simply used as a preliminary to Geophone listening, and in every case the final determination must be carried out by means of a Geophone at the face. It is essential that all men engaged in this form of listening should be trained and fully qualified to obtain results with all types of instruments.

Central Station.—This should be centrally situated in as quiet a spot as possible, preferably behind the lateral. It should be comfortably fitted up with switchboard, light, tables and chairs, and everything done to make the lot of the listener as pleasant as circumstances permit. Various types of switchboards have been devised, the type used generally depending upon the number of posts to be connected to the station.

A common form of board is similar to the circular rheostat control, the different posts being connected to studs on the board.

A second type that has been used is a diagrammatic plan of the mining system, studs being fixed at the end of each post in the plan, to which the detector in that particular part is connected, contact being made by inserting a plug; this type is supposed to quicken the interest of the listener as he is better able to visualize the probable position of the hostile working. In this form of board the plan must naturally not be made accurate or drawn to scale (*Plate* XXV.).

A trained and trustworthy listener must be placed in charge of the switchboard and made responsible for the general efficiency of the listening during his shift—with him should be one or more trained listeners for the purpose of investigating all sounds recorded through the switchboard. The number of listeners required depends on the size of the system and hostile mining activity of the sector.

The first duty of the listener in charge on going on shift is to test all detectors to ascertain whether they are in working order and are accurately recording sounds; this is done either by one of the listeners visiting the posts in turn and placing a watch against the detector, or attaching an electrical buzzer device to the back of each seismophone, the buzzer being controlled from the Central Station (*Plate* XXVI.).

With the latter method a code of signals can be arranged by means of which the listener in the station is able to direct the man in the post to proceed to any place necessary.

A log-book must be kept in which will be recorded every shift, when sounds were first detected, report of listener's investigation, and time sounds ceased. *Nil* reports should also be entered.

Too much importance cannot be attached to this, for by this means it can be ascertained how many faces are being worked at one time, whether the miners are being withdrawn from one face to another, and whether a face is being worked continuously—in fact, a carefully compiled daily listening-log is an invaluable asset in the determination of enemy mining activity.

Wiring and Listening-Posts.—Low-resistance twin-wire cable is generally used, though ordinary firing cable is quite satisfactory.

The general method of wiring is to have one common return wire running along the lateral, from which a tapping is taken to each detector; thus for 25 detectors only 26 separate leads would be needed.

The wires must be carefully insulated from one another, and a system of labelling adopted in case of breaks occurring.

Each listening post should bear a distinctive name-plate at the entrance, and must be kept in as clean and dry a state as possible.

The need for silence must be impressed on all listeners when entering posts.

In close-timbered galleries it is advisable to cut a niche half-way up the face sufficiently big to allow of the manipulation of the Geophones.

25. OFFICE RECORDS.

Great importance must be attached to the efficient correlation and filing of listening reports.

Reports should always be made out in duplicate, the original being sent to Headquarters.

A " Listening-Post " diary should be kept for each individual post, entries being made daily of all sounds that may have been heard during the previous 24 hours ; *nil* reports are also entered.

In addition to this, a listening-plan should be constructed, showing the whole mining front and the positions where the enemy have been heard working.

All *reliable* reports are plotted on this plan, the position being indicated by coloured flags and the date of working. Different colours are used for enemy working, active and inactive. In this way it can be seen at a glance how many hostile faces are known actually to be working, which are offensive and which are defensive, and, most important of all, at which places he is lying in waiting.

Without a proper method of listening-records at Headquarters it would be a simple matter to go on working blindly ahead, and possibly be blown by the enemy at a point where he might have been heard working previously, but where his existence had been forgotten.

Listening Officer.—If the hostile mining is very active, it is sometimes advisable to appoint a listening officer, who will naturally be a man specially chosen for the post.

The listening officer will supervise all the special listeners, organize the administration of the Central Chambers and generally act in advisory position to the C.O. in questions of mine-listening.

26. MINE-LISTENING INSTRUCTION.

Soon after the importance of mine-listening was recognized, a thorough course of instruction in mine-listening was found to be essential.

Mine-Listening Schools were therefore instituted, being so constructed that all mining sounds common to front-line work could be faithfully reproduced both for the instruction of the men and for the standardization and testing of listening instruments

The training should be both theoretical and practical, and only men with unimpaired hearing and bright intelligence should be chosen for such a course.

The eight-day listening course, of which particulars are given in Chapter V., para. 32, was the result of many months of experience, and was regarded as sufficient to produce a thorough and reliable listener.

Additional details of the course were as follows :—

Gallery Work.—The first day was devoted to becoming accustomed to various sounds, first with the naked ear and then with the single Geophone.

From the second day onwards several Geophone determinations were made daily from listening-posts underground, the working places being so selected that as much variety as possible was given to the listeners both as regards variety of ground, difference in direction and level, and change of those sounds common to mining.

Towards the end of the course two picks were worked together some distance apart, and the position of each had to be determined.

In every case the listener was required to book his results on a standard listening-form.

Central Listening Station.—Each man was shown the wiring and working of a Central Listening Station, and was required to connect up his own instruments.

Men were formed into Listening Patrols, the man in charge of the station determining from which gallery the sounds of working could be heard by means of the central switchboard.

On working being heard he despatched his listening patrol to determine the nature and direction of the sound by means of the double Geophone from the listening galleries themselves.

Examination.—Each man had to carry out a double Geophone determination from three posts, booking the results on a proper form drawn up by himself and plotting them on a plan. In addition he was subjected to a *viva voce* examination on the testing of listening sets, compass work, electrical instruments, and Central Listening Stations.

In reporting on a candidate considerable attention was paid to the results obtained by him during the course, a complete record of which was kept.

Three grades of efficiency were given, *viz.* :—

Very good, good, and fair, the percentage of marks for these being 76, 56, and 40 respectively.

A high standard for the grade " very good " was required owing to the importance which would naturally be attached to the listening reports of a man who had been placed in this category.

In addition to the ordinary tutorial class work, the galleries could always be used by more advanced students for the purpose of calibration and testing of instruments.

Listening Circle.—The Listening Circle forms a valuable and integral part of a Listening School and is most necessary for the elementary training of the listener, as it enables him to place reliance in his results. *Plate* XXVII. shows a plan and section of such a circle. A circular shaft about 9 ft. deep and 5 ft. wide is sunk with suitable means of excluding surface noises as far as possible.

This shaft is reached by the " Tapping Circle," which is about 5 ft. deep and 3 ft. wide, the whole listening circle being 50 ft. in diameter.

The " Tapping Circle " is divided into 32 sections marked by wooden tabs from o to + 15 and from o to — 15, a wooden stake being driven into the ground at each point for knocking on.

In the listening shaft similar pairs of numbers are placed at equal intervals forming a circle of about $2\frac{1}{2}$ ft. diameter. On any one of the stakes being struck in the " tapping circle " it is possible for the listener in the shaft to determine accurately from which point the noise is coming.

For example, suppose the striker is at + 13 and the listener has his two pots at 9, the left pot being in the negative semicircle—the sound will be heard in the left ear first. Suppose the two pots are next shifted to 15, the left pot being still in the negative semicircle, the sound will now be the first heard in the right ear. From the result of these observations the listener has learnt that the sound is between + 9 and + 15 ; he will then simply bracket his observations until at 13 he will hear the sound equally in both ears, and will call out the number 13. The numbers are denoted by + and — signs to enable the listener to signify from which side of the circle the noise is proceeding, *e.g.*, as long as the left Geophone is in the negative semicircle, the sound will be from the + division.

Care must be taken when tapping that the noise cannot be heard plainly by the listener in the shaft, or the value of the practice will be lost.

Listening Gallery.—The following is a description of a listening gallery for instructional purposes. It has been found to be extremely satisfactory, being economical in ground, and at the same time giving scope for a great variety of directions, levels, and sounds. The system can be used either in clay or in chalk.

In *Plate* XXVIII. shafts 1 and 2 are sunk to the requisite depth in order that ground of a homogeneous nature may be worked in and no surface sounds are liable to cause confusion.

No. 1 gallery is the listening gallery, and No. 2 gallery is the working gallery ; as will be seen, a " pillar and stall " method of working is adopted, that being found to be the most economical method.

Model listening posts are constructed on either side of the listening gallery, and it is possible in this manner to accommodate a large class of listeners at one time ; this is a great advantage, the necessity for

I

each individual having as many observations as possible being obvious.

With the working galleries as shown it is possible to reproduce sounds at any desired distance, direction, or level. This is extremely useful both from an instructional point of view, and for the testing of instruments.

Plate XXIX. shows the same listening posts put on to a plan of an imaginary front. This was given to the students at the conclusion of the course, and they were required to plot on it the position of the working faces which they determined during their examination. In conjunction with it, they were required to hand in a Listening Report with full particulars of their observations.

In all the posts electrical detectors were placed connected up to the Central Listening Station. It was thus possible to carry out actual listening patrols, combining the Central Station with the Geophone determinations.

CHAPTER V.

MINE SCHOOLS.

27. ORGANIZATION, ETC.

Formation.—Owing to the large number of casualties suffered by Tunnelling Companies in the summer of 1915, due to carbon monoxide poisoning underground, a qualified instructor in the use of mine rescue apparatus was sent out from England. A small school for training in mine rescue work was started at Armentières, followed, towards the end of the year, by further schools in the First and Third Armies, these schools being known as Army Mine Rescue Schools.

At the commencement of 1916 further schools were started for training in the use of mine-listening instruments, but it was soon discovered that to be really efficient these schools had to be centralized in each Army at some site where instruction in all mining subjects could be given, and at the same time supervision of the mine rescue work and mine-listening of Tunnelling Companies exercised.

On 1st July, 1916, the First Army Mine School was started and functioned as such until the conclusion of hostilities.

Mine Schools were opened later in other armies, and courses run intermittently on more or less the same lines ; but, owing to various reasons, such as the constant change of Army fronts, were not enabled to enjoy the same facilities for continuous training as that of the First Army.

The following notes on training are based on the syllabus of courses at the First Army Mine School.

Establishment.

Army Mine School (Authority: W.O. Letter 121/8751 (S.D 2) dated 16. 9. 16).

Captain (Officer Commanding)	1
Subaltern	1
	2 Officers
Serjeant (Mine Rescue Instructor) ...	1
Corporal ,, ,, ,, ...	1
Serjeant (Mine-Listening Instructor) ...	1
Corporals ,, ,, ,, ...	2
Storeman	1
Batmen	2
	8 other Ranks.

Objects of School.

(a). To train Tunnelling Company personnel in mine rescue work ; to repair, test, issue and maintain a reserve stock of mine rescue apparatus.

(b). To train Tunnelling Company personnel in the use of mine-listening instruments ; to repair, test, issue and standardize same.

(c). To train all officers in Tunnelling Companies in advanced mining tactics, trench surveying, and allied subjects.

(d . To train officers and other ranks of units other than Tunnelling Companies in the construction of mined dug-outs ; to instruct in the detection and removal of enemy traps.

(e). To train teams of men in the use of boring machines.

(f). To test and report on explosives, new instruments and engineering appliances, and carry out instructional demonstrations in the use of same.

(g). To form a centre for the exhibition of Military Engineering works for the benefit of representatives from Allied Armies.

28. GENERAL MINING COURSE FOR ALL PERSONNEL OF TUNNELLING COMPANIES.

Duration of Course : 10 days.

The object of the course was to give instruction in those subjects only which would be of practical use in mining warfare.

The course for officers was of a more advanced type than that given at the School of Military Engineering, Chatham, and no officer was accepted as a student unless he had had at least two months' experience in the trenches.

A full report was rendered to the Army on each student, special certificates being given for proficiency in mine rescue work.

29. SYLLABUS OF TEN DAYS' GENERAL MINING COURSE FOR OFFICERS.

General Mining.

Lecture 1.—Definitions and classification of craters and mines.
Radius of rupture and application of same to mining problems.
Formulæ for calculation of charges and size of craters.
Calculation of maximum camouflets.
Use of curves for determination of charges.
Demonstration of the use of formulæ in the working out of a mining scheme.

Lecture 2.—Geology of the front.
Importance of geological sections, with special reference to depth and variation of water-level.

Defensive mining on one or more levels, with principles underlying it.

Offensive-defensive mining for general attacks and for the assistance of infantry raids.

Defilade and enfilade craters.

Assistance of ordinary mining methods by use of boring machines.

Demonstration of the different methods of mining by the exhibition of actual mining plans of the front.

Lecture 3.—General points of importance for efficient co-operation with the infantry of the line.

General duties of the officer on shift.

Organization in case of attack.

Advice to infantry in mining operations.

Lecture 4.—Explosives and their use in warfare.

Description and advantages obtained from the use of Delay Action Fuses and Cordeau Détonant, with necessary precautions when using same.

Electric detonators and their use.

Correct method of testing exploders, detonators and leads.

Risks caused by testing with coils of low resistance.

Results of all recent investigations carried out at the school.

Tutorial.—Calculation of problems involving the use of formulæ for charges and craters.

Practical Work.

Mining War Game.—This type of " war game " proved of the greatest value both to instructors and students, many points of technical interest being brought out.

On more than one occasion a scheme tried in the " game " was reproduced successfully in the trenches.

The officers were divided into two parties, a senior officer being in charge of each side, and given actual plans of the front with aeroplane photographs and full particulars as regards existing galleries, listening-posts, and number of men available.

The two sides were opposed to one another and were given definite instructions as regards defensive and offensive work at the beginning of the game. A certain number of days' work was plotted every day, the instructor copying same on his key plan. Listening reports were issued by him daily as the opposing faces approached within listening range of one another, the opponents having to alter their scheme as the exigencies of the case demanded. In the event of a mine being blown, full particulars as to date, time, size of charge, amount of tamping, and the number of men employed had to be given. At the end of the course the two schemes were examined and criticized, and a verdict given.

Testing of Electrical Circuits and Exploders.—Complete resistance tests of leads and detonators. Efficiency tests of Service exploder.

Examination.—A three-hours' paper was set at the termination of the course, composed of questions on crater calculations, mine fighting, listening instruments and organization, explosives and electrical testing.

Practical Surveying.—Use of the Dumpy level, prismatic compass, theodolite, and periscopic theodolite. Plotting of enemy trenches by the use of aeroplane photographs and proportional compass.

Listening.

Lecture 1.—Particulars and use of the geophone, double geophone, seismostethoscope, telegeophone, seismophone and Western Electric
Care of apparatus.
Importance of accurate results.
Concrete examples of results obtained from accurate and systematic listening.

Lecture 2.—Duties of an officer.
Efficient organization of listening patrols.
Systematic arrangement of listening posts.
Organization of central listening stations.
Forms of listening reports, office records, and listening plans.
Graphical representation of listening reports.

Practical Work.—Practice with double geophone in listening circle and galleries.
Obtaining of direction from one or more posts.
Detection and direction of two picks.
Listening patrols.
Calibration of a Western Electric machine, and use of different forms of electric detectors.
Demonstration of the working of a central listening station.

Examination.—A searching examination was carried out, comprising tests in the listening circle, galleries, and with electrical instruments.
Management of patrols, and detection of a working place from several listening posts.

Mine Rescue Work.—Before this work was commenced, all members of the class were medically examined for heart trouble, bronchial trouble, or other organic weakness.

Theory.—Five lectures, each of three-quarters of an hour duration, were given, dealing with " Proto," " Salvus " and " Novita " apparatus ; first-aid in gas-poisoning cases ; properties and detection of mine gas, and organization of mining companies for efficient mine rescue work.

At the termination of the course a two hours' written examination was held on these subjects.

Practical Work.—Each officer was in charge of a squad of men.

The practices were carefully graded, starting with simple exercises in the open air, and finishing with mine rescue work in underground galleries in an irrespirable atmosphere.

Each member of the team had to clean and re-charge his apparatus after practices.

In the practical examination test, each man had to report on defective sets of apparatus, the officer having also to examine his squad of men to see their apparatus was properly adjusted and in good order before use.

Certificates.—The grade of work required to justify the granting of a certificate was as far as possible standardized both at Chatham and at the different mine schools ; it was not considered necessary for a man with a Chatham certificate to qualify a second time in France.

30. SYLLABUS OF TEN DAYS' GENERAL COURSE FOR OTHER RANKS.

Listening.

Lecture.—Detection of sounds with the naked ear.

Judging of nature of sounds and detection of same.

Constant need for careful investigations.

Difference of listening in clay and chalk.

Approximate distances that various sounds can be heard in different classes of ground.

General rules to be observed when listening.

Practical Work.—Daily practices in listening with the naked ear and detection of various working sounds.

Listening results and the correct method of recording results.

Practical Mining.—Timbering and mining in various forms of galleries.

General assistance in experimental work.

Mine Rescue Work (Theoretical and Practical).—Similar to the Officers' Mine Rescue Course, with the exception that eight short elementary lectures were given and a *viva voce* examination was held in the place of the written paper.

The practical part of the training was extremely severe in character, approximating as nearly as possible to the work men were called on to do in the trenches.

In selecting men for this course, companies were expected to send only the best type of men, physically fit and intelligent.

31. TIME-TABLE OF TEN DAYS' GENERAL MINING COURSE.

			Officers.	Other Ranks.
First Day.				
Mine Rescue Lecture	...	...	2 — 3	9.30—10
Mine Rescue Practice	...	...	10.30—12	10.30—12
Mine Rescue Practice	...	...	3 — 4.30	3 — 4.30
Listening	...	...	8 — 9	8 — 9
Listening Lecture ...	...	...	9 —10	———
Mining Lecture ...	...	...	12 — 1	———
Second Day.				
Mine Rescue Practice	...	...	9.30—11.30	9.30—11.30
Mine Rescue Lecture	...	...	2 — 3	12 —12.30
Listening	...	...	11.30—1	8 —9
Practical Mining ...	...	...	3 — 4.30	2 — 4.30
Third Day.				
Mine Rescue Lecture	...	...	2 — 3	12 —12.30
Mine Rescue Practice	...	...	9.30—11.30	9.30—12
Listening	...	...	11.30— 1	8 — 9
Practical Mining ...	...	...	———	2 — 4.30
Mining Lecture ...	...	...	3 — 4.30	———
Fourth Day.				
Mine Rescue Practice	...	...	9.30—11.30	9.30—12
Mine Rescue Lecture	...	...	2 — 3	12 —12.30
Lecture	...	...	11.30—1	8 — 9
Practical Mining ...	...	...	———	2.30— 5
Surveying	...	...	3 — 4.30	———
Fifth Day.				
Mine Rescue Practice	...	...	9.30—11.30	9.30—12
Mine Rescue Lecture	...	...	2 — 3	12 —12.30
Listening	...	...	11.30— 1	8 — 9
Practical Mining ...	...	...	3 — 4.30	2 — 4.30
Sixth Day.				
Mine Rescue Practice	...	...	9.30—11.30	9.30—12
Mine Rescue Lecture	...	...	———	12 —12. 30
Listening	...	...	11.30— 1	8 — 9
Practical Mining ...	...	...	———	2 — 4.30
Surveying	...	...	2 — 4.30	———
Seventh Day.				
Mine Rescue Practice	...	...	9.30—11.30	9.30—12
Mine Rescue Lecture	...	...	———	12 —12.30
Listening	...	...	11.30— 1	8 — 9
Practical Mining ...	...	...	———	2 — 4.30
Eighth Day.				
Mine Rescue Practice	...	...	10.30— 1	10.30— 1
Practical Mining ...	...	...	———	2 — 4.30
Listening	...	...	8 —10	8 —10
Ninth Day.				
Mine Rescue Practice	...	...	10.15—11.15	9.15—10.45
Mine Rescue Exam.	...	...	11.30— 1	2 — 5
Listening	...	...	9 —10	8 — 9
Practical Mining ...	...	...	2 — 4.30	———

Tenth Day.			*Officers.*	*Other Ranks.*
Mine Rescue Theory	...	...		9 —10.30
Mine Rescue Practice	...	...	11.45—12.45	11 —12.30
Practical Mining	...	...		2 — 4.30
Listening	...	...	9 —11.30	8 — 9
Mine Rescue Exam. (Practical) ...			8.15— 8.45	
Mining Examination	...	...	2 — 4.30	

32. SPECIAL EIGHT DAYS' COURSE OF LISTENING FOR OTHER RANKS.

The students for this course were most carefully selected from Tunnelling Companies.

The course consisted solely of lectures and practices with listening instruments, and was of a most thorough nature.

At the conclusion, all men with a Grade 1 Certificate were appointed as " Special Listeners " in the Tunnelling Companies, being excused all other duties.

The results obtained more than justified its institution, and the success which companies enjoyed in the determination of direction of hostile workings was largely due to the training men received at this course.

Lecture 1.—Detection of sounds with the naked ear.

Judging of nature of sounds and distance of same.

Need of careful investigations.

Difference of listening in clay and chalk.

Approximate distances that various sounds can be heard in different classes of ground.

General rules to be observed when listening.

Lecture 2.—The geophone, its use and abuse.

Care of the instrument.

Use of the double geophone for the deduction of direction and level.

Concrete examples of results obtained from accurate and careful listening.

Lecture 3.—Use of the magnetic compass in combination with the double geophone.

Advantages of listening to the same sound from more than one post.

Booking of results correctly and plotting of same on listening plans.

Lecture 4.—Use of electrical instruments as detectors in dangerous places and for use in tamping up with charges.

Description of the Western Electric, seismophone, and tele-geophones.

Listening patrols and the care of listening posts.

The organization of central listening stations.

Practical Work.—Detection and classification of sounds with the use of the double geophone in the listening circle and galleries.

Correct booking of results and plotting of the same.

Listening with electrical detectors from a central station.

Tracing defects in apparatus.

Examination.—Each man was subjected to a searching *viva voce* examination on all points covered by the course.

Pupils were trained to listen either in clay or chalk, according to the nature of the ground they were working in in the trench.

33. Syllabus of Mined Dug-out Course.

Object.—The object of the course was the training of officers and other ranks of artillery, engineer and other units in the construction and design of mined dug-outs.

The course was so arranged that, in addition to the students receiving a thorough training, the work performed by them was of practical use to the Army, being of a type similar to that performed by Tunnelling Companies.

Organization.—Students were posted into companies of eighty. Each company was divided into sections and squads, and was under the personal instruction and supervision of one officer and five N.C.O. instructors.

Care was taken that each man in the squad received instruction in all branches of the work, and a daily report on every man was made to the chief instructor.

General Course.

Lectures.—Three general lectures were given. The first lecture (1st day) was preliminary and general in character, dealing in an elementary manner with mining methods, materials and terms.

The second lecture (6th day) was more advanced, and dealt with the different methods of dug-out construction, with types of mining and timbering used.

The third lecture (10th day) dealt with the design of dug-out systems, special attention being given to questions of camouflage and gas protection.

Time-Table.—The length of each course was fourteen days, the time being allocated as follows :—

Inclined entrances	3 days.
Stepped entrances	2 days.
Galleries	3 days.
Chambers	5 days.
Lagging and strutting ...	1 day.

Officers' Course.

In addition to the general lectures, the following special lectures were given :—

(*a*). *Surveying* (*Theoretical*).—Uses of prismatic compass and Abney level as applied to dug-out surveying.

Corrections for magnetic deflections.

Plotting of results.

Siting of entrances.

(*b*). *Design of Dug-Outs.*—Design of dug-outs to meet given requirements.

Estimation of time, material and labour necessary.

Surveying (*Practical*).—Students were required to make a complete survey of a trench and dug-out system, with properly executed plan of the same.

In addition, it was necessary for them to submit a dug-out design to meet given conditions, with complete list of material, etc., required.

As much time as possible was spent on tours of the works under an officer instructor, in order to obtain a practical knowledge of methods of mining and timbering.

A written examination was held on the last day of the course.

Certificates and Reports.—Certificates were granted to all students whose standard of work was sufficiently high to justify the giving of same.

A report was made on the ability and work of every student attending the course.

Detection of Enemy Traps.—Specimens of known types of enemy traps were arranged in a dug-out, demonstrations being frequently held with regard to their effect, detection and removal.

It is of interest to record that the work carried out during these courses was of use during the German offensive in April, 1918, when the underground workings sufficed to provide sleeping space for over 1,000 men.

At one time the dug-outs were used as Divisional Headquarters, and a large amount of work was done by the students in constructing different types of dug-outs in the neighbouring defence lines.

34. MISCELLANEOUS MINE RESCUE WORK.

In addition to the ordinary courses, all mine rescue men were required to go through three-days' "refresher" courses from time to time.

If any man was found to have become unsuitable during the interval, his certificate was cancelled.

All apparatus in the trenches was returned periodically to the school to be re-charged and tested, and the officer in charge of mine rescue instruction paid frequent visits of inspection to the companies' rescue stations.

When it is realized that for many months no fewer than 120/100 cub. ft. cylinders of oxygen were used monthly, and that 450 " Proto " and 250 " Novita " sets were in constant use both in the school and in the Tunnelling Companies administered by it, it will be possible to form some idea of the magnitude of this special branch of training.

Experimental Work.—The experimental side of the school was one of its most valuable branches, and it was customary to test and report on all new explosives, boring machines and scientific instruments in general.

Among the many investigations undertaken, the following are typical examples :—

(i). Complete trial and comparison of the properties of ammonal, amatol and sabulite.

(ii). Testing of Explosive Formulæ by charges varying from 3,000 lbs. downwards.

(iii). Trial of the " Wombat " borer for different types of work.

(iv). Experiments on the Sympathetic Detonation of Explosives.

(v). Properties and use of Cordeau Détonant.

(vi). Selection and standardization of the geophone and seismophone from the many existing types of listening instruments.

(vii). Experiments for improving the " Proto " and " Novita " Mine Rescue Apparatus.

General Remarks.—The success of the school was undoubted, and it grew from a school originally for miners only to one where all branches of the Service were trained.

During the two and a half years the school was in existence over 500 officers and 5,500 O.R. were granted certificates of proficiency in various subjects. In the later stages classes of 400 students were in residence, necessitating a staff of eight officer and 30 N.C.O. instructors.

The school was handicapped by its small establishment, additional staff having to be attached from Tunnelling Companies.

In addition to the ordinary instructional work the school staff was at times called on to undertake special work for the Army, this work including an investigation of the collieries of the Lens Concession and the supervision of the construction of the Army Defence Line near Béthune by civilian labour during the German offensive in 1918.

INDEX.

PLATE I

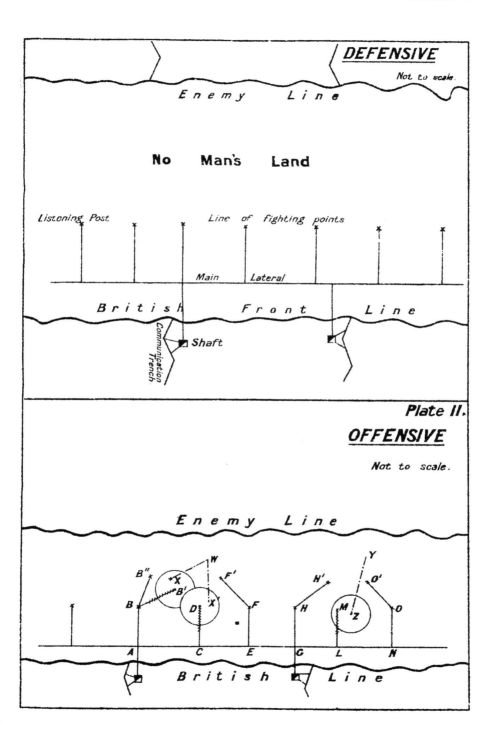

PLATE III

DIAGRAM SHOWING SYSTEM OF DRIVING GALLERIES.

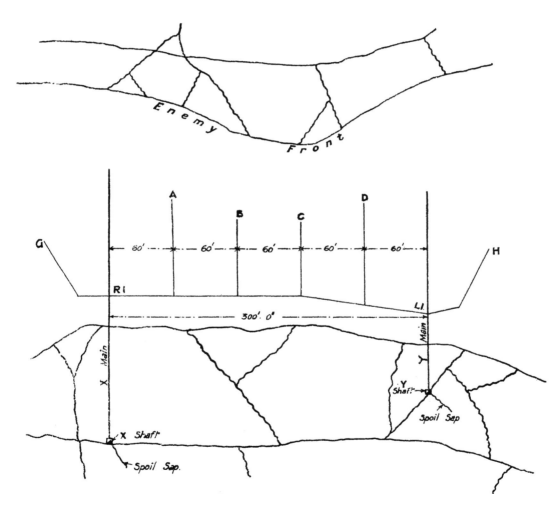

TWO GALLERIES DRIVEN FOR AN ATTACK ON THE TRIANGLE. S. OF LOOS. 30-6-1916   PLATE IV

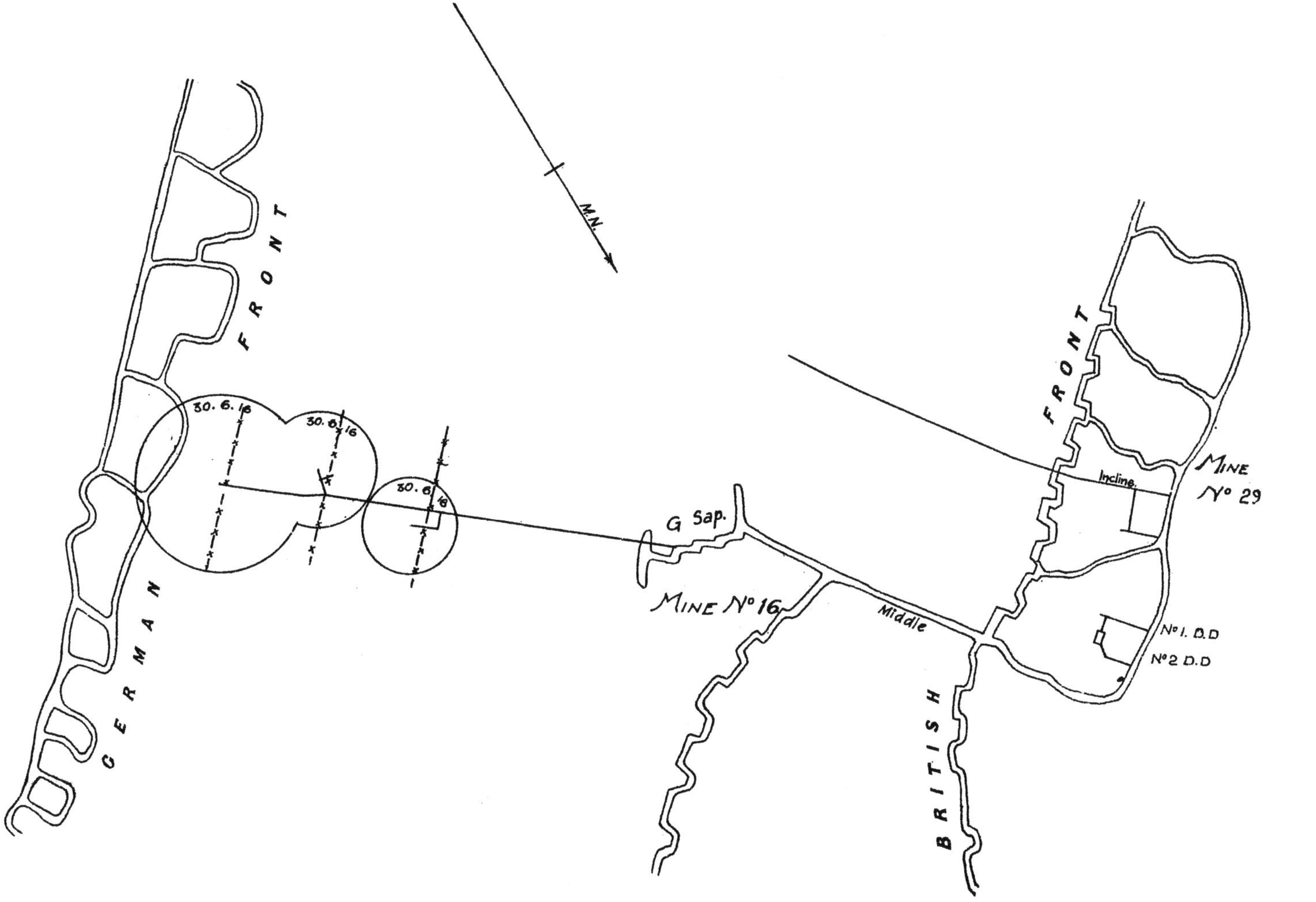

FRONT

BRITISH

Mine Nº 29

Incline

Nº 1 D.D
Nº 2 D.D

Middle

MINE Nº 16

G. Sap.

M.N.

30.6.16

30.6.16

30.6.16

FRONT

GERMAN

PLATE V

WHEEL-BARROW FOR MINES.

Not drawn to scale.

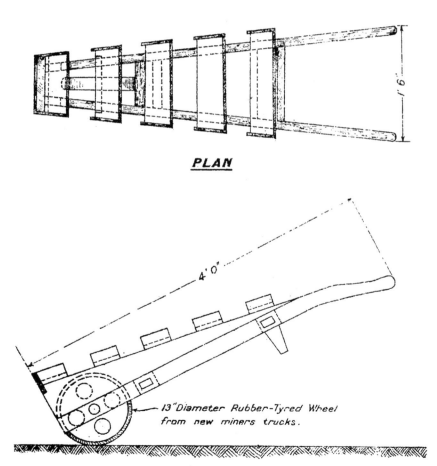

1' 6"

PLAN

4' 0"

13" Diameter Rubber-Tyred Wheel
from new miners trucks.

SECTION

PLATE VI

TRUCK FOR DOUBLE TRACK SHAFT.

INCLINE 1 IN 4.   GAUGE 2'0".   AVERAGE LOAD, 22 BAGS.

EACH TRIP TAKES 8 MINUTES AVERAGE HAULING.

LENGTH OF INCLINE 254 FEET.

Eye-bolt used for axle box to take eye of sprag.

Hook for sprag when truck is running down.

Sprag

5'0"

1" Planking

5" x 2" timber

Flanged wheels

Wire Rope

3" Ring

SIDE ELEVATION

PLATE VII

CHUTE.

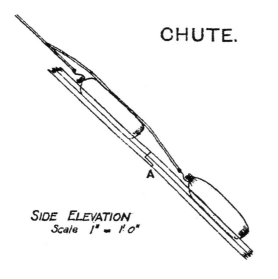

SIDE ELEVATION
Scale 1" = 1' 0"

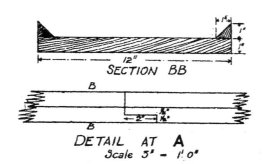

12"

SECTION BB

DETAIL AT A
Scale 3" = 1' 0"

TEMPLATE.

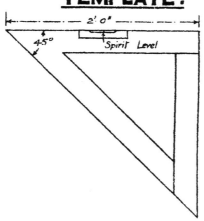

2' 0"

45°

Spirit Level

PLATE VIII

WINDLASS FOR DEEP VERTICAL SHAFTS.

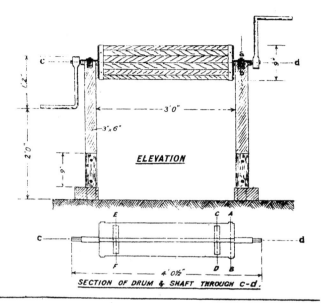

c ⎯ d

← 3' 0" →

3" x 6"

12"

2' 0"

1' 9"

ELEVATION

E   C A

c ⎯ d

F   D B

← 4' 0½" →

SECTION OF DRUM & SHAFT THROUGH c-d.

2" x ¾" Iron

END SECTION a-b.

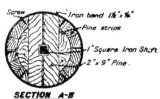

Screw — Iron band 1½" x ¾"

Pine strips.

1" Square Iron Shaft.

2" x 9" Pine.

SECTION A-B

Scale 2 inches to 1 foot.

1" x ¾" Iron straps well screwed
to 2" x 9" Core and passing through
hole in shaft.

One 2" x 9" bored to take screws
after Sections have been placed
together.

SECTION C-D

Section E-F same as C-D
but screws reversed.

ALTERNATIVE METHOD OF PREVENTING A SPINDLE
FROM TURNING IN A DRUM.

PUTTING FEATHERS
ON A
SPINDLE.

Feathers   Disc   Drum

The drum in both cases is made in two halves.

MAKING THE
SPINDLE
WITH A CRANK.

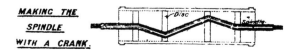

Disc   Spindle

PLATE VIII^A

WINDLASS USED FOR DEEP VERTICAL SHAFTS.

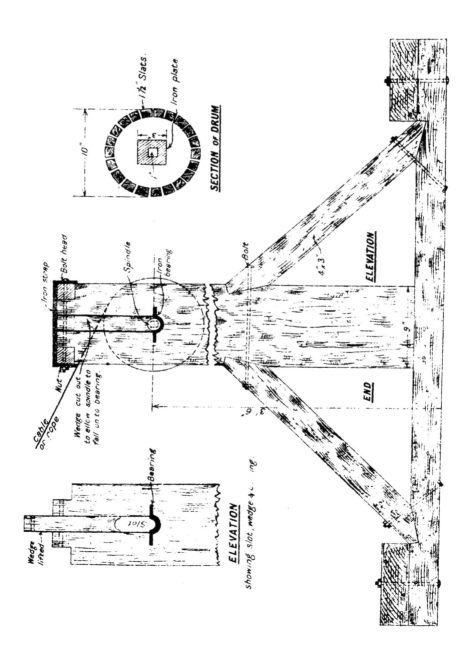

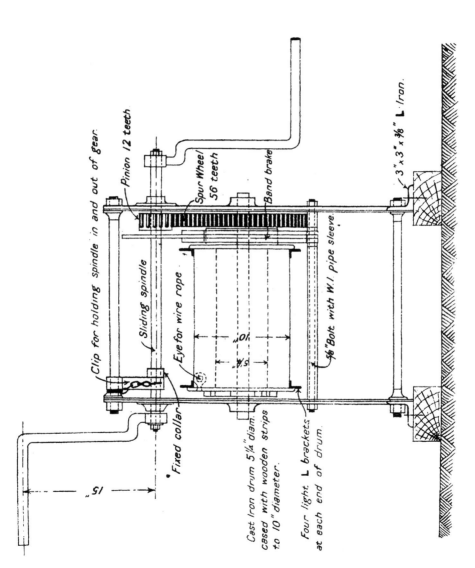

Clip for holding spindle in and out of gear.

Pinion 12 teeth

Spur Wheel 56 teeth

Band brake

Sliding spindle

Eye for wire rope

Fixed collar

3"×3"×⅜" L Iron.

⅝" Bolt with W.I. pipe sleeve.

Cast Iron drum 5¼" diam. cased with wooden strips to 10" diameter.

Four light L brackets at each end of drum.

10"

5¼"

15"

FRONT ELEVATION

PLATE X

MONO—RAIL SYSTEM.

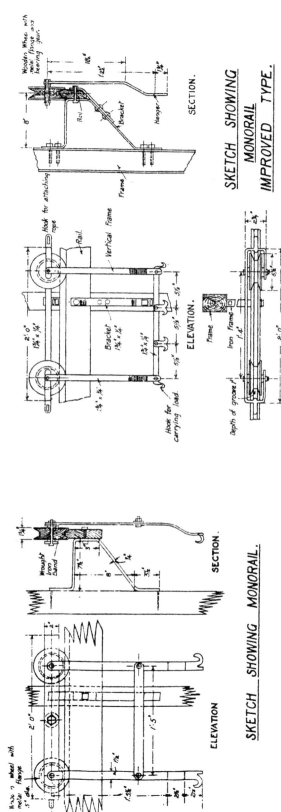

SKETCH SHOWING MONORAIL IMPROVED TYPE.

SECTION.

ELEVATION.

PLAN.

SKETCH SHOWING MONORAIL.

SECTION.

ELEVATION.

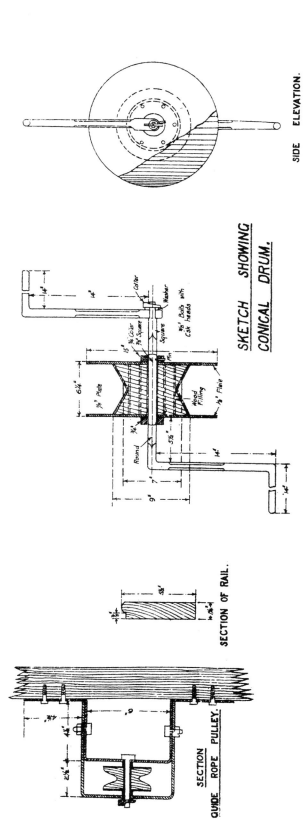

SIDE ELEVATION.

SKETCH SHOWING
CONICAL DRUM.

Collar

Washer

⅜″ Bolts with
CSk heads

¾″ Collar
Pin Square

Square

Pin

15″

6¼″ ⅛″ Plate

Wood
Filling

⅜″ Plate

14″

14″

¾″
Round

5⅝″

7″

9″

14″

14″

SECTION OF RAIL.

5¾″

SECTION
GUIDE ROPE PULLEY.

4½″

6″

4½″

4⅝″

PLATE XI

DIFFERENTIAL DOUBLE DRUM WINCH.

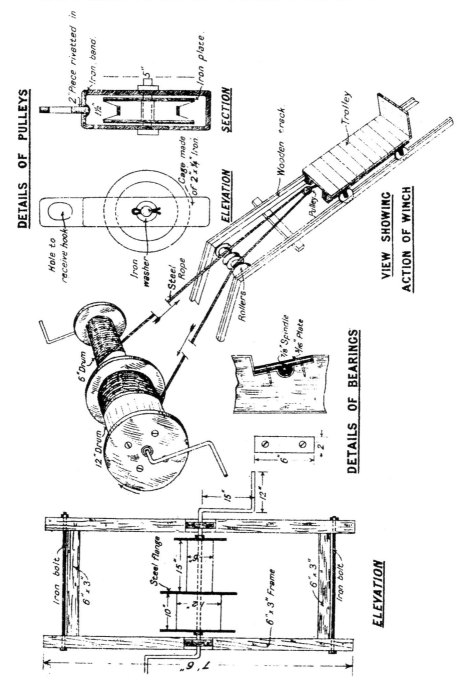

DETAILS OF PULLEYS

2" Piece rivetted in

Iron band.

Iron plate.

5"

1/2"

SECTION

Cage made of 2" x 1/4" Iron.

ELEVATION

Hole to receive hook

Iron washer

Steel Rope

Wooden track

Trolley

Pulley

Rollers

7/8" Spindle

3/16" Plate

DETAILS OF BEARINGS

VIEW SHOWING

ACTION OF WINCH

6" Drum

12" Drum

6"

2"

15"

12"

Iron bolt

6" x 3"

Steel flange

15"

9"

2"

10"

6" x 3" Frame

6" x 3"

Iron bolt

7' 6"

ELEVATION

PLATE XII

PLAN OF CRATER SHOWING ARRANGEMENT OF POLES TO CARRY CAMOUFLAGE.

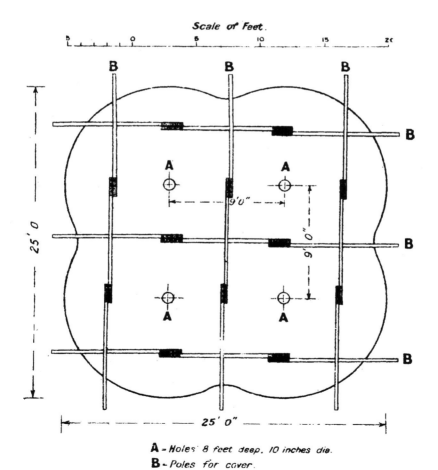

Scale of Feet.

A = Holes 8 feet deep, 10 inches dia.
B = Poles for cover.

PLATE XIII

TYPE OF REGULATOR DOOR IN MINE.

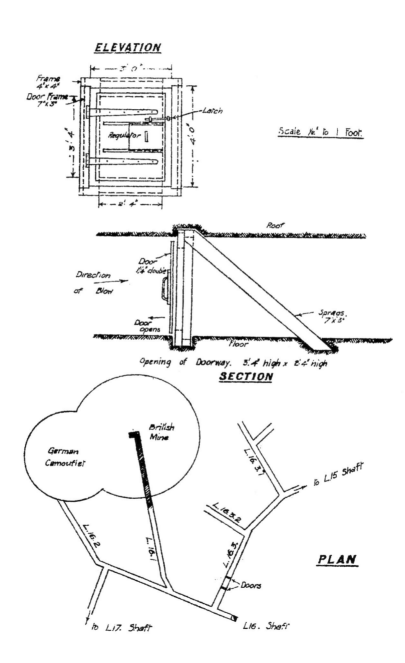

PLATE XIV

SKETCH OF MINE GAS DOOR.

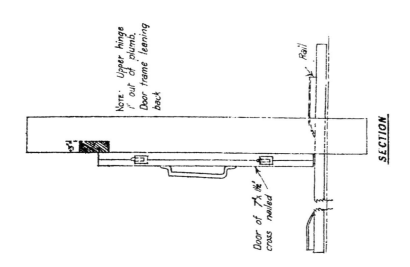

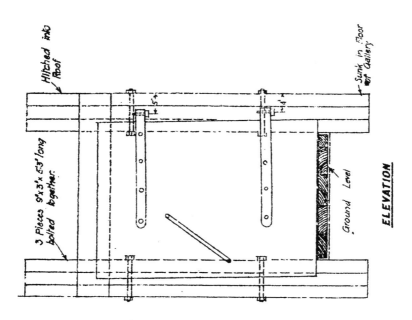

DEVON TUNNEL

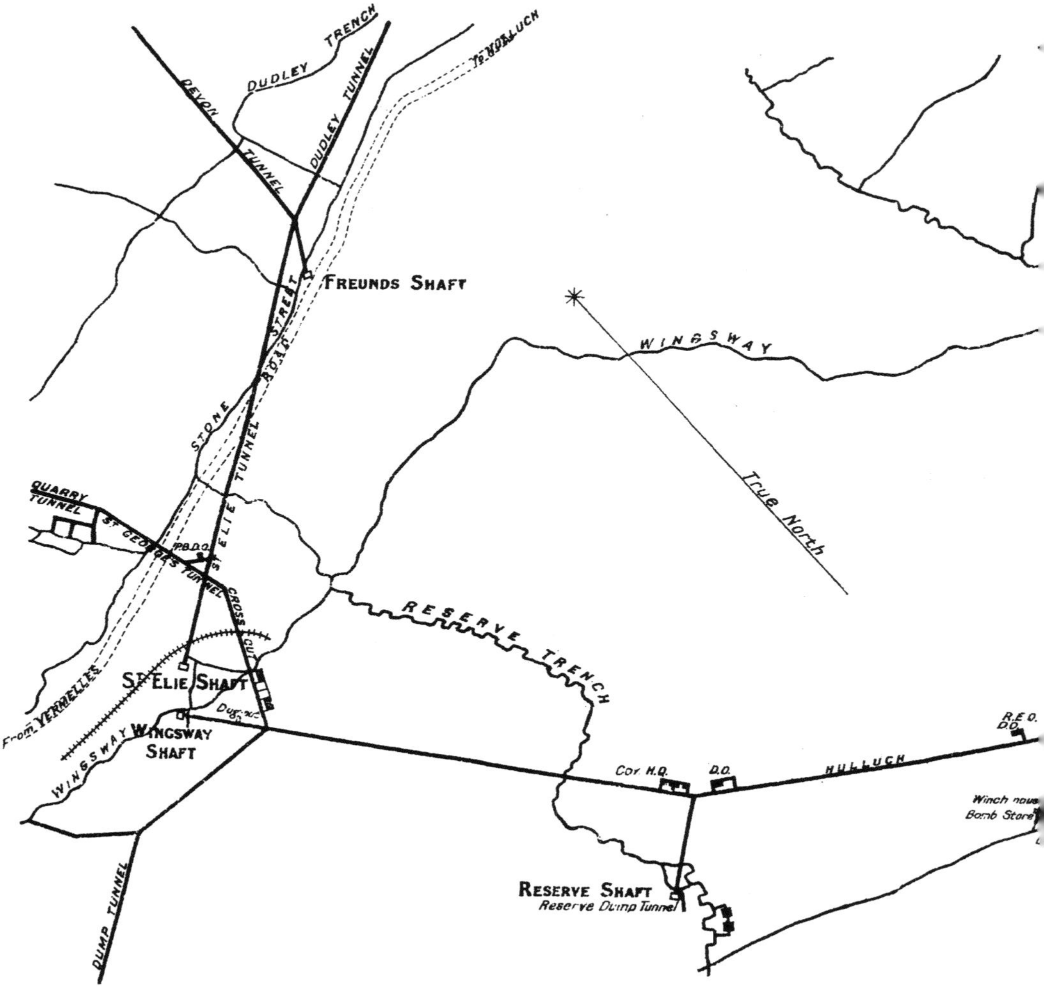

DUDLEY TRENCH

DUDLEY TUNNEL

To HULLUCH

FREUNDS SHAFT

WINGSWAY

STONE STREET ROAD

ELIE TUNNEL

True North

QUARRY TUNNEL

ST GEORGES TUNNEL

P.B.D.O.

CROSS CUT

RESERVE TRENCH

From VERMELLES

ST ELIE SHAFT

WINGSWAY SHAFT

Dug.

R.E.O. D.O.

Cor H.Q.

D.O.

HULLUCH

Winch house Bomb Store

DUMP TUNNEL

RESERVE SHAFT
Reserve Dump Tunnel

PLATE XV

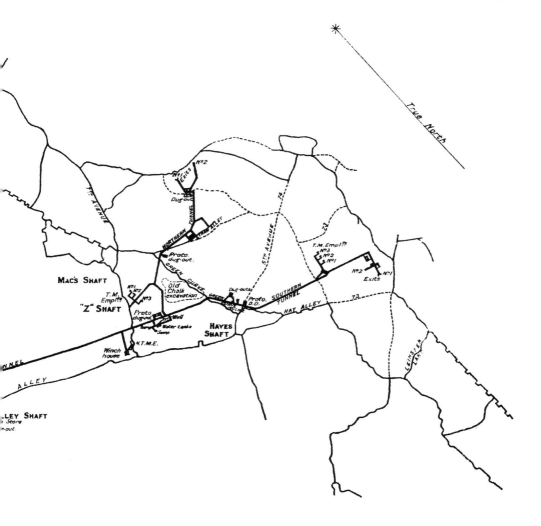

PLATE XVI

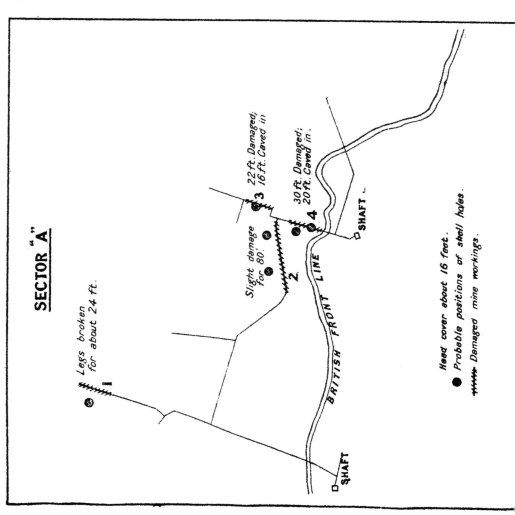

SECTOR "A"

Legs broken
for about 24 ft.

1

Slight damage
for 80.

2

22 ft. Damaged;
16 ft. Caved in
3

30 ft. Damaged;
20 ft. Caved in.
4

BRITISH FRONT LINE

SHAFT

SHAFT

Head cover about 16 feet.
● Probable positions of shell holes.
ϟϟϟϟ Damaged mine workings.

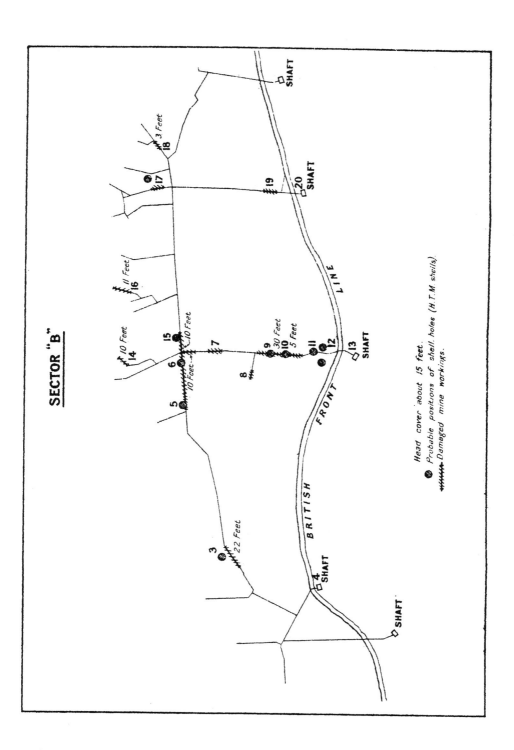

SECTOR "B"

● Head cover about 15 feet.
● Probable positions of shell holes (H.T.M shells).
⊢⊢⊢⊢ Damaged mine workings.

PLATE XVII.

SECRET.

Army Form W.3404. (*From A.F. B.213*).

WEEKLY MINE REPORT.

Date ....

.... Corps.

.... Division.

.... Tunnelling Company, R.E.

Strength of Company.	Officers.	O.R.
R.E.		
Permanently Attached Infantry		
Temporarily Attached Infantry		
Totals ...		

Designation of Working.	Trench No. or Name.	Map Reference.	Shaft or Gallery.			Footage for Week.	No. of Days Worked.	Nature of Ground.	REPORT.
			Depth.	Size Inside Timbers.	Total Footage.				Circumstances affecting progress. Results of listening. Mines and camouflets. General information.
1.	2.	3.	4.	5.	6.	7.	8.	9.	10.

WEEKLY PROGRESS REPORT.
(SERVICES OTHER THAN MINING).

.... Corps.

.... Division.

.... Tunnelling Company.

Date ....

Strength of Company.
(From A.F. B.213).

	Officers.	O.R.
R.E.		
Permanently Attached Infantry		
Temporarily Attached Infantry		
Totals ..		

Designation of Working.	Nature of Work or Service.	Map Reference.	Section Employed. No.	Days Worked.	Shifts per Day.	PERSONNEL O.R. Per Shift.		Average Working Party.	Probable Date of Completion.	REMARKS. Circumstances affecting Progress (Working Parties, Material, Equipment, Transport, Enemy Activity, etc.).
						R.E.	P.A.I.			
1.	2.	3.	4.	5.	6.	7.	8.	9.	10.	11.

(Dug-out progress to be shown by sketch).

PLATE XVIII.

SECRET.

For British Mine, use other side.)

MINE EXPLOSION REPORT (ENEMY).

...................ARMY.   ....CORPS.   ....DIVISION.

....................TUNNELLING COMPANY R.E.   SECTOR......................

DATE.....................................   TIME......................................

Location of Blow	
Nature of Ground	
Probable depth of Charge	
Probable object of Mine	
Underground damage	
Surface Effects	
Dimensions of Crater (if any)	
Infantry action regarding Crater : (Particularly stating whether any new positions occupied appear adequately protected underground)	
Gas Effects Underground	
Casualties :—Underground	
Surface	
General Remarks	

(Sketch attached.)

Date..   Signed......................................

FOR ENEMY MINE, USE OTHER SIDE.)   Army Form W3376

MINE EXPLOSION REPORT (BRITISH).

.... ARMY.   ....CORPS.   ....DIVISION.

.......................TUNNELLING COMPANY R.E.   SECTOR...........................

DATE...   TIME......................................

Location and depth of Charge	
Nature of Ground	
Details of Charge : (Size, class of explosive, form of packing and primers used.)	
Tamping : (Lengths of Solid and Air Spaces)	
Reasons and Authority for Mine	
Effects of Explosion :	
Dimensions of Crater	
Underground effects	
Estimated H.R.R.	
Surface effects	
Gas Conditions	
If against enemy gallery, estimated distance	
Infantry action regarding Crater : (Particularly stating whether any new positions occupied appear adequately protected underground)	
General Remarks	

(Sketch attached.)

Date...   *Signed*..

PLATE XIX.

Army Form W. 3414.

*ESTIMATE—*STOCK.

SPECIAL MINING STORES (APPENDIX " B.")

Month of..

Unit...   Date....................................

	RECEIPTS.	ISSUES.	BALANCE.	REQUIRE-MENTS.
TOOLS.				
Adzes, clay heads				
,, ,, handles				
Boring Machines, " Acme "				
,, ,, ,, drills for . . .				
Earth Augers, 10 in.				
,, ,, ,, extensions for . . .				
Jacks, Bottle, 3 ton				
,, ,, 5 ton				
Picks, Hardy, 2½ lbs.				
,, ,, 4 lbs.				
,, ,, helves for				
Rods, drain, 2 ft.				
Tools, grafting, 2 ft. 6 in. overall . . .				
,, ,, 3 ft. overall . . .				
Vertical Borers, 30 ft.				
,, ,, 50 ft.				
Wheels and Axles, pairs, 12-in. dia., 12-in. gauge. .				
INSTRUMENTS.				
Compasses, prismatic, 4 in.				
,, ,, tripods for . . .				
Detectors, sound, Geophone				
,, ,, Roger				
,, ,, Sadlier-Jackson . . .				
Periscopes				
Staves, Stanley's Mine, 6 ft closing to 20 in. .				
Telescopes				
Theodolites				

* Delete word not applicable.

	RECEIPTS.	ISSUES.	BALANCE.	REQUIRE-MENTS.
VENTILATING APPARATUS.				
Bellows, 3 ft. 6 in.				
,, 5 ft.				
Pumps, Holman				
,, ,, hose for				
LAMPS. *C.E.A.G.—*OLDHAM, complete				
,, ,, Accumulators for . .				
,, ,, Bulbs for . . .				
,, ,, Glasses, well for . . .				
,, ,, Pins, spring contact for .				
,, ,, Plates, insulating for . .				
,, ,, Rings, Packing for . .				
,, ,. Springs, pressure . . .				
,, ,. Screws, ,, . . .				
MINE RESCUE APPARATUS.				
Apparatus, Oxygen Reviving				
Canaries, or other small birds				
,, ,, ,, ,, cages for . .				
Cylinders, Storage, 100 c.f.				
Mice, White				
,, ,, cages for				
" Proto " Sets				
,, ,, Spare twin cylinders for . . .				
Pumps, Oxygen, Lever				
" Salvus " Sets				
,, ,, Spare cylinders for . . .				
·, ,, Cartridges for . . .				
Soda, Caustic, 4-lb. tins				
,, ,, 1-lb. ,, ...				
MINE RESCUE APPARATUS—SPARES.				

* Delete words not applicable.

(Signature)...
....

PLATE XX

DETAILS OF GEOPHONE.

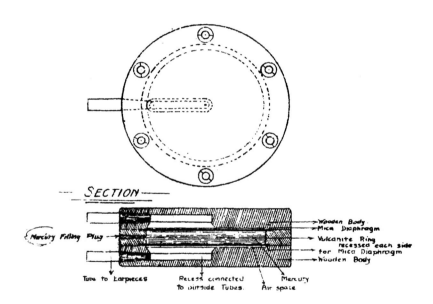

SECTION

Wooden Body.
Mica Diaphragm
Vulcanite Ring
recessed each side
for Mica Diaphragm
Wooden Body

Mercury Filling Plug

Tube to Earpieces

Recess connected
to outside Tubes.

Mercury

Air space

PLATE XXI

METHOD OF USE OF GEOPHONE.

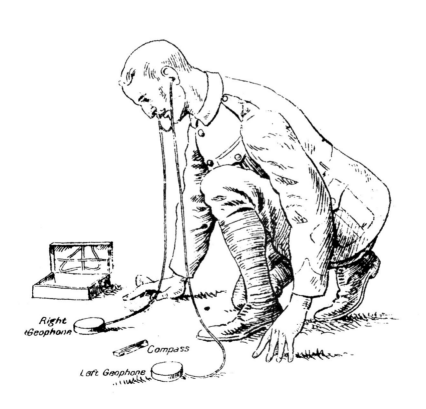

Right Geophone

Compass

Left Geophone

PLATE XXII

GEOPHONE SECTION DIAGRAM.

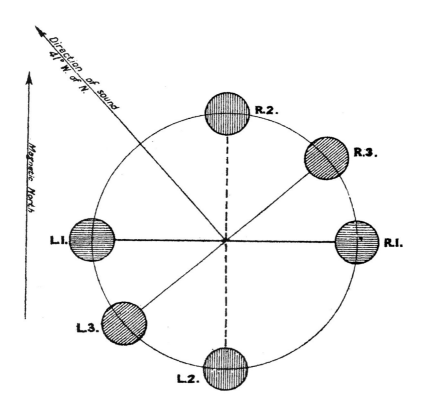

PLATE XXIII

THE WESTERN ELECTRIC.

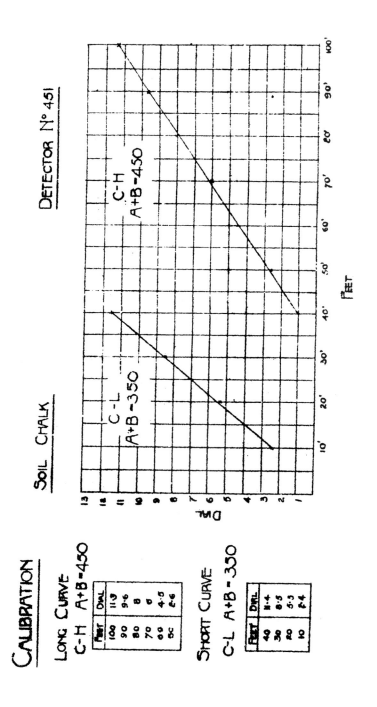

DETECTOR N° 451

SOIL CHALK

C-H
A+B=450

C-L
A+B=350

FEET

DIAL

CALIBRATION

LONG CURVE
C-H A+B=450

FEET	DIAL
100	11.3
90	9.6
80	8
70	6
60	4.5
50	2.6

SHORT CURVE
C-L A+B=350

FEET	DIAL
40	11.4
30	8.5
20	5.3
10	2.4

PLATE XXIV

THE SEISMOMICROPHONE.

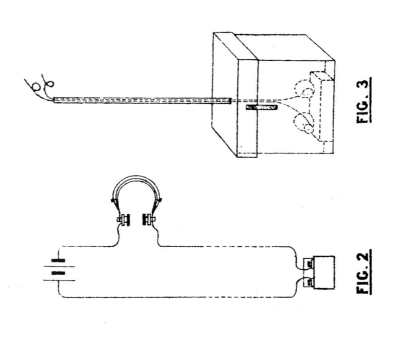

FIG. 3

FIG. 2

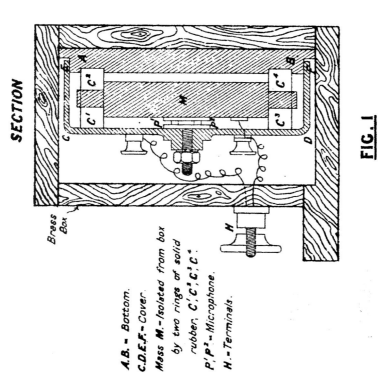

SECTION

FIG. I

A.B. = Bottom.

C.D.E.F. = Cover.

Mass M. = Isolated from box
by two rings of solid
rubber, C¹, C², C³, C⁴.

P¹, P² = Microphone.

H. = Terminals.

PLATE XXV

CENTRAL LISTENING STATION TABLE AND SWITCHBOARD.

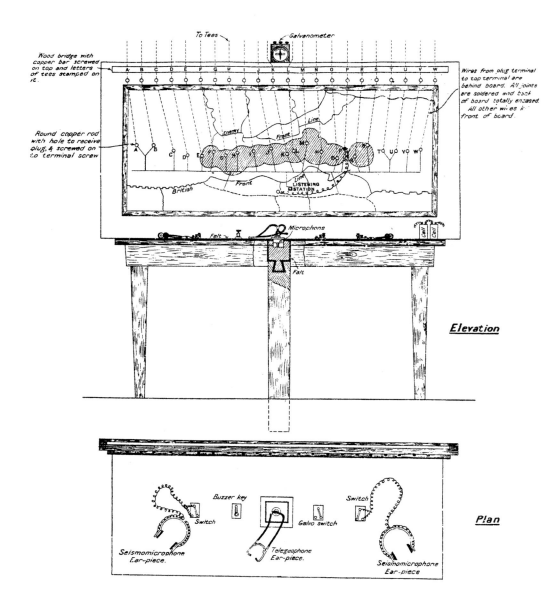

PLATE XXVI

BUZZER ATTACHMENT TO SEISMOMICROPHONE.

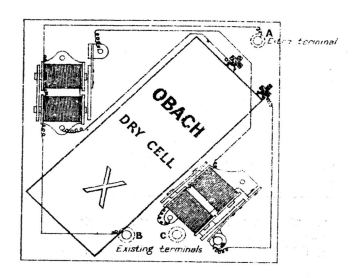

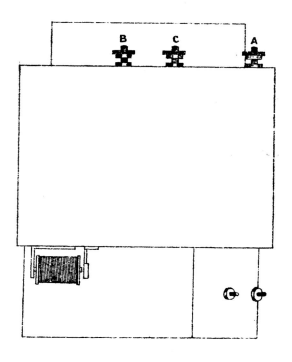

PLATE XXVII

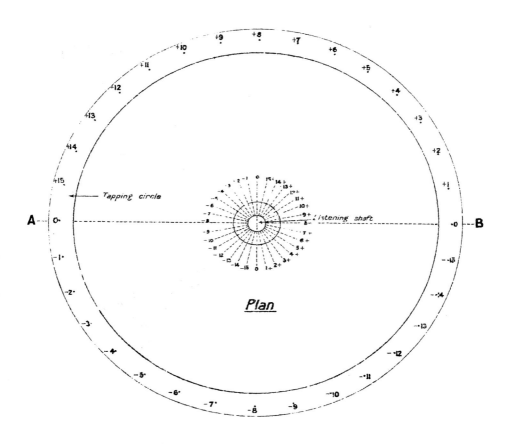

Plan

LISTENING CIRCLE

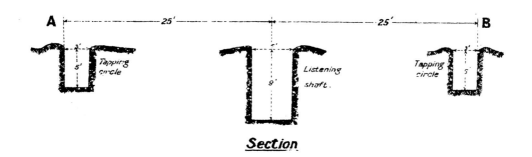

Section

PLAN OF SCHOOL LISTENING GALLERIES.

PLATE XXVIII

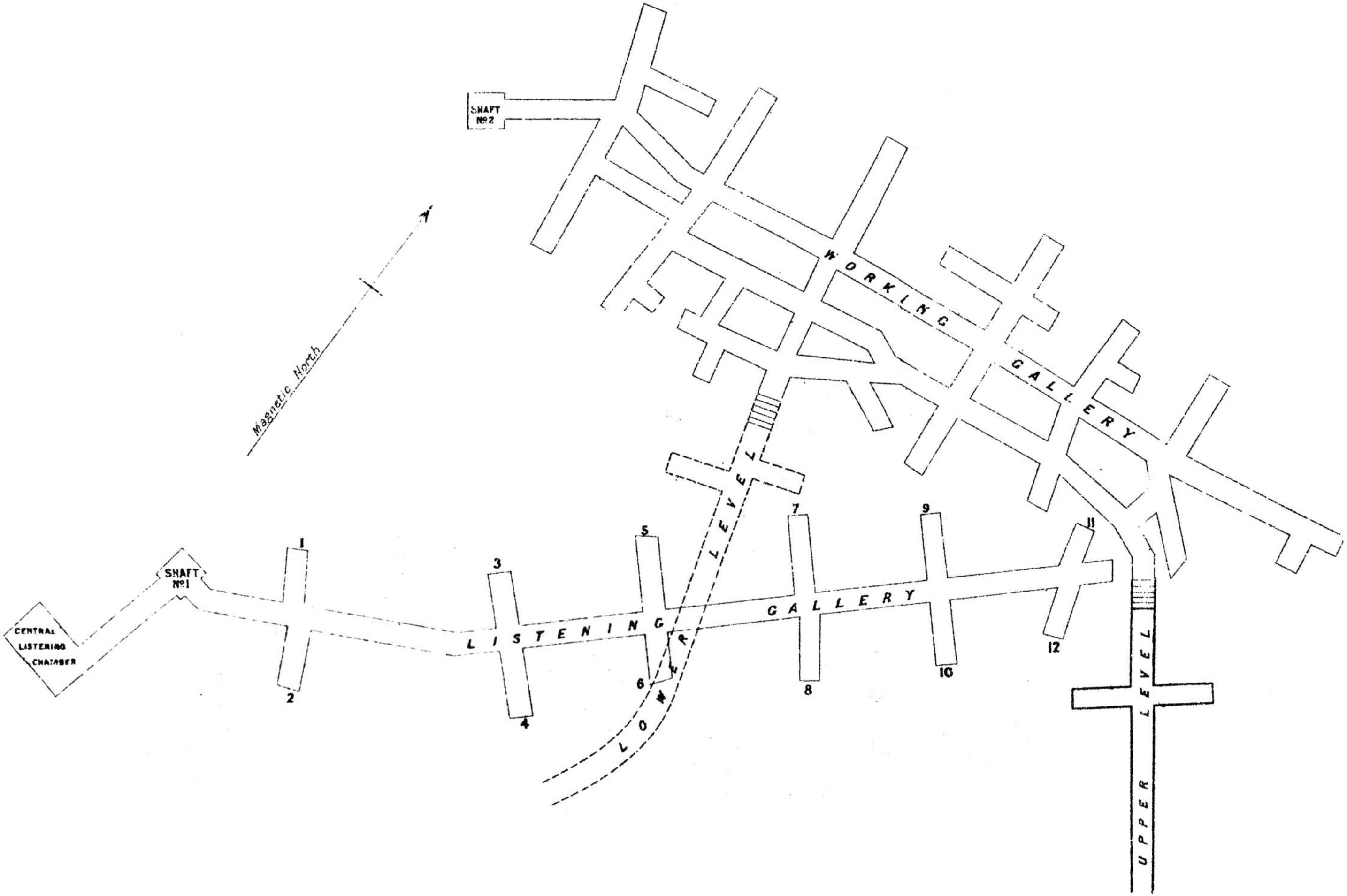

PLATE XXIX

LISTENING POSTS PUT ON
PLAN OF IMAGINARY FRONT.

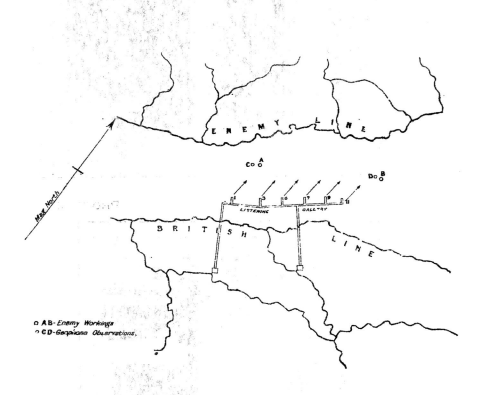

o AB - Enemy Workings
o CD - Geophone Observations.

PHOTO I.

GERMAN TRENCH THEODOLITE.

PHOTO II.

Photo III.

GEOPHONE.

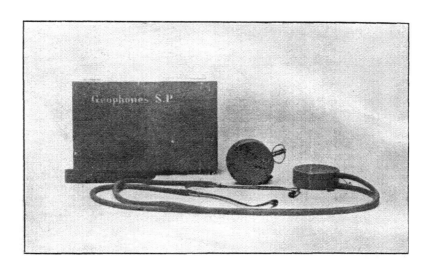

Photo IV.

WESTERN ELECTRIC MINING DETECTOR.